WHAT PEOPLE ARE SAYING ABOUT THE GREATEST MOMENT AND ITS AUTHOR

What is the greatest moment in the Bible? What event warrants this title? Dr. Harrel has woven Scripture upon Scripture, to lead us to the answer to this question. In the process, we will grow to understand our purpose and develop a greater passion for our God.

—*Susan Titus Osborn*
Author, International Conference Speaker,
Director of the Christian Communicator

Dr. Harrel has written an engaging book, The Greatest Moment. *It promises to take the reader on a journey through Scripture to discover what God's greatest moment is for each of us. I believe it will transform our understanding of what God's call truly is.*

—*Paul W. Smith*
Author, Ordained Minister, Managing Editor for Curriculum at
Gospel Publishing House

I have read with interest the opening chapters of Dr. Charles Harrel's new book. I was impressed with the passion and the tone of the writing. I'm sure it will be a winner.

—*Dr. Karl D. Strader*
Author, Pastor, Founder of Carpenter's Home Church in
Lakeland, Florida

As an editor of Christian publications, I have worked with Charles Harrel for many years, receiving his written words in devotional materials. He writes from the heart and always makes it plain how readers can apply the Word of God in everyday life. I highly recommend this author to the Christian community at large!

—*Gary Wilde*
Author, Pastor, Editor for *Devotions* at Standard Publishing

For those seeking to know God better and to love Him more, I encourage you to read and meditate on the wonders of God's Word that are shown so masterfully in Dr. Harrel's new book. I believe that you will enjoy and benefit from the marvelous insights the Lord has given him.

—Rev. Jerry Cooney
Bible Scholar, Evangelist, Founder of Holy Spirit Ministries

Charles Earl Harrel is a man of passion in all he does. He shines at unfolding the majesty of God piece by piece until revelation of truth emerges.

—Dr. Carol J. Robeson
Author of the *Strongman Series,* Inspirational Speaker,
Former Missionary to Latin America

Dr. Charles Harrel is a friend and colleague. But more important, he has been touched by and had an encounter with the Holy Spirit. The greatest moments in the Word of God have to be experienced personally. His book encourages such intimacy.

—Rev. Stephen Strader
Author, International Speaker,
Lead Pastor at Ignited Church in Lakeland, Florida

The Greatest Moment *delivers a message right from the heart of God with compassion and clarity. It will capture your attention and spark the awakening your soul is longing for.*

—Patricia L. Kuehl
Educator, Former Director of Christian Education
at Calvary Temple in Portland, Oregon

THE *Greatest* MOMENT

*God's Greatest Hour, Heaven's Highest Call,
and Your Moment of Destiny*

May you embrace all that God has for you!

DR. CHARLES EARL HARREL

Blessings, Dr. Charles Earl Harrel

Xulon ELITE

DEDICATION

To Laura Lee,
my beloved wife and
co-laborer in the harvest:

Thank you!

Without your support,
this book would not have been written.

To friends and family who helped with the book,
believed in it, and prayed for it to make a difference:

"I thank my God upon every remembrance of you"
(Philippians 1:3).

CONTENTS

INTRODUCTION

There is no greater discovery than seeing God as
the author of your destiny.
—Dr. Ravi Zacharias

O ne particular moment, surpassing all others, has been waiting
since the dawn of time for its unveiling. This event is the
greatest moment in the Bible. No other moment is greater, more
revered, or significant to humanity.

According to Isaiah, knowledge and understanding are established
by building precept upon precept, line upon line, a little here, a little
there (Isaiah 28:9–10). I use this same approach throughout the book.
Each chapter builds upon the previous chapter by connecting one
majestic moment to the other, until reaching the single greatest moment
in the Bible. When something is the greatest, it does not obtain this
ranking independently but is composed of all the parts preceding it.
After weaving all the parts together, a little-known moment will emerge
as the most important of all.

The same method of reasoning will help identify the Bible's greatest
word and Scripture. Does God's Word hold such absolutes? Yes, it does.
The Bible contains specific examples where circumstances, situations,

individuals, commandments, and other things are considered as the greatest. One of these things is an esteemed, awe-inspiring word and the other an unparalleled, all-inclusive Scripture, but more on that as the chapters unfold.

The book will lay a foundation for the greatest moment with sensational events and epic accounts from the Bible, qualifying them with certain rules that distinguish greatness. Using intriguing stories and unique word pictures blended with Scriptures, the chapters will lead you to this ultimate moment and conclude by revealing heaven's highest calling.

The apostle Paul wrote about this inspiring moment and how it influenced his own life. Abandoning everything else, Paul pressed toward the goal and the prize he discovered in this precious revelation. He based his writings on it, even his calling. Paul wanted this *one thing* more than life itself. "But one thing *I do,* forgetting those things which are behind and reaching forward to those things which are ahead, I press toward the goal for the prize of the upward call of God in Christ Jesus" (Philippians 3:13*b*–14).

What is this high call of heaven, and why was it so important to Paul? Is there more to faith, something richer, deeper? Did Paul sense a greater plan and purpose for his life? Will understanding the greatest moment and highest call stir our hearts as well? Yes, I believe it can. It must.

What Can You Expect?

You can expect to find great truths connected to great moments, to see a divine theme that points to one preeminent event planned before the foundation of the world, to have your faith encouraged and your spirit renewed, to see the need for true revival, and to help the

Church fulfill its original purpose and calling. Will reading this book accomplish all these things? I hope it does, and the apostle Paul might concur. For these are the same things "the greatest moment" revelation did for him.

Revelation often facilitates change. Therefore, ask the Lord to give you discernment as you read the chapters in this book. Let His Word rekindle your spirit and fill your soul with desire. "Then I said, 'I will not make mention of Him, nor speak anymore in His name.' But His *word* was in my heart like a burning fire shut up in my bones; I was weary of holding it back, and I could not" (Jeremiah 20:9). Jeremiah knew this fiery passion, and we can too. God's Word still enflames hearts with greater truths and deeper revelations, so allow the Holy Spirit to guide you. "However, when He, the Spirit of truth, has come, He will guide you into all truth; for He will not speak on His own *authority,* but whatever He hears He will speak; and He will tell you things to come" (John 16:13).

Will This Book Fill Some Need?

Yes, it will touch one of the most essential needs of all: to know the truth. Can such knowledge make a difference in your life? Absolutely, for truth is a great liberator, even more so, when that truth is spiritual. It not only sets devoted followers free from religious bondage, it releases them to embrace their heritage in Christ. "And you shall know the truth, and the truth shall make you free" (John 8:32). If your interests are more analytical, then these chapters will challenge your thinking with facts and biblical concepts. If you enjoy digging into the Scriptures, comparing verses, and studying Greek and Hebrew words for their meanings, then keep an open Bible nearby.

Great events can shape our destiny, and embracing the greatest moment will do the same. Most of all, I pray that the teachings in this book will reaffirm God's call on your life, encourage intimacy with God, and inspire you to reach out to a lost and needy world. If this sounds like a spiritual journey, it is—at least it was for me. Hundreds of years ago, travelers were given a special charge before embarking on a voyage. The word spoken over them was *Godspeed*.

Understanding *The Way of Greatness* is where this journey begins. I wish you Godspeed!

PART ONE:

GREATNESS UNVEILED

CHAPTER 1

THE WAY OF GREATNESS

The greatest gift of sight is to see as Christ sees.
—Dr. E. Clayton Calhoun

Major League Baseball tracks almost every detail of their sport, recording the greatest efforts by athletes, teams, and managers. The struggle to distinguish greatness plays out in every game of every season. Players compete to pitch the fastest ball, connect for the most hits, and earn the highest batting average. At the end of the season, each league recognizes the best manager, most valuable player, best relief pitcher, rookie of the year, team with the most wins, and these are just a few of the many categories for outstanding achievements. My favorite overall category is single season leaders for home runs.

In 1927, Babe Ruth hammered out sixty home runs. With this seemingly unbreakable record, Ruth became the greatest home run hitter for a single season. Many believed his record would never be broken. Then Roger Maris hit sixty-one homers in 1961. This accomplishment made Maris the greatest. Few thought his record would be surpassed. However, during the 1998 season, a homerun race developed between

Mark McGwire and Sammy Sosa. Perhaps you watched the contest that year, wondering who would end up becoming the new record holder for a season. Sosa finished with sixty-six homers, but McGwire slammed out seventy. Surely, McGwire's record would remain the greatest. Who could beat this mark? Yet three years later in 2001, Barry Bonds hit seventy-three homers to become the new home run champion.[1] For a moment, put aside any controversies and consider just the achievements.

All these baseball records were absolutes—the best there was or ever will be—until someone broke them. One day, a talented baseball player will top the current record, and then another ballplayer will exceed that. For some reason, the quest to become the greatest never reaches a permanent resolution.

Striving for Greatness

In 1876, Alexander Graham Bell introduced a device that could transmit a person's voice over a telegraph wire; his telephone became one of the greatest inventions of all time. Today we have smart phones and other such gadgets. Not only do they send and receive voice messages, they allow users to endlessly text one another, download music, watch videos, surf the Internet, take pictures, and who knows what else. Most cell phones have GPS technology, track family and friends, and feature a programed voice to give advice on important matters. No doubt, an ingenious inventor has a greater application pending. One day, we might even place a phone call to an astronaut on Mars or other distant planet.

Ironically, it doesn't matter whether it's the ultimate discovery, the most esteemed event, or the greatest athlete—something or someone always turns out greater. Eventually, though, we should arrive at an indisputable point where something really is the absolute greatest—and

17

nothing will ever be its match or equal. Determining this point of greatness sets the stage and focus of this book: recognizing, understanding, and embracing the greatest moment in the Bible.

This event reveals God's ultimate plan and purpose for humanity. It is the single, sovereign, most sensational moment in God's Word. It has no equal. All other moments in the Bible point to this one. To highlight this moment of moments, we will need a Scripture greater than all others—and the Bible holds such a verse. We will also need a greatest word, one that describes God in all His fullness—and the Scriptures contain such a word. Both of these will link together to define the greatest moment of all.

Can Something Be the Greatest?

Yes! According to the Bible, a person, commandment, word, situation, or event can be considered the greatest. There are several cases in point: We find one in Matthew 18:4, where Jesus explains that those who humble themselves as little children can become the greatest in the kingdom of God. In 1 Corinthians 13:13, Paul writes about three great words, with one of them regarded as greater than the other two.

On a different occasion, Jesus tells His twelve followers, who are involved in a heated debate, the greatest disciple is the one who serves the others (Mark 10:41–44). In Matthew 22:36–38, when asked about the foremost law in the Torah, Jesus does not hesitate to quote the greatest commandment of all (Deuteronomy 6:4–5). These are only a few cases that present something as the greatest. This book will offer more detail and other examples in the following chapters.

The Criteria for Greatness

Anyone can say, "I am the greatest" or "this event is the greatest," but making those statements do not make them true. The world's methods of determining greatness are usually biased; they do not reflect God's perspective: "'For My thoughts *are* not your thoughts, nor *are* your ways My ways,' says the LORD. 'For *as* the heavens are higher than the earth, so are My ways higher than your ways, and My thoughts than your thoughts'" (Isaiah 55:8–9).

God's ways are lofty indeed, and His benchmarks for greatness are established in heaven. No wonder humanity has difficulty sorting out the proper meanings. More often than not, the world's least significant circumstances end up having the most significance in the kingdom of God. This concept is the *less is more* principle, highlighted in the next chapter. Still, the world often ignores this divine contradiction. It assumes the most prominent person or most influential individual is also the greatest. However, God does not view greatness in this fashion and probably never will. So here we have it—God's criteria for greatness—God's way. This is the way of true greatness.

Balancing Understanding

Fortunately, we have certain guidelines that help determine and distinguish greatness. One of them is The Rule of the Greatest. This rule acts like a plumb line so the walls of understanding are built properly. A plumb line is a leveling apparatus with a weighted cord. According to a vision given to Amos, God used such a device to measure His people for uprightness (Amos 7:7–8). We will use ours to align truth and balance understanding.

Jesus gave His disciples a similar measuring tool. He wanted them to understand the *Parable of the Sower* before learning the lessons

19

from the other parables. "And He said to them, 'Do you not understand this parable? How then will you understand all the parables?'" (Mark 4:13). Proper understanding is important, but so is "rightly dividing the word of truth" (2 Timothy 2:15). We will need both.

Before we delve deeper into the ways of greatness, a refresher course on absolutes will help enlighten us. The Rule of the Greatest and other biblical guidelines are next.

Chapter 2

The Rule of the Greatest

To be filled with God is a great thing; to be filled with the fullness
of God is still greater; to be filled with all the fullness
of God is greatest of all.

—Adam Clarke

G rowing up, we learn to obey many rules in order to stay within
the boundaries determined by our society. Sometimes, teen-
agers have a harder time appreciating these necessary rules, and I was
no exception. However, my perception changed the day I enrolled in
a driver-training course offered at my high school.

Our instructor, also the head football coach, addressed our class
as if we were trying out for the starting lineup on the varsity team.
Actually, only three of us were on the football team. We had grown
accustomed to his gruff voice; the rest of the class had not. As he spoke,
they sank into their seats, wondering how to get an early transfer out
of his class. "Listen up you guys!" he shouted. "You'll not be driving
for me until you know the rules of the game."

I'm sure our instructor didn't mean to imply driving was a game, but everyone got his point. None of us wanted to sit on the sidelines that week, either. By the end of the course, we realized the importance of driver training and experience, but nothing proved more essential than knowing the rules of the road.

A Great Rule

God also has rules governing the boundaries of His kingdom. I call one of them, "The Rule of the Greatest." Elementary school teachers are often the first to introduce this basic rule generally associated with grammar. Miss Barnes, my fourth grade teacher, explained it this way: first start with a person, place, or thing that is great, and then add more to make it greater. Her lesson was my first exposure to comparative and superlative adjectives. I still remember her illustration about the three friends who dreamed of becoming great scientists. Their names were Jan, Stan, and Maryann.

Jan attended a prestigious college, studied hard, and became a great science teacher. I am sure there were other variables, but Miss Barnes always kept her illustrations simple. The second friend, Stan, went to the same institution and acquired the same knowledge as Jan. However, Stan attended graduate school where he learned more about science. Therefore, Stan was greater in his field of study. Greater will always include what is great, plus more.

Not wanting to be outdone, Maryann attended the same two colleges as her friends and then enrolled in a third school. She gained the knowledge of her first friend (who was great), the knowledge of the second friend (who was greater), and then accrued even more understanding from the third college. Consequently, Maryann became the greatest scientist of the three, at least in accumulated learning.

Although this example is simplistic, it illustrates the progressive nature and essence of greatness. This important rule, however, has applications beyond grammar.

A Great Scripture

Consider the following portions of Scripture found in John 3:16: "For God so loved the world…" These six little words reveal one of the greatest truths in the Bible. Our God is a God of love. Some Bible scholars have reasoned that *Love* in its truest form is a name for or title of our God—for God is love (1 John 4:8, 16). Not only is God love, He is the only one who passionately loves every person in this world. The first portion of this verse makes a great statement.

When we add: "For God so loved the world *that He gave His only begotten Son…*" The statement now becomes greater because it contains what is great, plus more. Not only does God love us, He manifested that love by sending us a precious gift—His only Son. Here we see a divine truth revealed: unselfish love begets lavish giving.

When we further add: "For God so loved the world that He gave His only begotten Son, *that whoever believes in Him…*" The statement becomes even greater and more precise because it reveals more about God's purpose. God loves us, has demonstrated His love, and now calls on us to exhibit faith in His only Son.

Thankfully, the verse does not stop there but goes on to say, "For God so loved the world that He gave His only begotten Son, that whoever believes in Him *should not perish but have everlasting life.*" The complete Scripture expresses the greatest meaning since it encompasses every truth preceding it, including the promise of eternal life.

This is how The Rule of the Greatest works. To regard a Scripture, a moment in time, or a single word as the absolute greatest, it must be all-inclusive. Depending on the category, it should embrace every attribute, hold the highest meaning, or reveal the complete purpose. John 3:16 is certainly one of the greatest Scriptures, but it is not the greatest. The Bible has even greater verses.

The Less Is More Principle

Just as rules of the road are necessary for driving the highways, biblical guidelines are essential for traveling through God's kingdom. Several of these guidelines comprise the *less is more* principle. In the parable below, Jesus explains how the least emerges as the greatest:

> Another parable He put forth to them, saying: "The kingdom of heaven is like a mustard seed, which a man took and sowed in his field, which indeed is the least of all the seeds; but when it is grown it is greater than the herbs and becomes a tree, so that the birds of the air come and nest in its branches." (Matthew 13:31–32)

A disagreement among Jesus' disciples, mentioned in the previous chapter, provides another look at this principle:

> And He said to them, "The kings of the Gentiles exercise lordship over them, and those who exercise authority over them are called 'benefactors.' But not so *among* you; on the contrary, he who is greatest among you, let him be as the younger, and he who governs as he who serves. For who *is* greater, he who sits at the table, or he who serves?" (Luke 22:25–27*a*)

These two examples are representative of greatness in the kingdom of heaven. Ironically, what humanity regards as less, God esteems as more.

A Helpful Checklist

Many biblical guidelines exist, but the following eight are uniquely suited for balancing and establishing truth according to God's viewpoint. These scriptural guidelines will serve as a checklist, summarizing the correct path to greatness.

- ✓ The greatest lord is servant of all (Mark 10:42–44; Matthew 20:26–28; John 13:5–16).
- ✓ The most humbled are the most exalted (Matthew 23:12; Luke 18:10–14; Matthew 18:4).
- ✓ The least things are the greatest (Luke 9:48; Ephesians 3:8; 1 Corinthians 12:22–24).
- ✓ We lose life to find it (Matthew 10:39; Luke 9:23–24).
- ✓ Death is gain; loss is victory (Philippians 1:21; 1 Corinthians 15:54–55; Philippians 3:8).
- ✓ The last will be first (Mark 9:35; Matthew 20:16; Luke 13:30).
- ✓ Few are greater than many (Judges 7:6–7; 1 Samuel 14:6; Deuteronomy 32:30–31).
- ✓ The weakest are the strongest (2 Corinthians 12:10; Joel 3:10; Judges 6:15–16).

Refer to this checklist as you journey through the sensational moments in this book. They will help you recognize the events and people that are truly the greatest. Only in God's kingdom can the last be first, loss become gain, and the least moment turn out as the greatest of all. These spiritual contradictions, and others like them, will help us discern things according to God's perspective.

Follow the Moments

We have seen how to use The Rule of the Greatest and reviewed eight biblical guidelines that help determine, validate, and distinguish greatness. Now it is time to layer the Bible's greatest words, Scriptures, and events upon each other—and follow their path to the greatest moment.

To set the proper groundwork, we must venture back to eternity past, a time before the foundation of the world.

PART TWO:

MOMENTS FROM CREATION

CHAPTER *3*

BEFORE THE FOUNDATION
OF THE WORLD

I will open My mouth in parables;
I will utter things kept secret from the foundation of the world.
—Matthew 13:35

When I was four years old, I helped my father build an addition for our one bedroom house. At the time, I didn't realize what he was doing when he began digging in the backyard, but it looked like fun so I offered to help. Using my yellow toy shovel to dig holes and my plastic bucket to haul away the dirt, I worked right alongside my dad. Sometimes, he even let me use his wheelbarrow. It took a while to learn the proper balance, but when I did, I enjoyed pushing this one-wheeled cart around because it made me feel older, like a grownup.

After a few weeks of excavation, Dad and I finished three trenches about twice the length of my swing set, forming a boxlike shape at the back of the house. Then we dug a smaller ditch running down the middle, connecting both ends. We nailed some boards together and put them inside the trenches. By the time the first delivery truck arrived with a load of sand, gravel, and these heavy bags of gray stuff, I could see a pattern developing. Even before we poured the foundation or framed one wall, I realized what my father had planned: a new bedroom for my sister and me.

God's plans were also taking shape before the universe was framed. Although most history from the early days of eternity remains a mystery, not everything is a secret. Some of His greatest revelations appear in reverse order: "*I am* God, and *there is* none like Me, declaring the end from the beginning, and from ancient times *things* that are not *yet* done" (see Isaiah 46:9, 10). God placed specific verses in our Bibles that allow glimpses into eternity past. These prophetic Scriptures hold important truths and give clues to God's intentions—long before the foundation of the world.

Loved before the Foundation

"Father, I desire that they also whom You gave Me may be with Me where I am, that they may behold My glory which You have given Me; for You loved Me before the foundation of the world" (John 17:24).

Love is multifaceted. It is one of the greatest feelings or emotions ever, but love is also a commitment. It is the main reason why people get married, volunteers reach out to help the homeless, and missionaries move to foreign lands to share their ministries. Love, however, isn't just a human trait—it's a divine one—an attribute in which our heavenly Father excels. Love is as eternal as God Himself. If we were to use one word to describe God, the word would be love, "for God is love" (1 John 4:8).

In eternity past, long before humanity existed, God loved His Son and His Son loved Him. Their mutual bond embraced holiness, righteousness, trustworthiness, and perfect love. This loving relationship would set the pattern for every foundation God built.

The Trinity Revealed

"Come near to Me, hear this: I have not spoken in secret from the beginning; from the time that it was, I was there. And now the Lord GOD and His Spirit have sent Me" (Isaiah 48:16).

Isaiah, one of the most credible prophets in the Bible, reveals a precious truth about God's nature from eternity past. "And now the Lord GOD *[Heavenly Father]* and His Spirit *[Holy Spirit]* have sent Me *[Son of God]*" (48:16b, emphasis mine). For a lack of better terms, we call this divine association the Trinity. God is one God, yet somehow He manifests Himself in three persons or identities: Father, Son, and Holy Spirit. All are tangible, separate, and share total unity. I really cannot explain this miraculous relationship, although in the past I have made several attempts.

One Sunday while preaching a sermon on the mystery of Godliness, I tried to illustrate the Trinity. I told my congregation God was like an apple—one fruit with three parts: the core, the fruity middle, and the peel. Feeling really anointed, I further elaborated: God is also like water, which can be liquid, steam, or even an ice cube. Then, right in the middle of my explanation, I heard God speak to my heart. In essence, He said, *I am many things, Charles, but I am not like an ice cube or an apple. Please stop using those terms to describe My majesty.* After the longest pause, I concluded my sermon and invited our church members to join me at the altar. Although I believe in the doctrine of the Trinity, that day was the last time I attempted to analyze or dissect the oneness of God. Some things are better left alone in all their awe and splendor.

In another prophecy, Isaiah mentions both the LORD and his Redeemer. "Thus says the LORD, the King of Israel, and his Redeemer, the LORD of hosts: 'I *am* the First and I *am* the Last; Besides Me *there is* no God'" (Isaiah 44:6).

Whenever LORD appears in small caps, like in the previous verse, the Bible is referring to the proper name of God, written *YHWH*.[2] The Authorized Version uses all caps: LORD, for the same indication. Since God's proper name is very holy, devout followers would not speak it aloud, so they substituted *Adonai* (my Lord) in its place. Later on, the Hebrew vowel points for *Adonai* were added to the consonants of *YHWH* to remind readers to use *Adonai* when saying His name. Certain biblical scholars believed this formed the name Jehovah. Other experts felt the transliteration should be Yahweh. The name debate continues unabated. As for this book, we will use the more pronounceable name of Yahweh in place of *YHWH* whenever applicable.

Having resolved the name issue for now, let us take a closer look at Isaiah's prophetic word: "Thus says the LORD, the King of Israel, and his Redeemer, the LORD of hosts" (v. 6). In this passage, Isaiah describes two persons of the Trinity: the LORD (Yahweh), the King of Israel, and his Redeemer *(ga'al),* the LORD (Yahweh) of hosts. Although some Bible versions vary on wording and placement, which is normal for translations, the Authorized, New Revised Standard, New American Standard, English Standard, Darby, and other qualified versions concur: Yahweh and his Redeemer appear to be two distinct Lords that share the name *YHWH*. The Scriptures later reveal this Redeemer to be the Christ, the Son of the living God (see Matthew 16:16). Perhaps more revealing is the passage from John's gospel: "In the beginning was the Word, and the Word was with God, and the Word was God" (John 1:1).

The New Testament has even more revelations concerning the triune nature of God. The ones below come from the Gospel of John, chapters 14 through 17:

→ The Son refers to God as My Father (14:7, 23; 15:24).

→ His Father shares His glory and authority with His Son (17:1–2, 5, 22).

→ The Father and His Son are one and function in total unity (14:9–11; 17:21–22).

→ The Spirit of truth comes from God in the Son's name (14:26; 15:26).

→ The Helper guides, teaches, and comforts (14:26; 16:13).

→ The Spirit is eternal with holy attributes (14:16; 16:8, 14).

The Father, Son, and Holy Spirit share the same divine nature and triunity, and They have done so even before the Creation began. Yet for the most part, the mystery of the Godhead remains a glorious secret from ages past.

Slain before the Foundation

"All who dwell on the earth will worship him, whose names have not been written in the Book of Life of the Lamb slain from the foundation of the world" (Revelation 13:8). This Scripture contains a truth within a truth. It mentions a book registry in heaven authored by the Lamb of God and then tells us the Lamb was slain from the foundation of the world. The indication is this slaying happened beforehand. The New International Version says, "the Lamb who was slain from the creation of the world." Several translations concur, including *Nestle Aland 26th Edition Greek New Testament,* which shows the Lamb has already been slaughtered:[3]

βιβλίῳ	τῆς	ζωῆς	τοῦ	ἀρνίου	τοῦ	ἐσφαγμένου	ἀπὸ	καταβολῆς	Κόσμου.
small book	*of the life*		*of the lamb*		*the*	*one having been slaughtered*	*from*	*foundation*	*of world.*

No matter how we read it, something transpired before the dawning of the universe, something critical to God's plan.

If the Lamb of God was truly slain, then some aspect of death resulted. That's what a slaying is—a certain type of death. Perhaps this event occurred when the Father introduced His plan for redemption and asked His Son to serve as the sacrificial ransom. Maybe it was a trial run for Golgotha. No doubt, the Spirit of truth played an integral part in whatever happened that day. Angels who existed before the Creation may have witnessed this special moment, but I can only speculate about the details or its importance.

When my cousin, Dalton Ray, and I were eight years old, we made promises to each other and signed these agreements with our blood. We considered these oaths unbreakable. Although some might consider it a game, to us cousins it was serious business. Even today, I still honor the promises I made to him. Perhaps the slaying mentioned in Revelation 13:8 refers to a special agreement or blood oath given by the Lamb and accepted by God. Maybe the Son sacrificed His will: "Abba, Father,... not what I will, but what You *will*" (Mark 14:36). Either way, some type of slaying took place prior to Calvary.

What seems certain, however, is that God and His Son reached the final moment of decision, a point of no return. They must commit now or abort their plans. Which plans? All of them: creation, redemption, salvation, the greatest moment. God would put everything on the line, including His only Son. The stakes would be high, the rewards glorious. Once they started, a divine chain reaction would take place. The Son of God would become the Lamb of God, and through death, give His life as a ransom for many. His choice would forever change eternity. Apparently, His sacrifice began long before the foundation of the world.

"But with the precious blood of Christ, as of a lamb without blemish and without spot. He indeed was foreordained before the foundation of the world, but was manifest in these last times for you who through Him believe in God, who raised Him from the dead and gave Him glory, so that your faith and hope are in God" (1 Peter 1:19–21).

The "In Him" Decision

"He chose us in Him before the foundation of the world, that we should be holy and without blame before Him in love" (Ephesians 1:4*b*). Long before the creation of the world, God made a decision to use an inward relationship for salvation. The fulfillment of His plans would focus around this one choice. God would be with us through Christ who is in us. This would be His greatest hope for humanity. "The mystery which has been hidden from ages and from generations, but now has been revealed to His saints. To them God willed to make known what are the riches of the glory of this mystery among the Gentiles: which is Christ in you, the hope of glory" (Colossians 1:26–27).

Before the World Existed

We often picture eternity past as a dark, empty place, devoid of life; but in truth, many tangible things existed there. God's glory was one of them. "So now, Father, glorify me in your own presence with the glory that I had in your presence before the world existed" (John 17:5 NRSV).

What ancient glory did God share with His Son before the world existed, and how did this glory manifest itself? The Scriptures do not elaborate. Still, I am reasonably sure that God did not hang around in eternity past and do nothing. Therefore, if God revealed His glory in ages past, then great and marvelous things must have happened. His résumé of glorious deeds undoubtedly tracks backward, long before our universe began.

Angels also lived in eternity past. How far back they go or when God made them, no one really knows. Still, angels watched in awe as God laid the foundations of the earth, and they shouted for joy (Job 38:4, 7). The Bible says they were created to serve God. "Praise the LORD, you his angels, you mighty ones who do his bidding, who obey his word" (Psalm 103:20 NIV). God made seraphim, cherubim, numerous ranks of angels, and at least one archangel. Some are messengers, others are warriors, many are guardians, and according to Jacob (Genesis 32:24), one angelic being, probably the Lord Himself, appeared as a wrestler. Collectively, we know them as the heavenly host. Several Scriptures refer to angels as morning stars or sons of God (Job 1:6; 38:7). Like sons, God gave them the freedom of choice. Sadly, one third of their number chose to rebel against Him (see Revelation 12:3–9).

Before recorded time, hosts of angels sang about the glory of God. Their praises echoed through an ageless eternity, containing additional secrets and wonders.

In Ages Past

The Scriptures mention three more things that existed in ages past: a prepared kingdom, hidden wisdom, and the deep things of God.

Let's touch on God's kingdom first. Here again, we see a truth placed within the context of another truth.

"Then the King will say to those on His right hand, 'Come, you blessed of My Father, inherit the kingdom prepared for you from the foundation of the world'" (Matthew 25:34). Most Christians believe in a heavenly kingdom, but according to the Bible, the King created and prepared His kingdom in eternity past. This glorious realm is not a figurative domain, nor a temporary residence, but a permanent place all true believers can inherit. And it has been ready and waiting since the foundation of the world.

God also ordained wisdom but kept this knowledge hidden in eternity past. Wisdom and knowledge, though similar, have one main difference: Knowledge is something we know. Wisdom perceives what to do with what we know. The discovery of atomic energy was a knowledge issue. What to do with this powerful energy becomes a wisdom issue. Seemingly, wisdom is more important than knowledge. Such are the mysteries of God. They contain great truths, but how will we handle them—with wisdom or indifference? Maybe that's why God revealed His ancient wisdom in bits and pieces and only when it suited His purpose and timing. "However, we speak wisdom among those who are mature, yet not the wisdom of this age, nor of the rulers of this age, who are coming to nothing. But we speak the wisdom of God in a mystery, the hidden *wisdom* which God ordained before the ages for our glory, which none of the rulers of this age knew; for had they known, they would not have crucified the Lord of glory" (1 Corinthians 2:6–8).

Concerning the deep things of God, we should thank the Holy Spirit since He is the one who teaches them to us. I believe the Bible holds many deep truths; one of them is the greatest moment. As you prayerfully consider the Scriptures, truths, and moments highlighted in this book, ask the Holy Spirit to reveal all the mysteries of God. "These are the things God has revealed to us by his Spirit. The Spirit searches all things, even the deep things of God" (1 Corinthians 2:10 NIV).

The Works Were Finished

"For we also have had the good news proclaimed to us, just as they did; but the message they heard was of no value to them, because they did not share the faith of those who obeyed…. And yet his works have been finished since the creation of the world" (Hebrews 4:2–3 NIV). Apostle Paul would later describe some of these works in his epistle to the Ephesians.

> Blessed *be* the God and Father of our Lord Jesus Christ, who has blessed us with every spiritual blessing in the heavenly *places* in Christ, just as He chose us in Him before the foundation of the world, that we would be holy and blameless before Him. In love He predestined us to adoption as sons through Jesus Christ to Himself, according to the kind intention of His will, to the praise of the glory of His grace, which He freely bestowed on us in the Beloved. In Him we have redemption through His blood, the forgiveness of our trespasses, according to the riches of His grace. (Ephesians 1:3–7 NASB)

All these works of God, and others not mentioned yet, began long before the creation of our universe. How it all happened, I can only guess. Nevertheless, the Lamb of God was slain, we were chosen in Him, our adoption papers were drawn up, and God prepared a divine kingdom—all before the foundation of the world. These things would set the stage for what followed, including the greatest moment of all. You may well see that moment referenced in the previous passage. But for now, other moments are waiting their turn. God was ready to speak His first word into a deep void of apparent nothingness. Countless ages of darkness would end in a moment of dazzling glory.

CHAPTER 4

GOD SPEAKS A WORD

Nothing with God can be accidental.

—Henry Wadsworth Longfellow

Have you ever observed the midnight sky on a cloudless night? The view is dazzling, as countless stars shine against a backdrop of total blackness. These specks of light glisten in bold patterns when unhindered by the glare of city lights. It is easy to be drawn in and sit silently transfixed, watching the twinkling horizon for hours. Such tiny shimmerings in the night provide a small glimpse of something much larger, offering only a hint of what they truly represent.

One might be a distant sun, burning brightly in the middle of the Milky Way galaxy. Another may not be a star at all, but a neighboring planet reflecting light within our own solar system. Maybe the twinkling nightlight is not one but many stars, forming their own galaxy billions of light years away. These stellar bodies not only illuminate the evening horizon but also the minds of those who pause for a moment and ponder the vastness of the universe itself.

"Lift up your eyes and look to the heavens: Who created all these? He who brings out the starry host one by one and calls forth each of them by name. Because of his great power and mighty strength, not one of them is missing" (Isaiah 40:26 NIV).

Through the years, many have attempted to count and name this starry host. Early astronomers identified stars with proper names. Today, the International Astronomical Union recognizes them by their catalog information and coordinates. Even after thousands of years of observation, the total number of stars in the heavens remains unknown. How they came into being is another question — one in which scientific theories can only speculate.

What's Really out There?

With the help of orbital telescopes, better methods of magnification, space probes, and gravitational lensing, the windows into space have opened wider. Telescopes such as Hubble and Kepler have been instrumental in these efforts, enabling us to see farther out into space than ever before. Astronomers now estimate we have 225 billion galaxies in the observable universe.[4] They determine this total by counting galaxies in a small area of sky and then multiplying that number to account for the remaining regions. No doubt, the total will increase as exploration methods improve, making distant stars and smaller galaxies easier to detect.

The Milky Way, our home galaxy, has about 400 billion stars.[5] Of course, this figure is an estimate too. One would think counting the stars would quell our curiosity, but now thanks to the transit method, we also count exoplanets, which are planets orbiting stars outside our solar system. If a planet transits in front of a distant star, the visual brightness of the star drops a minute amount. Although not viewable at this distance, its presence can be inferred. Astronomers have located thousands of these exoplanets: some confirmed, others candidates pending validation. NASA logs each new discovery in their exoplanet archive.[6] God, however, does not need to estimate counts or analyze data. According to Isaiah, He knows the exact number of galaxies, stars, and planets in His universe (Isaiah 40:26).

When astronomers mention the whole universe, they are usually referring to the observable universe. If someone traveled at the speed of light, it would take almost fourteen billion years to reach that vista. Until someone discovers warp technology or how to bend space and time, any such trip is out of the question.

Still, my interest is piqued. I'm curious about what lies beyond the last star or the farthest-most galaxy in our universe. The outer reaches of space are obviously extensive. But does the cosmos have a limit or boundary? If so, where does the threshold end? On the other hand, what if space has no boundaries and spreads out endlessly, forever. Where is it going? More importantly, how did this vast, infinite region come into existence in the first place? These questions, mind-boggling as they are, point us back to one of the greatest statements in the Bible: "In the beginning God created the heavens and the earth" (Genesis 1:1).

The Beginning of Things

Theoretical physicists tell us space as we know it, emerged from some unverified anomaly known as the Big Bang. According to this popular theory about the creation of the universe, all matter, energy, space, and even time itself, began at this epicenter of nothingness. Using the scientific method of analysis, they speculated that energy and matter were confined into one tiny spot in the universe, just a few millimeters across. Then for an unexplained reason, this ancient, extremely hot, unknown type of energy or matter exploded in some fashion, spreading outward at tremendous speeds. Experts in cosmology believe this singularity happened about 13.8 billion years ago. For them, this event marked the birth of the universe. Their view, of course, is only a theory.

Cosmologists have other theories as well. One of these proposes a cyclic model where the universe was born not just once but multiple times, in endless cycles of fiery death and rebirth. Though controversial, this theory parallels the Bible on one point: One day, our world will experience a rebirth—the planet will melt with fervent heat and the heavens dissolve by burning fire—and we will see a new heaven and a new earth (Revelation 21:1; 2 Peter 3:10, 13).

At this point, it might be best to contrast the difference between a theory and the truth. Theories are humanity's best guess regarding a certain subject, based on scientific fact and secular conjecture. Most theories need updating from time to time as new discoveries and information become available. Truths are different. They are constant, unwavering, and not dependent on human analysis. The truth is simply the truth, with or without the facts to prove it, and biblical truth is the highest truth of all. God reveals these truths to us, spiritual or otherwise, through the Holy Scriptures.

So what existed before this Big Bang? Secular scientists will sidestep this issue, offer supposed concepts, or say nothing existed. Still, something must have been out there first that facilitated this unprecedented event. According to *Astronomy: The Definitive Guide,* there was no bang, no explosion, just an unfolding of some type, coming from a region no larger than a period.[7] For comparison purposes, here is the size (.) of this so-called area.

To me, God's narrative of Creation seems more believable. Nevertheless, for the sake of argument, let us say a small amount of ancient, unknown, extremely hot energy or matter exploded or unfolded in some fashion, thereby creating space and time. How did this tiny speck of "whatever" prevail in the nothingness of time and space? When did it arrive? What mode of transportation did it use? Was our little speck waiting long before unfolding or exploding? And what caused it to turn cataclysmic? Maybe the more pertinent question is—did someone create it? To me, the "Bang" theory sorely needs a spiritual rewrite that includes God and the variable called faith. "By faith we understand that the worlds were framed by the word of God, so that the things which are seen were not made of things which are visible" (Hebrews 11:3).

The Face of the Deep

According to the Bible, which deals with truth and not theories, the pre-universe contained a vast region of emptiness devoid of light. "The earth was without form, and void; and darkness *was* on the face of the deep. And the Spirit of God was hovering over the face of the waters" (Genesis 1:2). In the beginning of things, our planet had no shape or substance, which means it didn't exist. However, the face of the deep did, and the Spirit of God moved through this place of deep emptiness, hovering over endless seas of empty space. The Hebrew word *rachaph* is translated hover, but it can also mean shake or flutter.[8] As the Spirit shook and hovered over the face of the waters, one of the most enlightening moments of Creation awaited its unveiling.

The Scriptures confirm that the face of the deep prevailed before God spoke His first word, long before any theorized Big Bang. This deep void, which we now call outer space, was real and tangible. We can still look up into the night sky and see a portion of this void but never the end of it. Since the Lord made everything, then He must have made the darkness as well. This place, however, was not as dark as it seemed. "Even the darkness is not dark to You, and the night is as bright as the day. Darkness and light are alike *to You*" (Psalm 139:12 NASB). Out of this perfect darkness, God spoke His first word—at least the first one we know about.

First Word, First Day

"And God said, Let there be light: and there was light. And God saw the light, that it was good: and God divided the light from the darkness. And God called the light Day, and the darkness he called Night. And the evening and the morning were the first day" (Genesis 1:3–5 KJV).

Can you imagine what it would be like to see light burst forth from darkness? During one of our family vacations, we visited the Carlsbad Caverns in New Mexico. These caves are truly amazing. When we arrived at the central cavern, our guide turned off all the lights. The place went pitch-dark. I couldn't see my hand in front of my eyes or my parents standing beside me. After a few seconds, which seemed like minutes, our guide flipped the switch back on again. Light ripped away the darkness in a moment of dazzling brilliance. It hurt my eyes, but I enjoyed the demonstration. Perhaps the first day of Creation had a similar impact.

The Bible says the angels watched as God created the heavens and the earth: "Where were you when I laid the earth's foundation?… while the morning stars sang together and all the angels shouted for joy?" (Job 38:4–7 NIV). I wonder if these angels had to shield their eyes on the dawning of the first day. Seeing light engulf the darkness of space must have been a glorious experience for them. But what was that light?

According to the Bible, this light was not sunlight or moonlight because God would create the sun and moon on the fourth day. Was it a supernatural phenomenon, an unknown anomaly, or the unveiling of a divine presence? One can only wonder. Still, God is the light of the world, and one day in heaven He will do away with our need for sunlight or conventional lighting: "And there will be no more night; they need no light of lamp or sun, for the Lord God will be their light, and they will reign forever and ever" (Revelation 22:5 NRSV). It is entirely possible the light mentioned in Genesis 1:3 was not created; instead, it simply manifested or illuminated itself: "Then God said, 'Let there be light'; and there was light" (v. 3).

The first day ended well, but God had more planned: a full week of festivities and miracles were on the docket.

Just Getting Started

"And God said, Let there be a firmament in the midst of the waters, and let it divide the waters from the waters. And God made the firmament, and divided the waters which *were* under the firmament from the waters which *were* above the firmament: and it was so. And God called the firmament Heaven. And the evening and the morning were the second day" (Genesis 1:6–8 KJV). The waters above the firmament (or heavens) were probably the vast seas of outer space.

On the third day, God made oceans and formed dry patches of ground. "And God said, Let the waters under the heaven be gathered together unto one place, and let the dry *land* appear: and it was so. And God called the dry *land* Earth; and the gathering together of the waters called he Seas: and God saw that *it was* good" (Genesis 1:9–10 KJV).

Everything proceeded as planned: great miracles were followed by even greater ones. "For this is what the LORD says—he who created the heavens, he is God; he who fashioned and made the earth, he founded it; he did not create it to be empty, but formed it to be inhabited" (Isaiah 45:18*a* NIV). Emptiness would never rule the day again.

By the end of the third day, plants, trees, grasses, and herbs of every kind covered the earth. A few days later, it contained sea creatures, fish, and birds. On the sixth day, God created every kind of land animal and creature. He also made insects of every shape and design—all with their part to play in the cycle of life. It's hard to fathom it all. Can you imagine the planning that goes into making a mosquito prototype? Such a pesky little creature and effective too! It can fly almost undetected, land on an unsuspecting target, drill a hole, suck out some blood, and leave before the victim realizes what happened. By the time you hear a z-z-z-z sound in your ear, it's too late; the stealthy mosquito has completed his mission. And some say God doesn't have a sense of humor. His flair for style, His wit, and His divine goodness are seen in every creative word He uttered while designing our universe. "The heavens declare the glory of God; and the firmament shows His handiwork" (Psalm 19:1).

Above and beyond the Firmament

After years of comparative measurements, scientists now believe the firmament (or universe) is expanding at an ever-increasing rate—a fact not lost to the Scriptures: "*It is* He who sits above the circle of the earth,... who stretches out the heavens like a curtain, and spreads them out like a tent to dwell in" (Isaiah 40:22). "Indeed My hand has laid the foundation of the earth, and My right hand has stretched out the heavens; *when* I call to them, they stand up together" (Isaiah 48:13). Only God knows the extent of the universe, where it is going, and how far it will expand. Apparently, the heavens are more extensive than astronomers realize.

The Bible tells us the Lord ascended far above all the heavens (Ephesians 4:10). So apparently, there are other heavens. The first heaven is the earth's atmosphere. The second is probably the realm of the stars, planets, black holes, quasars, and other space phenomenon. The third heaven, according to Paul's writings, lies beyond the first two and includes a place called Paradise (see 2 Corinthians 12:2–4). Only a divine, supreme Deity could create such a place. It is beyond anything we can imagine. "But as it is written: '*Eye has not seen, nor ear heard, nor have entered into the heart of man the things which God has prepared for those who love Him*'" (1 Corinthians 2:9).

The eternal resting place we call heaven is real, and it has many wonders to reveal. Are there other heavens beyond that, other wonders? No doubt there are. What about other universes or dimensions? No one really knows, but if such places do exist, one thing is certain—the Lord God would rule over those domains as well. Moreover, to offer us peace of mind, God says we have nothing to fear from gods or demigods. He has not seen one of them in or beyond His heavens.

I am the first and I am the last, and there is no God besides Me. Who is like Me? Let him proclaim and declare it; yes, let him recount it to Me in order, from the time that I established the ancient nation. And let them declare to them the things that are coming and the events that are going to take place.

Do not tremble and do not be afraid; have I not long since announced *it* to you and declared *it?* And you are My witnesses. Is there any God besides Me, or is there any *other* Rock? I know of none. (Isaiah 44:6*b*–8 NASB)

The Word of the Lord

"By the word of the LORD the heavens were made, and all the host of them by the breath of His mouth. He gathers the waters of the sea together as a heap; He lays up the deep in storehouses. Let all the earth fear the LORD; let all the inhabitants of the world stand in awe of Him. For He spoke, and it was *done;* He commanded, and it stood fast" (Psalm 33:6–9).

The words God spoke created everything in the universe, but He was not finished. He needed to decorate the earth—spruce the place up a bit—make it more hospitable. A pleasant garden would be perfect.

CHAPTER 5

A GARDEN IS PLANTED

There is not one blade of grass, there is no colour in this world,
that is not intended to make us rejoice.
—John Calvin

My next-door neighbor had a garden; so did the couple across the
street. In fact, everyone on our block had one. Most of them
grew vegetable gardens. A few residents owned vineyards with various
grapes and berries. One yard featured a small orchard of orange trees.
It didn't seem to matter if people were homeowners or renters; if they
had any space in their yard, they raised a garden. When one lives in an
agricultural area like Reedley, California, having a garden is a given.

All my neighbors were hospitable, too, always willing to share some
of their harvest with needy friends. They usually gave away their extra
zucchini. It came in many forms: zucchini bread, zucchini pie, stuffed
zucchini, batter-dipped and pan-fried, and endless dishes of zucchini
casserole. I soon tired of eating it. Finally, I decided to plant my own
vegetable garden and stock it with zucchini squash; then I could hon-
estly say, "No thanks!" to all their offerings of zucchini benevolence.

Being a novice gardener, however, created problems. I had no idea what to do, so I improvised. My neighbors shook their heads in disbelief as I used a ruler to measure seed depth and spacing between rows. I spent hours in my garden, tilling the ground with a shovel, pulling weeds that sprang up out of nowhere, and watering each plant using a plastic bucket. It took hours to get the recommended amount of moisture to each plant. To my neighbors, I must have looked like a foolish amateur, which was probably a good assessment of my horticultural skills. I only wanted my garden to succeed and look beautiful—a place I could show to my friends with pride. Sadly, most of the plants died. Thinking back on my efforts, I should have asked for advice from a master gardener.

Planting Paradise

On the third day of Creation, God made all the vegetation on the earth and gave it a unique way to grow and reproduce called photosynthesis. Plants, grasses, and trees would take in water and carbon dioxide, converting it into breathable oxygen and edible nutrients. The whole process operated by light—an ingenious idea. Someday, a space probe may visit another habitable planet in our galaxy and find evidence of plant life. If it does, then God would have created those plants as well. "All things were made through Him, and without Him nothing was made that was made" (John 1:3).

However, one spot on earth was unique. God did not create it; He planted it. "The LORD God planted a garden eastward in Eden" (Genesis 2:8*a*). According to John Gill's *Exposition of the Bible,* this planting occurred on the third day. Other qualified scholars and Bible commentaries also concur with John Gill's view. Moreover, the Hebrew word, *nata*ʿ, indicates an actual planting (to place seeds or rootstock in the ground for agricultural purposes).[9] How it all happened, I have no idea, but the place must have looked beautiful: a paradise with lawns, decorative shrubbery, shade trees, various fruits, vineyards, and delicious vegetables of every kind. God placed His garden east of Eden where a river watered and nourished it.

Eden's River and Garden

"Now a river went out of Eden to water the garden, and from there it parted and became four riverheads" (Genesis 2:10). Over the years, many have asked where Eden was located. If we use two of these four riverheads (or tributaries) as reference points, then we have two possibilities—depending on whether "head" in riverhead refers to the source or mouth of these rivers. Head, *ro'sh* in Hebrew, also translates as front, principle, division, or beginning.[10] It can mean the beginning of a branch moving downstream or the beginning going upstream. Both interpretations are feasible.

If going upstream (the source), then Eden would be somewhere in eastern Turkey, because that is where we find the headwaters for two known tributaries. This interpretation would place one boundary of Eden southwest of Mount Ararat. If moving downstream (the mouth), then Eden would lie somewhere in Lower Mesopotamia, which includes parts of Iraq and Iran. The latter interpretation seems more likely. Either way, the garden was located eastward in Eden, perhaps placing it as far east as Kuwait near the tip of the Persian Gulf.

Four Tributaries, One Source

The source river flowed eastward through Eden to the garden and supplied four tributaries. "The name of the first *is* Pishon; it *is* the one which skirts the whole land of Havilah, where *there is* gold. And the gold of that land *is* good. Bdellium and the onyx stone *are* there. The name of the second river *is* Gihon; it *is* the one which goes around the whole land of Cush. The name of the third river *is* Hiddekel; it *is* the one which goes toward the east of Assyria. The fourth river *is* the Euphrates" (Genesis 2:11–14).

We can easily identify two tributaries by name and location. They are the Hiddekel, known as the Tigris, and the Euphrates. These rivers still empty their waters into the Persian Gulf. The locations of the other two, Gihon and Pishon, are more speculative. Dr. Juris Zarins and other noted researchers believe the Pishon includes parts of the Wadi Rimah and Wadi Batin watercourses. Geological surveys show these dry riverbeds follow the route of an ancient river that once connected to the Tigris and Euphrates delta. Regarding the Gihon, it could be the modern-day Karun River, which also empties into the Persian Gulf.[11]

These four tributaries in Eden branched off from an unknown source river: "and from there it parted and became four riverheads" (Genesis 2:10*b*). The Euphrates, the longest river in southwest Asia, and the Tigris are still major watercourses. Eden's source river must have been huge, in that it supplied both these tributaries, plus two others. For some reason, though, the primary river remains unnamed in Genesis. One would think the principal water supply would be the better reference. Nevertheless, the names of these four tributaries give us clues about the real nature and identity of this main river.

→ ***Pishon*** means *increase*.

→ ***Gihon*** means *bursting forth*.

→ ***Hiddekel*** (Tigris) means *rapid*.

→ ***Euphrates*** means *fruitfulness*.[12]

If Eden's main river flowed into the above named tributaries, and these tributaries exhibited life-bearing attributes, then maybe the main river also had these traits.

Ezekiel's River of Life

Ezekiel describes another river during the Millennium. It has special features too: The river will be deep, wide, healthy, and its waters will bring life to whatever it touches. It flows from the temple of God in a future-day Jerusalem. Some believe Ezekiel's river is only symbolic, but there's nothing to suggest this passage or context is anything but real. In some ways, the river described below is similar to the unnamed river from Genesis. Here is Ezekiel's narrative:

> Then he brought me back to the door of the house; and behold, water was flowing from under the threshold of the house toward the east, for the house faced east. And the water was flowing down from under, from the right side of the house, from south of the altar.

> He brought me out by way of the north gate and led me around on the outside to the outer gate by way of *the gate* that faces east. And behold, water was trickling from the south side. When the man went out toward the east with a line in his hand, he measured a thousand cubits, and he led me through the water, water *reaching* the ankles.

> Again he measured a thousand and led me through the water, water *reaching* the knees.

> Again he measured a thousand and led me through *the water,* water *reaching* the loins.

Again he measured a thousand; *and it was* a river that
I could not ford, for the water had risen, *enough* water
to swim in, a river that could not be forded. (Ezekiel
47:1–5 NASB)

"*When it* reaches the sea, *its* waters are healed. And it shall be *that*
every living thing that moves, wherever the rivers go, will live. There
will be a very great multitude of fish, because these waters go there; for
they will be healed, and everything will live wherever the river goes"
(Ezekiel 47:8*b*–9).

John's River of Life

In Revelation, the apostle John describes yet another river. It is also
a life-giving river, which contains pure, clear water coming from the
throne of God. John's river has the same properties as the millennial
river described by Ezekiel and the unnamed river found in Genesis.
The tree of life, first found in Eden, is now linked to John's miraculous river of life.

"And he showed me a pure river of water of life, clear as crystal,
proceeding from the throne of God and of the Lamb. In the middle of
its street, and on either side of the river, *was* the tree of life, which bore
twelve fruits, each *tree* yielding its fruit every month. The leaves of the
tree *were* for the healing of the nations" (Revelation 22:1–2).

The three rivers described in Genesis, Ezekiel, and Revelation are
similar. They were tangible, substantial, promoted life and healing, and
they nourished a nearby tree (or group of interconnected trees) with
the same attributes. There is something eternal about these rivers, and
I believe they are one and the same: "a pure river of water of life" (v.
1). How it all works, I do not know. It seems obvious, though, that this

river is not your normal, everyday water source. It has the touch of life upon it and the nature of Christ through it.

Two Trees of the Garden

"And out of the ground the LORD God made every tree grow that is pleasant to the sight and good for food. The tree of life *was* also in the midst of the garden, and the tree of the knowledge of good and evil" (Genesis 2:9). The garden was indeed a wonderful paradise. Besides trees with apples, oranges, pears, and fruits of every kind—there were two fruit trees with special attributes—one dispersed life, the other knowledge. One of them was off-limits.

The Tree of Life

The source river in Eden, which John and Ezekiel later described as possessing life, watered the trees in God's garden, including the tree of life. Genesis doesn't describe this life-giving tree or give its proximity to the river, but Revelation does. Here is what John witnessed from the future: "In the middle of its street, and on either side of the river, *was* the tree of life, which bore twelve fruits, each *tree* yielding its fruit every month. The leaves of the tree *were* for the healing of the nations. And there shall be no more curse, but the throne of God and of the Lamb shall be in it, and His servants shall serve Him" (Revelation 22:2–3).

In this passage, John describes a tree called the tree of life. Although only one tree, it looks like twelve separate trees. The twelve tree sections produce different fruits, each tree bearing its own fruit at the proper time each month. John's encounter goes on to disclose something truly amazing: the leaves from this tree can provide healing for everyone in every nation. His description reveals a remarkable tree with a root system that allows it to grow on each bank of the river of life. This additional information gives us a detailed view of the tree of life, first mentioned in Eden.

Ezekiel describes a similar arrangement of trees along the banks of his millennial river: "Along the bank of the river, on this side and that, will grow all *kinds of* trees used for food; their leaves will not wither, and their fruit will not fail. They will bear fruit every month, because their water flows from the sanctuary. Their fruit will be for food, and their leaves for medicine" (Ezekiel 47:12). Ezekiel's group of trees sounds like the twelve-part tree mentioned in Revelation by John. Furthermore, the roots appear to run underneath the river and connect to trees on the opposite bank. Ezekiel's trees also have different fruits for each month and leaves containing medicinal properties. These trees are likewise nourished by a supernatural river of life, one too deep and wide to cross (see Ezekiel 47:5).

Obviously, the tree from Genesis, the group of interconnected trees in Ezekiel, and the twelve-part tree in Revelation are one and the same: the tree of life. What a precious gift for Eden! God did not restrict access to the tree of life (see Genesis 1:29; 2:16), so eating its life-giving fruit or making tea from its medicinal leaves were definite options. Only later did God classify the "life" tree as off limits (Genesis 3:22, 24). Eating from the "knowledge" tree in the garden, however, was a different matter.

The Tree of Knowledge

"Of every tree of the garden you may freely eat; but of the tree of the knowledge of good and evil you shall not eat, for in the day that you eat of it you shall surely die" (Genesis 2:16b–17). The serpent had a different take on God's only rule for the garden: "For God knows that in the day you eat of it your eyes will be opened, and you will be like God, knowing good and evil" (Genesis 3:5). As usual, the serpent lied by telling a deceptive, half-truth.

The tree of knowledge had several unique features: the fruit looked appealing, tasted good, and increased one's knowledge. However, it had two drawbacks: this new understanding involved evil, and the fruit caused death in some fashion.

Gaining knowledge is admirable, even helpful, but it should not be our ultimate goal in life. According to the last chapter of Ecclesiastes, it is better to live each day listening to the voice of God and following His advice. Timothy tells us that knowledge without truth is a dead end—a fact overlooked by the serpent and those whose minds are corrupted through deception (see 2 Timothy 3:7–9). Humanity would do well to stay away from the tree of knowledge of good and evil. Sadly, the first humans chose otherwise.

A Voice That Walked

Eden held many wonders including the walking voice of God: "And they heard the voice of the LORD God walking in the garden in the cool of the day" (Genesis 3:8a KJV). Voice in this passage is the Hebrew word *qowl*. It can be translated voice, noise, sound, thunder, proclamation, thunderings, or fame.[13] How this voice walked, I cannot even imagine, but considering it was the *qowl* of God, it must have been spectacular. Still, I don't think the "voice or sound" snuck into the garden, unannounced. Rather, it came thundering in, whirlwinds swirling, sounding like a mighty rushing wind, proclaiming God had entered the garden (compare with Acts 2:2).

We know God's voice walked during the cool of the day, but when did that part of the day begin? In the low desert regions of Southern California, the cool of the day came in the early morning before the blazing sun heated up the valley floor. At my favorite campground in the Mount Hood wilderness of Oregon, it arrived midafternoon when a refreshing breeze blew through the canyons, cooling the temperature. In my hometown, the cool of the day began at eventide, after the hot sun disappeared below the San Gabriel Mountains. So I guess it depends on your locale, unless of course, the phrase has another meaning.

The Hebrew word for cool is *ruwach*. It can mean spirit, wind, breath, blast, or air.[14] Therefore, the "cool" of the day could also be translated "spirit" of the day or "wind" of the day. Although wind can help air temperatures feel cooler, I believe the interpretation goes deeper. In Eden, the *ruwach* of the day occurred whenever the *qowl* of the Lord walked in the garden. In this context, *ruwach* is the "breath" of God's presence, the Holy Spirit Himself. Every time God's voice thundered through the garden, the breath of His Spirit followed. God's Spirit would breathe on other moments in Bible history as well.

- Mount Sinai where God's goodness passed by Moses (Exodus 33:19–23; 34:5–7)
- Elijah and his thundering encounter at the cave near Mount Horeb (1 Kings 19:11–12)
- Pentecost when the Spirit came with the sound of a rushing mighty wind (Acts 2:1–2)

We call these events theophanies: manifestations of God or God's presence that are tangible to our senses. Some theophanies appear in human form, others do not. The pillar of cloud in the wilderness and the burning bush on Mount Horeb are examples of the latter. The Bible documents many such appearances of God.

My Garden Encounter

The Adventist hospital in my city has a nice garden spot. Nearby, you will find a little park bench, sitting on the manicured lawn underneath a stand of shady fir trees. Dark green shrubbery complements the surroundings. A few oak trees line the nearby sidewalk. The spot is peaceful: a great place to stop, reflect, and put the busyness of the day behind. I had gone there every day for two weeks to wait on God in prayer. Mostly, I sat in silence with my Bible in hand. I was desperate to hear from God. Things in my life, at home, and in my ministry had changed, and I needed answers, direction.

I will never forget that Friday afternoon. The temperature hovered near ninety degrees, but the humidity made it feel much hotter. Finally, the sun disappeared below the horizon, allowing the cooler air to drift in. Then out of nowhere, a rushing wind swished by, bending treetops and whirling branches. Showing no sign of stopping, the gusts built in intensity. I closed my Bible and prepared to rush to the safety of my Chevy Suburban when, from a couple blocks away, I noticed a shape approaching at a rapid pace. I almost believed God Himself had decided to walk down the sidewalk with an answer to my prayer. The moment was surreal.

When the person got closer, I recognized Pat, a former member at my church. The odds of being at this one spot when she walked by were astronomical. Pat didn't know I would be there, nor did she live in the Portland area any longer. She must have been visiting someone at the hospital. One minute either way, and I would have missed her.

Pat came over to the bench, offered me a heartfelt greeting, and then began sharing a message she had received in prayer. The words came from Pat but the "voice" came from God. The Lord had drawn me to this garden spot to hear His *qowl*. And hear it I did. In a way, it came walking down the sidewalk in the cool of the day. Interestingly, the prophetic word had to do with writing this book. "Thus speaks the LORD God of Israel, saying: 'Write in a book for yourself all the words that I have spoken to you'" (Jeremiah 30:2).

Eastward in Eden

The garden eastward of Eden was indeed a paradise, prepared for every contingency. Eden's garden provided delicious foods, housed a petting zoo filled with exotic animals, and in the cool of the day, a voice walked the garden paths. A great river meandered through the area and nourished all the plants, including a tree of providence. One day, Eden, its garden, the river of life, and the tree of life would disappear. The voice would no longer walk there. For now, though, the prospects looked good. God's garden had turned out just the way He wanted it—and on schedule. He had planted and decorated this place with divine foresight. Perhaps something greater was on the agenda.

CHAPTER *6*

THE GREATEST MOMENT
OF CREATION

The heaven, *even* the heavens, *are* the LORD's;
but the earth He has given to the children of men.
—Psalm 115:16

My family comes from Oklahoma where clay soil abounds, especially red clay. At twelve years old, I visited Leedey, Oklahoma with my family for the annual Bar X Ranch reunion. I noticed an outcropping of reddish clay everywhere I looked, and it seemed to stick to everything. It encrusted every pair of boots at the ranch. By the time our trip ended, my white tennis shoes had turned a muddy red. After several washes, they still showed a red tinge; even my shoestrings were discolored. Red clay soil is not exclusive to Oklahoma; one can find it throughout the United States and in many regions around the world.

Most farmers and gardeners know that clay is difficult to plow, much less fertile, and not conducive for harvest yields—but it does have other uses. The Garden of Eden may have contained a patch of red clay near the riverbank, and since clay is ideal for sculpting designs, God could have used it to form the first man.

Adam: The Red One

"And the LORD God formed man *of* the dust of the ground" (Genesis 2:7*a*). God called the first man Adam. In the Open Bible Cyclopedic Index, Adam means *red earth*.[15] Strong's Enhanced Lexicon further reveals the Hebrew noun, '*adam,* comes from the verb, '*adam,* which translates as *dyed red*.[16] Names in the Bible often held special significance beyond the name itself. They could reveal the nature of a person or other distinguishing characteristic.

When God called the first man Adam—his name inferred at least one characteristic—an individual made from *red earth*. Therefore, if Adam had a distinctive skin color at all, it probably looked red like his name implied. In speculation, what if the "dust of the ground" (or red earth) that God used to form Adam held a shade of crimson red. Since red often represents redemption, the color might foreshadow Calvary, as well as being a type and shadow for the last Adam, Jesus Christ. Either way, red clay or otherwise, God's man-molding project turned out well.

Eve: The Living One

"And the LORD God said, '*It is* not good that man should be alone; I will make him a helper comparable to him.' And the LORD God caused a deep sleep to fall on Adam, and he slept; and He took one of his ribs, and closed up the flesh in its place. Then the rib which the LORD God had taken from man He made into a woman, and He brought her to the man" (Genesis 2:18, 21–22).

Eve's name, *Chavvah* in Hebrew (pronounced khav-vaw), meant *life or living*.[17] Adam appropriately named his wife, the living one, for she became the mother of all human life. Adam also called her woman, *'ishshah* in Hebrew (pronounced ish-shaw).[18] If God used more clay to make Eve, then she likely had Adam's *red earth* skin tones. What a couple they made! In those days, they were not worried about fashion, so running around without clothing seemed natural. Without laundering concerns, they had more time to tend the garden, figure out how to have children, and accomplish God's purpose for their lives.

The First Blessing

"Then God blessed them, and God said to them, 'Be fruitful and multiply; fill the earth and subdue it; have dominion over the fish of the sea, over the birds of the air, and over every living thing that moves on the earth'" (Genesis 1:28).

In the Old Testament, parents passed the blessing on to their children. The blessing was more than a prayer or simply wishing someone good luck. It represented an anointed, often prophetic, act of faith. The blessing, once given, became a heritage that followed individuals the rest of their lives.

In essence, the Lord God was Adam and Eve's father, so He had the honor of releasing the first parental blessing. The blessing also entailed a few instructions: be fruitful and multiply, populate the earth, bring it under control, and take responsibility for its care, which involved watching out for the animals' welfare. Adam and Eve passed this blessing along to their children. It continued down the line of human descendants, growing in importance, scope, and revealing a greater purpose for humanity.

Made in His Image

"Then God said, 'Let Us make man in Our image, according to Our likeness;'… So God created man in His *own* image; in the image of God He created him; male and female He created them" (Genesis 1:26–27).

What is the image of God? Daniel saw Him as the Ancient of Days. He appeared as a burning bush to Moses. Jacob perceived Him as a fierce wrestler. God is a divine Spirit, and He can take any shape or likeness He chooses. He often uses a familiar image, consistent with the look, customs, and fashion of the day. Some people picture God with a human persona, believing He is a divine papa or spiritual daddy. Yes, God is our Abba Father (Mark 14:36), but we must remember He is also the Lord God Almighty. We are made in His image. He is not made in ours.

However, God's image does reveal certain human attributes: He has two eyes to see our needs, two arms to reach out in compassion, two legs to walk with us in the cool of the day, a face to express love and concern, lips for smiling and speaking truth, and a mouth and lungs to breathe life into lifeless situations.

The Breath of Life

"And the LORD God… breathed into his nostrils the breath of life; and man became a living being" (Genesis 2:7). One of the words for man in Hebrew is *'iysh* (pronounced eesh).[19] We find *'iysh* used in Genesis 2:23 and in over a thousand other verses. The word sounds like the noise people make when they exhale. Maybe that's what happened. God exhaled and life for humanity began. The final moments of Creation must have been glorious.

Word Picture: Eden Afternoon

My uncle is a renowned artist. When he wants to illustrate something, he paints a picture using canvas and oils, one of his favorite mediums. His work is not an exact copy but a representation of what he sees and feels. Likewise, my words below are simply a word picture, a representation of what might have happened on the sixth day of Creation.

No one watched the events unfold, at least no humans. The afternoon had turned to early evening by the time God knelt down at the riverbank. The river that flowed by Him was clean and pure, teeming with life. A gentle wind blew through the garden, tickling the field grasses in the meadow. When it reached the riverbank, it stopped and hovered over the surface of the waters. A large tree grew nearby, nourished by water from the river. It contained life too. The Lord scooped up some red clay and began forming a new but familiar design. He added several handfuls of water from the river and mixed it with the clay until the consistency felt pliable. He shaped His design with great care, occasionally stopping as if reflecting in thought.

In the distance, God noticed a beautiful-looking creature standing beside another tree, watching in earnest, hoping to see some fault in the workmanship. God ignored him. He knew about Satan's deceitful tricks and saw through all his deceptive disguises. When the Lord finished His molded sculpture, He closed His eyes and sat still for the longest time. The price would be costly, almost too high to pay. His actions today would set up a chain reaction that would affect all humanity, even eternity itself.

God looked again at the tree of life, then back at the creature standing by the tree of knowledge. Yes, there would be much turmoil, suffering, and pain, but He saw no other way. The plan had been conceived long before the foundation of the world—no turning back now. God knew this one divine moment would lead to the greatest moment of all. The Lord bent over, His face almost touching the face of the *red earth* man. He took in a deep breath and then exhaled slowly. His breath made a gentle *eesh* sound. Suddenly, two eyes opened and the man sat up, stretching his arms and legs. God smiled and said to him, *Hello, Adam. Would you like to go for a walk? I have a wonderful idea to discuss with you. I think you might like her.*

"Then God saw everything that He had made, and indeed *it was* very good. So the evening and the morning were the sixth day" (Genesis 1:31).

The Greatest Moment of Creation

"Thus the heavens and the earth, and all the host of them, were finished. And on the seventh day God ended His work which He had done, and He rested on the seventh day from all His work which He had done. Then God blessed the seventh day and sanctified it, because in it He rested from all His work which God had created and made" (Genesis 2:1–3).

On the seventh day, God took a well-deserved day of rest, even though He never tires. In six days, He had fashioned everything in the universe. Apostle John would later confirm that God's Son, the Word, performed the miracles during the Creation. "In the beginning was the Word, and the Word was with God, and the Word was God. He was in the beginning with God. All things were made through Him, and without Him nothing was made that was made" (John 1:1–3).

When the Lord made the heavens and the earth, He was laying the groundwork for something greater: God created a sun to rule the day and a moon to light the night, planted a garden, filled it with animals—all His efforts and everything else prepared the earth for what He truly longed to make. God had saved the best moment for last. With some dirt, the breath of life, and a borrowed rib, Adam and Eve became the greatest moment of Creation.

God had even greater moments planned, but before unveiling them, He would need to build a nation of holy people.

PART THREE:

MOMENTS FROM THE PATRIARCHS OF ISRAEL

CHAPTER 7

MAKING A NATION: ABRAHAM

> Vision is the key to leadership.
> Unless you have a vision of where you're going,
> you are not going to get there.
> —Father Theodore Hesburgh

Things looked promising in the beginning. God's creation of the world unfolded as expected. The earth turned out beautiful. Eden and its garden were a package deal with everything included—a paradise beyond imagination. Adam and Eve made the perfect couple. Even God's covenant seemed simple enough: populate the earth, rule it, watch over all the animals, take care of the garden, harvest whatever food you need, but most importantly—don't eat fruit from the tree of knowledge of good and evil.

However, after listening to some bad advice from a talking serpent, Adam and Eve tasted the forbidden fruit. Their experience was enlightening but a fateful mistake. Serious consequences ensued, forcing man and woman to leave the garden paradise forever. God's first covenant with humanity failed in short order. Sin had begun.

Disobedience spread quickly through the world, the effects devastating. "Then the LORD saw that the wickedness of man *was* great in the earth, and *that* every intent of the thoughts of his heart *was* only evil continually. And the LORD was sorry that He had made man on the earth, and He was grieved in His heart. So the LORD said, 'I will destroy man whom I have created from the face of the earth, both man and beast, creeping thing and birds of the air, for I am sorry that I have made them'" (Genesis 6:5–7).

Humanity's future looked quite grim. Their spiritual condition had sunk to new lows. All day long, they contemplated wickedness—every single thought embraced evil—and their sinful actions followed suit. A cataclysmic flood seemed the only solution. Fortunately, for all of us, Noah found grace in the eyes of the Lord (v. 8).

Someone Missed the Point

Even after a fresh start with Noah, his family, and replacement animals from the ark, God's covenant to replenish the earth experienced a setback. It seems the local inhabitants, all relatives of Noah, decided to forget the covenant, establish a permanent settlement, and build a skyscraper. Perhaps they needed a project to gratify their need for unity and recognition. "And they said, 'Come, let us build ourselves a city, and a tower whose top *is* in the heavens; let us make a name for ourselves, lest we be scattered abroad over the face of the whole earth'" (Genesis 11:4). Their tower turned out to be a construction project of disobedience and rebellion.

"But the LORD came down to see the city and the tower which the sons of men had built. And the LORD said, 'Indeed the people *are* one and they all have one language, and this is what they begin to do; now nothing that they propose to do will be withheld from them. Come, let

Us go down and there confuse their language, that they may not under-stand one another's speech.' So the LORD scattered them abroad from there over the face of all the earth, and they ceased building the city" (Genesis 11:5–8). The baffled workers dispersed, naming the place Babel (Babylon or confusion). With things back on track, God was ready to implement His next great moment—making a great nation.

Birthing a Nation

"I will make you into a great nation" (Genesis 12:2*a* NIV). To estab-lish a nation of devoted followers, God needed someone who would leave everything behind, including all family ties, and journey to the land of Canaan. This person must have leadership ability, obey His words, and exhibit great faith. God knew exactly who He wanted for the job—Abram.

Abram, later known as Abraham, was born in Ur of the Chaldees. Ur has several possible locations, but most commentaries place the city in southern Mesopotamia, near the mouth of the Euphrates on its western bank. Abram and his relatives would later emigrate from Ur to Haran, traveling through an area known as the Fertile Crescent on their way to Canaan (Genesis 11:28–31; 12:1–4; 15:7; Nehemiah 9:7).

The principal deity of Ur was Nanna, the so-called moon god. Nanna worship was prevalent throughout ancient Mesopotamia. If a traveler encountered a carved pillar depicting two hands reaching toward a crescent moon, it was probably a Nanna shrine.[20] The carnal ministry of cult prostitution often associated with these shrines undoubtedly added to their popularity.[21] Worshipers also referred to their deity as *Sin* or *Su'en* and sometimes as the *Shining Boat of Heaven*. They saw him as the originator of life, guardian of humanity, and lord of destinies.[22] All of these titles were disgusting to the true God of heaven and earth. No wonder the Lord God wanted Abram to leave Ur.

Get out of There

"And Terah took his son Abram and his grandson Lot, the son of Haran, and his daughter-in-law Sarai, his son Abram's wife, and they went out with them from Ur of the Chaldeans to go to the land of Canaan; and they came to Haran and dwelt there" (Genesis 11:31).

It appears Abram took a detour halfway to Canaan, stopping in the city of Haran. Perhaps the layover was due to low finances, big city distractions, or medical concerns like taking care of Terah, his elderly father. But staying in Haran was not part of God's plan. Besides, Abram still had his extended family with him—something God knew just wouldn't work. To establish a new nation of faith, He needed Abram to make a complete break and leave his family behind.

According to Joshua 24:2, Terah, the father of Abraham, served false gods. Others in Abram's family did the same. Abram's grandfather, Nahor, probably worshiped idols as well. More than anything else, all ties to idol worship needed to go. When Terah died, the influence of idolatry in the family ended, and God could remind Abram of his former calling. Notice the "had said" in the following passage:

> Now the LORD *had said* to Abram: "Get out of your country, from your family and from your father's house, to a land that I will show you.
>
> I will make you a great nation; I will bless you and make your name great; and you shall be a blessing.
>
> I will bless those who bless you, and I will curse him who curses you; and in you all the families of the earth shall be blessed." (Genesis 12:1–3, italicized emphasis mine)

Back on Track

"So Abram departed as the LORD had spoken to him, and Lot went with him. And Abram *was* seventy-five years old when he departed from Haran. Then Abram took Sarai his wife and Lot his brother's son, and all their possessions that they had gathered, and the people whom they had acquired in Haran, and they departed to go to the land of Canaan. So they came to the land of Canaan" (Genesis 12:4–5). Abram had no sooner set foot in Canaan when the Lord appeared and reminded him of His promise, not just a voice this time but an actual visitation from God: "To your descendants I will give this land" (12:7). Abram, obviously impressed, built his first altar at Shechem. This place would later hold special significance for God's people (see Genesis 33:17–20; Joshua 20:1, 7; 24:1, 25–28).

Although Abram had finally left his family behind as God instructed, he still traveled with Lot, his deceased brother's son. I often wonder why Abram took his nephew with him when God had already commanded him to leave the relatives. As it turned out, keeping Lot became a major liability. When the herdsmen of Lot quarreled with the herdsmen of Abram, the ensuing strife caused Lot and Abram to part ways. The decision was difficult for both parties. Afterwards, God encouraged Abram with a greater promise—one that revealed a plan for a perpetual nation:

> The LORD said to Abram, after Lot had separated from him, "Now lift up your eyes and look from the place where you are, northward and southward and eastward and westward; for all the land which you see, I will give it to you and to your descendants forever.
>
> I will make your descendants as the dust of the earth, so that if anyone can number the dust of the earth, then your descendants can also be numbered." (Genesis 13:14–16 NASB)

Fortunes of War

When Lot moved out of Abraham's camp, he chose the eastern plains of Jordan. He ended up in the suburbs of Sodom—a poor choice to say the least—for Sodom was known for its wickedness and carnal practices. Not long after Lot moved there, a war broke out and an alliance of rebel kings captured him. When Abram heard the news, he gathered a war party to rescue his nephew.

"Now when Abram heard that [Lot] was taken captive, he armed his three hundred and eighteen trained *servants* who were born in his own house, and went in pursuit as far as Dan. He divided his forces against them by night, and he and his servants attacked them and pursued them as far as Hobah, which *is* north of Damascus. So he brought back all the goods, and also brought back his brother Lot and his goods, as well as the women and the people" (Genesis 14:14–16).

Man from Salem

On the way home from the battle, Abram met a mysterious holy man who seemed to know him. Apparently, someone else in this desert worshipped the true God of heaven as well. Somehow, this priestly king from Salem understood God's plans for Abram, and when he prophesied over Abram, his words sounded familiar, like those of Yahweh Himself. Abram could only wonder. Even the refreshments offered Abram, common for hospitability purposes, seemed to hold a deeper meaning. "Then Melchizedek king of Salem brought out bread and wine; he *was* the priest of God Most High. And he blessed him and said: 'Blessed be Abram of God Most High, possessor of heaven and earth; and blessed be God Most High, who has delivered your enemies into your hand.' And [Abram] gave [Melchizedek] a tithe of all" (Genesis 14:18–20).

According to Hebrews 7:17–21 and Psalm 110:4, the order of Melchizedek is the priestly order to which Christ belongs. Most commentators believe Salem *(Shalem)* is the same place as Jerusalem *(Yâruwshalaim)*. Both have the same root word meaning of peace.[23] This connection identifies Melchizedek as a priestly king of peace. It reminds me of another title, Prince of Peace, given to the Son of God. Moreover, Melchizedek means "king of righteousness" (Hebrews 7:2). That may explain why Abram tithed to Melchizedek and not to the king of Sodom (Hebrews 7:3–4). It could also clarify why this priestly king from Salem served Abram bread and wine, the same elements that would later represent Christ (see Luke 22:19–20). No doubt, the appearance of Melchizedek was another Old Testament theophany.

A Child Promised

The prophecies Abram received from God held a common theme: His descendants would be as numerous as the sands in the desert, his offspring would inherit huge amounts of land forever, God would bless him and make him a well-known celebrity, and somehow he would become a philanthropist and bless all the families in the world. Sure, it could happen, but there was a big problem. One must have descendants in order to fulfill all these great and wonderful prophecies—and Abram had none. In fact, he and his wife were not able to conceive children, even though they had been trying most of their married life.

As the prophetic words from God poured in, Abram became increasingly concerned. This next one added frustration and a little agitation:

> After these things the word of the LORD came to Abram
> in a vision, saying,

"Do not fear, Abram, I am a shield to you; your reward shall be very great."

Abram said, "O Lord God, what will You give me, since I am childless, and the heir of my house is Eliezer of Damascus?" And Abram said, "Since You have given no offspring to me, one born in my house is my heir."

Then behold, the word of the Lord came to him, saying, "This man will not be your heir; but one who will come forth from your own body, he shall be your heir."

And He took him outside and said, "Now look toward the heavens, and count the stars, if you are able to count them." And He said to him, "So shall your descendants be." (Genesis 15:1–5 NASB)

When Abram saw the multitude of stars that night a new level of faith stirred in his heart, and against all hope (Romans 4:18), he believed God could give him an heir. Abram wasn't sure how God would accomplish this feat, but for now, he would hold off on any adoption plans or giving his power of attorney to Eliezer of Damascus. "And [Abram] believed in the Lord; and He accounted it to him for righteousness" (Genesis 15:6).

Abram's wife, Sarai, however, had her own ideas on how to bring God's word to pass. All too often, we try to help God's promises materialize. Believers would do better if they left the prophecy confirmation business to Him. Nevertheless, after patiently waiting for ten years, Sarai, who remained barren, suggested a substitute plan to her husband. "So Sarai said to Abram, 'See now, the Lord has restrained me from bearing *children*. Please, go in to my maid; perhaps I shall obtain children by her.' And Abram heeded the voice of Sarai. Then Sarai, Abram's wife, took Hagar her maid, the Egyptian, and gave her to her husband Abram to be his wife, after Abram had dwelt ten years in the land of Canaan" (Genesis 16:2–3).

In the legal custom of the day, a barren woman could give her handmaiden to her husband as a second wife, but any child born from that union became the first wife's child. "So Hagar bore Abram a son; and Abram named his son, whom Hagar bore, Ishmael. Abram *was* eighty-six years old when Hagar bore Ishmael to Abram" (Genesis 16:15–16). The name Ishmael means *God hears*.[24] Yes, God heard Abram and Sarai's cry for a child, but Ishmael was their solution to the childless dilemma, not His.

Father of Many Nations

Each new prophetic word grew in scope, encompassing even more promises than the ones before:

> Now when Abram was ninety-nine years old, the LORD appeared to Abram and said to him, "I am God Almighty; walk before Me, and be blameless. I will establish My covenant between Me and you, and I will multiply you exceedingly."
>
> Abram fell on his face, and God talked with him, saying, "As for Me, behold, My covenant is with you, and you will be the father of a multitude of nations.
>
> No longer shall your name be called Abram, but your name shall be Abraham; for I will make you the father of a multitude of nations.
>
> I have made you exceedingly fruitful, and I will make nations of you, and kings will come forth from you." (Genesis 17:1–6 NASB)

Adding to his prophetic résumé, Abram will become a kingmaker and founder of nations. God's accord with Abram will continue, descendant to descendant, down his generational line. Furthermore, it will be an everlasting covenant where the land of Canaan remained their eternal possession. Obviously, Abram would need a name and title change to coincide with these added responsibilities. Instead of being Abram (exalted father), he will be Abraham (father of multitudes). He would somehow go from a childless, over the hill, hundred-year-old man to become a king and father of many nations.

God had similar plans for Abram's wife. Instead of being Sarai (princess), she will be Sarah (noblewoman). Likewise, she would go from a childless, seemingly barren, ninety-year-old woman to become a queen and mother of many nations.

> Then God said to Abraham, "As for Sarai your wife, you shall not call her name Sarai, but Sarah *shall be* her name. I will bless her, and indeed I will give you a son by her. Then I will bless her, and she shall be *a mother of* nations; kings of peoples will come from her."

> Then Abraham fell on his face and laughed, and said in his heart, "Will a child be born to a man one hundred years old? And will Sarah, who is ninety years old, bear *a child?*"

> And Abraham said to God, "Oh that Ishmael might live before You!"

> But God said, "No, but Sarah your wife will bear you a son, and you shall call his name Isaac; and I will establish My covenant with him for an everlasting covenant for his descendants after him." (Genesis 17:15–19 NASB)

As for Ishmael, he grew up to be an accomplished archer. Later in life, he married an Egyptian woman and fathered twelve princes who in turn founded many of the nomadic tribes. Sometimes called Bedouins, the Ishmaelite people inhabited the wide desert areas of Northern Arabia (see Genesis 37:25, 28). Ishmael, however, was not the child of promise. That honor would belong to another individual named Isaac.

Abraham the Intercessor

After his uncle rescued him, Lot returned to the city of Sodom. Little did he know that Sodom had run out of chances and so had the sister city of Gomorrah. The wickedness of their sins cried out to God in heaven. However, God is merciful so He sent a scouting party of three angels to visit the city. God wanted a firsthand report. One of the angels turned out to be Yahweh Himself. "Then the men rose from there and looked toward Sodom, and Abraham went with them to send them on the way. And the LORD said, 'Shall I hide from Abraham what I am doing, since Abraham shall surely become a great and mighty nation, and all the nations of the earth shall be blessed in him?'" (Genesis 18:16–18).

Abraham knew all too well the evils of Sodom, and he worried about his nephew who lived there. "And Abraham came near and said, 'Would You also destroy the righteous with the wicked? Suppose there were fifty righteous within the city; would You also destroy the place and not spare *it* for the fifty righteous that were in it?'" (Genesis 18:23–24). It's a good question, especially if one is trying to understand the ways of God. On one hand, God is just and therefore requires account-ability, but on the other, He is merciful. Assuming God was not bent on needless destruction—Abraham continued his intercession—whittling the number down from forty-five to forty, then to thirty, and then to twenty. He stopped bargaining at ten righteous people: "Then he said, 'Let not the Lord be angry, and I will speak but once more: Suppose ten should be found there?' And He said, 'I will not destroy *it* for the sake of ten'" (Genesis 18:32).

Why did Abraham stop at ten people? That's a question for eternity. Maybe Abraham believed he had allowed for every contingency. When we look at the progression of his prayer, it seems likely God would have spared the city for five righteous people, maybe even for one. To Abraham, further intercession seemed unnecessary. If Abraham allowed for Lot, his wife, his two daughters and their husbands—the total stood at six. If his nephew's friends were righteous, the count might go even higher. Maybe some of the in-laws had abandoned idolatry and joined the faith. Certainly, Lot's loyal herdsmen were still following God. And if Lot had witnessed to others in town about Yahweh, Abraham could add these numbers to the tally as well. Achieving his quota of ten righteous people should have been easy. Abraham only needed four in addition to his nephew's family. Unfortunately, the totals fell short.

After the two angels arrived in Sodom, men from the city made an unholy request and tried to enter Lot's house. One of the angels advised Lot, his wife, and their two daughters to leave town immediately—saying, "Escape for your life! Do not look behind you nor stay anywhere in the plain. Escape to the mountains, lest you be destroyed" (Genesis 19:17*b*). Before leaving, Lot requested a different refuge: Zoar, a little city south of the Dead Sea. The angels granted his request, but sadly, only Lot and his two daughters reached the safety of Zoar. His wife disobeyed the angel, looked back, and became a pillar of salt. In the end, Sodom and Gomorrah were both destroyed by fire and brimstone, a judgment from God long overdue. Still, were it not for Abraham's prayers and God's mercy, even Lot would have perished.

Trip to Mount Moriah

Abraham had reached the century mark (Genesis 21:5) by the time Isaac was born. Finally, things were working out for the better. The sheep business had picked up. Trading was profitable. God's promises made a little more sense. Even the family squabbles had settled down after sending Hagar and Ishmael off to make their own way in the world. Although God had a plan and purpose for Ishmael, Isaac was the promised child (Genesis 17:19), and Abraham and Sarah loved him more than life itself. Yes, it was a time to relax a bit, enjoy their only son, and teach him the patriarchal business.

"Now it came to pass after these things that God tested Abraham, and said to him, 'Abraham!' And he said, 'Here I am.' Then He said, 'Take now your son, your only *son* Isaac, whom you love, and go to the land of Moriah, and offer him there as a burnt offering on one of the mountains of which I shall tell you'" (Genesis 22:1–2).

Personal Sidebar

Have you ever thought about the worst possible thing that could happen to you? Just for a moment, consider what it would be like to have your son or daughter hate you; become horribly crippled; face abuse; catch an incurable disease; or lose all your money, your job, or even your own life. Well, nothing compares to losing your only child, with little hope of ever having another one. Abraham faced this scenario. I don't know how he did it, but he obeyed God, without hesitation, and packed up for a final camping trip to Mount Moriah with his only son. Some say Abraham knew what would happen on that lonely, barren hill, but I think otherwise. I believe he faced the most difficult day of his life. Sometimes, going through a crisis is the only way we can understand the purposes of God.

Encounter with Yahweh-Yireh

> Then they came to the place of which God had told
> him; and Abraham built the altar there and arranged the
> wood, and bound his son Isaac and laid him on the altar,
> on top of the wood. Abraham stretched out his hand and
> took the knife to slay his son.
>
> But the angel of the LORD called to him from heaven and
> said, "Abraham, Abraham!" And he said, "Here I am."
>
> He said, "Do not stretch out your hand against the lad,
> and do nothing to him; for now I know that you fear
> God, since you have not withheld your son, your only
> son, from Me."
>
> Then Abraham raised his eyes and looked, and behold,
> behind *him* a ram caught in the thicket by his horns;
> and Abraham went and took the ram and offered him
> up for a burnt offering in the place of his son. (Genesis
> 22:9–13 NASB)

"And Abraham called the name of the place, The-LORD-Will-Provide; as it is said *to* this day, 'In the Mount of the LORD it shall be provided'" (Genesis 22:14). Before the day ended, Abraham caught a glimpse of Calvary. He may not have understood everything or anything, but he did see it—a type and shadow of God's redemption plan. One day, another Father would lay His only begotten Son upon an altar. His sacrifice would be a precious gift to save humanity. On that day, the price will be high, but *YHWH Yireh,* The-LORD-Who-Provides, will pay it in full.

Father of Faith

Three major religions admired and respected Abraham and his contributions to society. The Jewish people referred to him as "Father Abraham" (Luke 16:24; John 8:56). Paul, an apostle to Christian believers, called him "the father of us all" (Romans 4:16). Islam considered him an esteemed prophet and patriarch.[25] Abraham certainly influenced secular and religious history. Many people still regard him as the father of faith, and according to the writer of Hebrews 11, he used that faith to obey God.

> By faith Abraham, when he was called, obeyed by going out to a place which he was to receive for an inheritance; and he went out, not knowing where he was going.
>
> By faith he lived as an alien in the land of promise, as in a foreign *land,* dwelling in tents with Isaac and Jacob, fellow heirs of the same promise; for he was looking for the city which has foundations, whose architect and builder is God.
>
> By faith Abraham, when he was tested, offered up Isaac, and he who had received the promises was offering up his only begotten *son.* (Hebrews 11:8–10, 17 NASB)

Working out the Details

Earth's inhabitants had made many mistakes up to this point, and even though they would make many more, God still loved them. He would honor His covenants to humanity and bless all the families of the world through Abraham as promised. As time marched on, these covenant blessings passed from Abraham unto Isaac, from Isaac unto Jacob, from Jacob unto Joseph, until the descendants of Abraham filled the land of Goshen in Egypt.

This young Hebrew nation was getting larger, growing up fast, but they were not maturing in the right place. Goshen cramped their style, and Pharaoh's rules were too harsh. They needed a mass exodus back to Canaan, a guide who knew the right path through the desert, and someone who could explain their true heritage and purpose. Most of all, they required an experienced priest who could talk with God face to face and clarify the ground rules. God had just the right person in mind—Moses.

CHAPTER 8

ORGANIZING THE COVENANT: MOSES

Talking to men for God is a great thing,
but talking to God for men is greater still.
—E. M. Bounds

The deserts of Southern California are fun places to explore, as long as one carries a canteen and watches out for rattlesnakes, scorpions, tarantulas, and the occasional mountain lion. My favorite spot is near Joshua Tree National Park. I enjoy hiking the trails, searching ravines for rocks and fossils, panning for gold flakes in dry riverbeds, and sleeping outside so I can watch the stars pass overhead. The low deserts are hot during the day but cool down fast after sunset. Darkness sets in quickly, so I always build my campfire pit ahead of time and stock it with plenty of firewood.

On one such trip to the desert, I noticed an unusual sight. Off in the distance I saw smoke drifting up from a dry creek bed. Who would set up their tent or fire pit there? If it rained during the night, a cloudburst could easily wash the campsite five miles down the canyon. Being concerned and somewhat curious, I decided to have a look. About two hundred yards away, I realized it wasn't a plume of smoke from an unattended campfire—but a lone smoke tree, rooted in the dry soil.

Smoke trees *(Dalea spinosa)* grow in the deserts of Southern California, Arizona, Nevada, and other arid regions in the Sonoran Desert. When the new growth emerges, the grayish-toned branches can look like a plume of smoke, especially from a distance. Smoke trees prefer hot summers and mild winters. They are usually found along sandy flats, arroyos, and washes—close to an ample water supply.[26] Because of its dry appearance, it is difficult to tell if a smoke tree is dead or alive without a closer look. Plants that share the common name of smoke tree can range in size from a bush to a small tree. The one I saw in the desert was almost twenty feet high. Apparently, it thrived in the middle of this dry wash by tapping into hidden moisture beneath the soil.

While seeking the warmth of a friendly fire, weary travelers or confused miners have mistaken smoke trees for the real thing. However, when Moses turned aside, he did not see a mirage but an actual bush on fire, which is not unheard of in a dried-out, combustible wilderness. What made this particular *bush-on-fire* event so intriguing was a fire that didn't consume the bush. Since smoke is the usual byproduct of fire, Moses may have seen a smoke cloud rising in the distance as well.

The Bush Burns

Much had happened to Moses prior to his encounter with the burning bush. Born into the tribe of Levi, Moses had an inauspicious beginning. After Moses turned three months old, his mother, Jochebed, put him in an ark made of bulrushes and placed it along the Nile River.

She hoped to save him from Pharaoh's edict to kill all Hebrew male infants. Divine providence came into play when Pharaoh's daughter found the child's ark in the reeds near the riverbank. "So she called his name Moses, saying, 'Because I drew him out of the water'" (Exodus 2:10*b*). His name in Hebrew, *Mosheh,* means drawn out.[27]

Moses grew up in the courts of Pharaoh. As a prince of Egypt, he learned about *Ra* and the other Egyptian gods. At forty years old, Moses disputed with a taskmaster about the treatment of a Hebrew slave, killed the taskmaster, and then ran from the authorities who wanted him for murder. He escaped into the wilderness of Midian; later, he married a local girl named Zipporah and fathered two sons. However, nothing he had experienced thus far would compare with meeting the one true God on a hilltop. "Now Moses was tending the flock of Jethro his father-in-law, the priest of Midian. And he led the flock to the back of the desert, and came to Horeb, the mountain of God. And the Angel of the LORD appeared to him in a flame of fire from the midst of a bush" (Exodus 3:1–2*a*). Moses did not actually see the Angel, only the flaming bush and perhaps some smoke.

I Am Who I Am

Unlike other bushes, this one could speak. After calling his name a couple times, a voice from within the bush told Moses to remove his sandals because he stood on holy ground. The voice then introduced Himself as the God of his father, Amram, and the God of Abraham, Isaac, and Jacob (Exodus 3:6). After a brief historical update, God asked Moses to go back to Egypt, get a release order from Pharaoh, and bring the Hebrews back to the mountain.[28]

At first, Moses declined the job offer; after all, he was a wanted criminal in Egypt. Besides, he had never excelled in diplomatic relations or public speaking. God, however, seemed quite insistent, so Moses agreed but with one main concern:

> Then Moses said to God, "Behold, I am going to the sons of Israel, and I will say to them, 'The God of your fathers has sent me to you.' Now they may say to me, 'What is His name?' What shall I say to them?"
>
> God said to Moses, "I AM WHO I AM"; and He said, "Thus you shall say to the sons of Israel, 'I AM has sent me to you.'" (Exodus 3:13–14 NASB)

I find it interesting that God used the name I AM, not *YHWH* when commissioning Moses for the rescue outreach to Goshen; only later did He add the name Yahweh (*YHWH*) to His directive as LORD God (v. 15). The single and distinct name of *YHWH* was first spoken by Eve in Genesis 4:1, but in earlier verses, the Bible only referred to the Lord as either *'Elohiym* (God) or *YHWH 'Elohiym* (LORD God).[29] All these names are holy and precious, but if God has an official name in heaven, He may not be limited to only one.

Individuals can have many names or surnames representing their full name; maybe God does too. He is God, after all—no one named Him. He can be the unnamed God (see Genesis 32:29–30; Judges 13:17–18, 22) or choose whatever name He wants. In fact, He may have countless names—some not yet revealed—a point worth pondering, since great is the mystery of godliness (1 Timothy 3:16). Nonetheless, God gave Moses the name: I AM WHO I AM. In Hebrew it is *Hayah 'Aher Hayah* (pronounced haw-yaw, ash-er, haw-yaw).[30] Of all the names or titles of God, I like this one the best. It creates a memorable word picture: God will be whoever or whatever He wants to be. To face down Pharaoh, Moses would need a miracle-working *Hayah* on his side.

Outreach to Goshen

The Hebrew people were no longer honored guests in Goshen. The freedoms they enjoyed during the time of Joseph had gradually slipped away. The pharaohs had grown leery of Hebrew prominence and decided to implement a harsher diplomacy: force the Hebrews into a life of bondage and endless brick making. God's people were now little more than common slaves. By the time Moses returned from the backside of the desert as God's appointed deliverer, forty more years had passed, and the treatment of Hebrews had only worsened.

With the name I AM in his heart and on his lips, Moses entered Goshen, armed with two traveling miracles: a staff that transformed into a snake and a *restore-leprous-hand* wonder (see Exodus 4:1–7). After first delivering God's message to the Hebrews and demonstrating His miracle power, Moses moved on to Pharaoh, taking his brother as his spokesperson.

"Afterward Moses and Aaron went in and told Pharaoh, 'Thus says the LORD God of Israel: Let My people go, that they may hold a feast to Me in the wilderness.' And Pharaoh said, 'Who *is* the LORD, that I should obey His voice to let Israel go? I do not know the LORD, nor will I let Israel go'" (Exodus 5:1–2). Moses and Aaron even showed Pharaoh the *staff-into-snake* miracle, but it only hardened his heart (Exodus 7:9–13). It took ten more divine wonders to convince Pharaoh to release the Hebrews. The last one, a plague of death, proved both significant and destructive.

Moses instructed the Hebrews to take blood from an unblemished lamb and apply it to the sides and tops of their doorframes. "For I will pass through the land of Egypt on that night, and will strike all the firstborn in the land of Egypt, both man and beast; and against all the gods of Egypt I will execute judgment: I *am* the LORD. Now the blood shall be a sign for you on the houses where you *are*. And when I see the blood, I will pass over you; and the plague shall not be on you to destroy *you* when I strike the land of Egypt" (Exodus 12:12–13). This event became a yearly celebration of remembrance called the feast of Passover. God would give the Israelites six more festivals. Prophetically, all of them pointed to greater moments.

Returning to the Mountain

On the way out of Egypt, Moses put the slip on Pharaoh's army and left them to drown in the Red Sea, chariots and all. As instructed, Moses brought the Hebrew refugees to Mount Sinai to reconnect with their God (Exodus 3:12; 19:17). The place had changed a bit. The mountain no longer featured a small bush on fire; instead, the entire summit burned like a volcano with clouds of smoke enveloping it.[31]

> And Moses brought the people out of the camp to meet God, and they stood at the foot of the mountain. Now Mount Sinai *was* all in smoke because the LORD descended upon it in fire; and its smoke ascended like the smoke of a furnace, and the whole mountain quaked violently. When the sound of the trumpet grew louder and louder, Moses spoke and God answered him with thunder. The LORD came down on Mount Sinai, to the top of the mountain; and the LORD called Moses to the top of the mountain, and Moses went up. (Exodus 19:17–20 NASB)

The Ten Commandments

"And when [God] had made an end of speaking with him on Mount Sinai, He gave Moses two tablets of the Testimony, tablets of stone, written with the finger of God" (Exodus 31:18). Writing on the stones might have looked something like the ancient Hebrew script below, which shows the first of the Ten Commandments. One day, someone may discover the Ark of the Covenant or choose to reveal its location.[32] We could then peek inside and see God's actual handwriting (see 1 Kings 8:9).

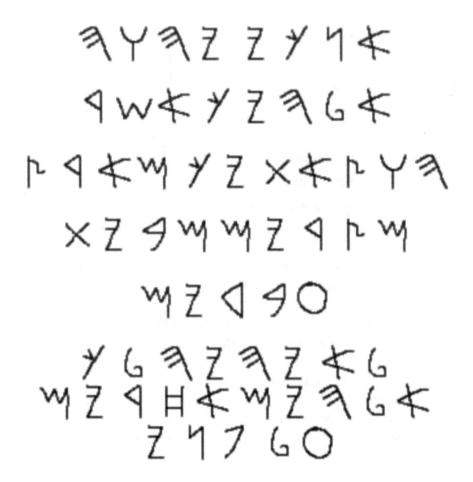

Exodus 20:2–3: The Parallel Hebrew Old Testament by John Hurt. Used by permission. Paleo-Hebrew before 585 B.C.E.

Ancient Hebrew is one of the oldest written languages. The Paleo-Hebrew script evolved from a variation of Old Canaanite script used by the Israelites during their early history. It dates back to the tenth century B.C.E., perhaps earlier. Paleo-Hebrew writing did not use vowel marks, as does the modern script shown below. Again, here is the first commandment from Exodus 20.

אָנֹכִי יְהוָה אֱלֹהֶיךָ, אֲשֶׁר הוֹצֵאתִיךָ מֵאֶרֶץ מִצְרַיִם מִבֵּית עֲבָדִים: לֹא יִהְיֶה לְךָ אֱלֹהִים אֲחֵרִים, עַל פָּנָי.

I *am* the LORD thy God, which have brought thee out of the land of Egypt, out of the house of bondage. Thou shalt have no other gods before Me.

A Hebrew–English Bible According to the Masoretic Text and the JPS 1917 Edition by Mechon Mamre. Used by permission.

God first spoke the Ten Commandments to the Israelites gathered at the foot of Mount Sinai (see Exodus 20:18–19; Deuteronomy 5:4–5, 22–23). Later, Moses climbed the mountain, and God gave him the written version on two tablets of stone. God's finger wrote these commandments on both sides of each stone. Unfortunately, an angry Moses destroyed the first set of stones after he witnessed the people dancing foolishly before a golden calf. His brother, Aaron, had built this idol while Moses tarried on the mountain in God's presence. The tablets were a great loss, but God was understanding and merciful. "And the LORD said to Moses, 'Cut two tablets of stone like the first *ones,* and I will write on *these* tablets the words that were on the first tablets which you broke.' So he cut two tablets of stone like the first *ones.* Then Moses rose early in the morning and went up Mount Sinai, as the LORD had commanded him; and he took in his hand the two tablets of stone" (Exodus 34:1, 4).

The Ten Commandments below are a combined list from Exodus 20:1–17 and Deuteronomy 5:6–21. Since the commandments are not numbered in the Bible, some religions and denominations group them differently.

I.

I am *YHWH* your God. Have no other gods before me.

II.

Thou shalt not make a graven image.

III.

Thou shalt not take the name of *YHWH* your God in vain.

IV.

Remember the Sabbath day. Keep it holy.

V.

Honor your father and your mother.

VI.

Thou shalt not murder.

VII.

Thou shalt not commit adultery.

VIII.

Thou shalt not steal.

IX.

Thou shalt not bear false witness.

X.

Thou shalt not covet.

Show Me Your Glory

Then Moses said, "I pray You, show me Your glory!"

And He said, "I Myself will make all My goodness pass before you, and will proclaim the name of the LORD before you; and I will be gracious to whom I will be gracious, and will show compassion on whom I will show compassion."

> But He said, "You cannot see My face, for no man can see Me and live!"
>
> Then the Lord said, "Behold, there is a place by Me, and you shall stand *there* on the rock; and it will come about, while My glory is passing by, that I will put you in the cleft of the rock and cover you with My hand until I have passed by.
>
> Then I will take My hand away and you shall see My back, but My face shall not be seen." (Exodus 33:18–23 NASB)

Before Moses made the second trip up the mountain, he asked God to show him His glory, rendered *kabowd* in Hebrew. God's *kabowd* is not just His glory but also His honor, splendor, reverence, abundance, dignity, and reputation.[33] His glory embraces *all that He is*. Sadly, God declined the request because looking at His unfiltered glory is too extreme for mere mortals. Instead, God would allow Moses to see "all My goodness" or *tuwb*, which in Hebrew means His goods, property, prosperity, fairness, joy, and gladness.[34]

In addition to revealing all His goodness, God promised to proclaim His name, called *shem* in Hebrew. *Shem* is not just the name but also the reputation, fame, and glory represented by the name.[35]

> The Lord descended in the cloud and stood there with him as he called upon the name of the Lord. Then the Lord passed by in front of him and proclaimed, "The Lord, the Lord God, compassionate and gracious, slow to anger, and abounding in lovingkindness and truth; who keeps lovingkindness for thousands, who forgives iniquity, transgression and sin; yet He will by no means leave *the guilty* unpunished, visiting the iniquity of fathers on the children and on the grandchildren to the third and fourth generations." (Exodus 34:5–7 NASB)

I can only imagine what it felt like to see "all of God's goodness" pass by Moses. As His glory *(kabowd)* drew near, God covered Moses with His hand, protecting him in the cleft of a nearby rock—for if Moses saw *all that God was*—it would have killed him instantly. Next, Moses heard the *shem* of *YHWH* proclaimed, "The LORD, the LORD God" (v. 6). His glorious reputation and fame filled the mountaintop and the heavens: Yahweh, Yahweh God is merciful, compassionate, patient, full of goodness and truth, gracious, willing to forgive but requiring justice (vv. 6–7). Then, if that weren't enough, God removed His hand to let Moses view the backside of His presence. No wonder the face of Moses glowed when he returned from the mountain (Exodus 34:29–30). Although God allowed Moses to experience more than anyone else had, He did not let Moses see the face of His presence.

Faces of God's Presence

When God said, "You cannot see My face" (Exodus 33:20), He was referring to His *paniym*. Likewise, when God told Moses, "My Presence will go *with* you" (Exodus 33:14), He again referred to His *paniym*. In Hebrew, God's *paniym* (pronounced paw-neem) is His face or His Presence.[36] Dictionaries define presence as the existence, occurrence, or the personality of someone. It relates to essence—what makes something what it is—the most important qualities. Even more intriguing: *paniym* is a plural word, rendered singular. It could also be translated as faces.

Moreover, the word translated "showbread" (Numbers 4:7) is also the word *paniym*. The New American Standard Version translates it as "the bread of the Presence." The New Revised Standard Version does the same. The literal translation, *lehem happānîm,* is "bread of the face."[37] Some references make it plural, calling it "bread of the faces." Interestingly, the tabernacle showbread table held twelve loaves of showbread: "And you shall take fine flour and bake twelve cakes with it. Two-tenths *of an ephah* shall be in each cake. You shall set them in two rows, six in a row, on the pure *gold* table before the LORD" (Leviticus 24:5–6).

These loaves were very holy. Besides the obvious connection to the twelve tribes of Israel, the showbread represents a deeper truth about the manifest presence of God: His face is always before His people — and we are always before Him.

In Exodus 33:22, when the *paniym* of God's *kabowd* passed by, Moses remained hidden, unable to view it. Later, when he ventured out, he experienced only the afterglow. Apparently, the glorious face of God is not viewable, at least not right now, but like Moses, we can still see and experience the faces of His *tuwb* and *shem* in all their wonder.

Law of Moses

As time passed, God gave Moses other commandments, which Judaism calls the Law of Moses. The Law included the Ten Commandments, civil statutes, religious rituals, seven festivals, and prophetic words. Faith, repentance, forgiveness of sins, worship, and sacrificial offerings also had their part. The first five books of the Old Testament, sometimes called the Books of Moses, are known as the Pentateuch in Christianity and the Torah in Judaism. In a general sense, torah, which means instruction or teaching, includes all the Hebrew Scriptures.

In later Judaism, torah not only came to mean the written Torah but also the oral Torah. The latter includes a collection of rabbinic texts that form two lengthy religious documents called the Palestinian Talmud and the Babylonian Talmud. The Babylonian Talmud is considered more authoritative. Both Talmuds contain *Mishnah* (the Hebrew code of laws) and *Gemara* (the commentary).[38]

Blessings of the Law

According to the Fifth Book of Moses, if the people followed all God's commandments and ordinances, they could enjoy the blessings of God.

> Now it shall be, if you diligently obey the LORD your God, being careful to do all His commandments which I command you today, the LORD your God will set you high above all the nations of the earth. All these blessings will come upon you and overtake you if you obey the LORD your God:
>
> Blessed *shall* you *be* in the city, and blessed *shall* you *be* in the country.
>
> Blessed *shall be* the offspring of your body and the produce of your ground and the offspring of your beasts, the increase of your herd and the young of your flock.
>
> Blessed *shall be* your basket and your kneading bowl.
>
> Blessed *shall* you *be* when you come in, and blessed *shall* you *be* when you go out. (Deuteronomy 28:1–6 NASB)

Word Picture: Portfolio of Blessings

The blessings for obedience probably made more sense to those who lived three thousand years ago. I'm not sure if modern-day people relate to having one's basket and kneading bowl blessed. Therefore, in an effort to make the meanings more applicable, I have updated the terminology while staying true to the message. A contemporary version of the remaining blessings might read as follows:

God will embarrass your enemies and scatter them seven different ways. He will fill your garages with goods and improve the listing on your real estate. Your neighbors will see God's favor on you and watch in awe. You will have many pets, numerous children and grandchildren, a large orchard, and a full vegetable garden. The Lord will increase your retirement accounts. Even the rain will water your garden when needed. In fact, God will bless everything you do, whether you are working or taking a vacation. You will get all the promotions at work and rise to the top ranks of society. However, you must always follow the right path and stay true to God (adapted from Deuteronomy 28:7–14).

The other choice, of course, was not to follow the commandments of the Lord. That, however, would result in a long list of horrible afflictions and disasters known as the curses of disobedience, all of them most unpleasant (see Deuteronomy 28:15–68).

None Like Moses

"But since then there has not arisen in Israel a prophet like Moses, whom the LORD knew face to face, in all the signs and wonders which the LORD sent him to do in the land of Egypt, before Pharaoh, before all his servants, and in all his land, and by all that mighty power and all the great terror which Moses performed in the sight of all Israel" (Deuteronomy 34:10–12).

The Lord also spoke to Moses, face to face, as a person does with his best friend (Exodus 33:9–11). Moses was the greatest prophet to arise in Israel: greater than Abraham, Isaac, Jacob, or any other patriarch. He was greater than Adam (the first person), greater than Noah (the first preacher), even greater than Enoch (the first raptured saint).

Moses gathered the descendants of Abraham and organized them into a chosen nation of holy people (Deuteronomy 7:6–8). He received

99

the Law and gave it to the people so they could follow God and prosper. Without Moses' efforts and intercession, the Ten Commandments might have been lost for good. Thankfully, God wrote another copy. These ten simple statutes have influenced civil laws more than any other document, religious or otherwise. God's covenant with Moses was the best thing to happen to the tribes of Israel in years. Even so, this covenant only served as a tutor until a better one came along (Galatians 3:24).

In the meantime, God would introduce His next great moment—a kingdom of united tribes—something the judges of Israel could not accomplish. Perhaps a king would be the right answer. It was not exactly God's first choice or preference, but if He picked a sovereign for the job, this ruler would need to have a shepherd's heart.

CHAPTER 9

RULING A KINGDOM: DAVID

The first step to leadership is servanthood.
—John C. Maxwell

B efore the end of the second bell, the last few students shuffled in and took their seats. After greeting my class, I collected homework assignments, asked two teens in the back to stop talking, and began teaching my lesson for that day. Out of the corner of my eye, a familiar face appeared, peeking through the back door window. The school principal motioned me to come to the door—obviously another one of his *this-is-too-important-to-wait* meetings. I told my class to review their notes while I conferred with the principal for a few minutes. Upon my return, I noticed my wonderful students had tampered with my chalkboard outline.

My world history class had erased the entire lesson and replaced it with a new list of kings and emperors. Napoleon Bonaparte was now Linoleum Blown-apart. They had changed every name in a matter of minutes. Such misdirected talent, but I got their point. Apparently, my students were having problems differentiating between the numerous names and titles of monarchs—a daunting task for any student of medieval history. I decided to try something different. Next week, I brought in a board game called *Kingmaker* and set it up in the middle of the classroom.

Andrew McNeil created *Kingmaker.* The game first came out in Britain, followed by a second edition produced by Avalon Hill in the United States in 1975. *Kingmaker* is based on the War of the Roses (1455–1487) in English history. The game depicts a civil war between royal families and others who competed for the English throne. Using military and political powers, the players try to influence royalty and control various factions. They support certain heirs while trying to eliminate others. Eventually, someone wins the hearts of the people and becomes their true king.[39]

The board game helped my students understand which rulers were corrupt or honorable, and how they became that way. My classroom outline of sovereigns reminded me of the long list of kings in Israel and Judah: some considered good, others bad. Biblical scribes wrote meticulous histories concerning their monarchs in Kings and Chronicles. Trying to sort out the differences between these Jewish rulers is not an easy task, either. One ruler, though, stood out above all others. He had a heart for God and knew the difference between greatness and humility. His name was David.

Merciful King

We find the words, "Son of David, have mercy," in the Gospels, and each time they come from people calling out to Jesus of Nazareth. The Jews believed any true son of King David or any messiah of royal ancestry would be a man of mercy like David. So how did David earn this reputation for being merciful?

"Now when King David came to Bahurim, there was a man from the family of the house of Saul, whose name *was* Shimei the son of Gera, coming from there. He came out, cursing continuously as he came. And he threw stones at David and at all the servants of King David" (2 Samuel 16:5–6*a*). To say Shimei, a King Saul supporter, was angry with King David would be an understatement. He rejected and despised David, calling him a bloodthirsty scoundrel and other derogatory names. Shimei did not understand the spiritual circumstances or that God had removed King Saul because of his disobedience. His words toward King David were seditious and treasonable, and David could have ordered his commander to execute him on the spot. Instead, David showed mercy and left him alone. As David moved down the road, Shimei continued cussing, throwing stones, and showing his dissidence by kicking up dust.

In another situation, David extended kindness to Mephibosheth, a grandson of King Saul. After his grandpa, his uncles, and his father, Jonathan, perished in battle, Mephibosheth lived in isolation and obscurity. Having two crippled feet didn't help matters. Although he was an heir of King Saul, David had no legal obligation to take care of him. In fact, David could have considered Mephibosheth an enemy of the state. Instead, David showed mercy. "So David said to him, 'Do not fear, for I will surely show you kindness for Jonathan your father's sake, and will restore to you all the land of Saul your grandfather; and you shall eat bread at my table continually'" (2 Samuel 9:7). David also appointed Ziba, one of Saul's servants, to oversee his needs.

David also showed mercy to King Saul who was looking for rest area facilities at Rocks of the Wild Goats.

> He came to the sheepfolds on the way, where there *was* a cave; and Saul went in to relieve himself. Now

> David and his men were sitting in the inner recesses of the cave.
>
> The men of David said to him, "Behold, *this is* the day of which the LORD said to you, 'Behold; I am about to give your enemy into your hand, and you shall do to him as it seems good to you.' " Then David arose and cut off the edge of Saul's robe secretly.
>
> It came about afterward that David's conscience bothered him because he had cut off the edge of Saul's *robe*. So he said to his men, "Far be it from me because of the LORD that I should do this thing to my lord, the LORD's anointed, to stretch out my hand against him, since he is the LORD's anointed."
>
> David persuaded his men with *these* words and did not allow them to rise up against Saul. And Saul arose, left the cave, and went on *his* way. (1 Samuel 24:3–7 NASB)

Although David had just saved the king's life, Saul still hated him. He hunted for David at every opportunity, bent on capturing or killing him. One day, King Saul took three thousand of his best men and chased David into the Wilderness of Ziph. Saul made camp and unwisely fell asleep in his tent without posting guards. David showed mercy and restraint by preventing Abishai, a captain in his squad of thirty, from harming an overtired and overconfident King Saul.

> David then arose and came to the place where Saul had camped. And David saw the place where Saul lay, and Abner the son of Ner, the commander of his army; and Saul was lying in the circle of the camp, and the people were camped around him. Then David said to Ahimelech the Hittite and to Abishai the son of Zeruiah, Joab's brother, saying, "Who will go down with me to Saul in the camp?"

> And Abishai said, "I will go down with you." So David
> and Abishai came to the people by night, and behold,
> Saul lay sleeping inside the circle of the camp with his
> spear stuck in the ground at his head; and Abner and
> the people were lying around him.
>
> Then Abishai said to David, "Today God has delivered
> your enemy into your hand; now therefore, please let
> me strike him with the spear to the ground with one
> stroke, and I will not strike him the second time."
>
> But David said to Abishai, "Do not destroy him, for who
> can stretch out his hand against the LORD's anointed and
> be without guilt?" (1 Samuel 26:5–9 NASB)

King Saul tried to kill David numerous times without any rational or justifiable reasons, but each time David responded with mercy. He used constraint when Saul twice threw spears at him. Then Saul tricked David into a suicide mission to obtain a wedding dowry of Philistine foreskins, hoping the enemy soldiers would slay him. He not only survived the encounter, he went on to marry Saul's daughter. And if that weren't enough, Saul ordered his son, Jonathan, to kill David; instead, Jonathan told David to hide and stay vigilant. Saul sent messenger after messenger to track David down and murder him (1 Samuel 19:11–20). Then one day in desperation, Saul traveled to Samuel's house in Ramah and tried to capture David unaware. This effort failed too. In all these things, David showed restraint, kindness, honor, and most of all, mercy. David even played music to soothe Saul's troubled spirit after God rejected him as king. How could we consider David anything but merciful?

A Man after God's Own Heart

"And Samuel said to Saul, 'You have done foolishly. You have not kept the commandment of the LORD your God, which He commanded you. For now the LORD would have established your kingdom over Israel forever. But now your kingdom shall not continue. The LORD has sought for Himself a man after His own heart, and the LORD has commanded him *to be* commander over His people, because you have not kept what the LORD commanded you'" (1 Samuel 13:13–14).

Samuel told King Saul that God rejected him for his disobedience and had already picked a new king with a heart like His own. Instead of repenting, Saul became angry, directing most of his anger toward David. Although Samuel did not name the replacement king, Saul might have assumed it was David. Afterward, God sent Samuel to Bethlehem where he found David and officially anointed him for the job. Was David any different from Saul? Both kings made mistakes; both sinned. King David even committed adultery with another man's wife, and when she became pregnant, he conspired to have her husband murdered to cover up his infidelity. Later, David let pride motivate him to number the people of Israel, which resulted in a severe judgment from God (1 Chronicles 21:1, 8).

If we consider his faults, how then did David have a heart like God's? There were two reasons: First, David loved mercy. He understood why God desired mercy more than sacrifice (see Hosea 6:6). He could be merciful because God had shown him mercy. Second, David did *all of God's will*. Although he experienced moral failure, made mistakes, and sinned against God and others, David still accomplished everything God willed for Israel during his reign. "He raised up for them David as king, to whom also He gave testimony and said, '*I have found David* the *son* of Jesse, *a man after My* own *heart,* who will do all My will'" (Acts 13:22b). David had a heart for other things, too, including worship.

Man of Worship

David loved to worship. He played his harp and sang songs unto God, something he learned to do as a young shepherd while keeping watch over his father's flock. After they crowned him king, David brought the Ark of the Covenant to Jerusalem. "Then David and all the house of Israel played *music* before the LORD on all kinds of *instruments* of fir wood, on harps, on stringed instruments, on tambourines, on sistrums, and on cymbals" (2 Samuel 6:5). The praise service encountered a few complications, but after they remembered the correct way to transport the ark, they resumed the procession, stopping every six steps (about eighteen feet) to offer sacrifices to the Lord. "And so it was, when those bearing the ark of the LORD had gone six paces, that [David] sacrificed oxen and fatted sheep. Then David danced before the LORD with all *his* might;... leaping and whirling before the LORD" (2 Samuel 6:13–14a, 16b).

David erected a tent on Mount Zion and placed the ark inside. People called the tent, the tabernacle of David, and Jerusalem, the City of David. In the wilderness, the tabernacle of Moses kept the ark hidden behind a veil in the Holy of Holies (Exodus 26:33–34). The tabernacle of David had no such veil, so anyone passing by could see the Ark of the Covenant in all its glory.[40]

David also instituted a new kind of worship. It not only involved singing, it included structured and spontaneous praise; clapping hands; bowing down; raising uplifted hands; playing cymbals, tambourines, and stringed instruments of every kind; and dancing unto God. David appointed thousands of singers and musicians who took turns ministering before the Lord, day and night (1 Chronicles 23:5). This unique style of worship and ministry continued until the construction of Solomon's temple. David also exempted the musicians' guild from regular employment so they could pray and worship full time: "These are the singers, heads of the fathers' *houses* of the Levites, *who lodged* in the chambers, *and were* free *from other duties;* for they were employed in *that* work day and night" (1 Chronicles 9:33).

In Acts, Apostle James connects the tabernacle of David to the Church. His reference comes from Amos who prophesied that Davidic worship would return in the last days. "After this I will return, and will build again the tabernacle of David, which is fallen down; and I will build again the ruins thereof, and I will set it up: That the residue of men might seek after the Lord, and all the Gentiles, upon whom my name is called, saith the Lord, who doeth all these things" (Acts 15:16–17 KJV).

Psalms of David

Many psalms were first written for use in the tabernacle of David. The Book of Psalms contains one hundred fifty psalms—almost half are attributed to David. His psalms embrace worship, praise, warfare, and intercession. No doubt, his experiences as a shepherd, warrior, and king influenced them. Several of them are prophetic in nature. The Psalms reveal why David was a man after God's own heart. For centuries, his words have encouraged and drawn us closer to God. One of the most endearing psalms is "The LORD, the Psalmist's Shepherd."

> The LORD is my shepherd,
> I shall not want.
> He makes me lie down in green pastures;

He leads me beside quiet waters.

He restores my soul;

He guides me in the paths of righteousness

For His name's sake.

Even though I walk through the valley of the shadow of death,

I fear no evil, for You are with me;

Your rod and Your staff, they comfort me.

You prepare a table before me in the presence of my enemies;

You have anointed my head with oil;

My cup overflows.

Surely goodness and lovingkindness will follow me all the days

of my life,

And I will dwell in the house of the LORD forever.

—Psalm 23:1–6 (NASB)

Psalm 23 was the first and only psalm I memorized as a child. I always thought it was about a shepherd, "I shall not want." Years later, I realized the old English wording meant not having any wants (needs or lacks). After my understanding changed, Psalm 23 took on a new meaning. I realized that David, a shepherd himself, wrote this psalm from the sheep's perspective, not the shepherd's point of view. Many call it the shepherd's psalm, but in reality, it is the sheep's song about its life under the watchful eye of a faithful and trusted shepherd.

The last song, Psalm 150, is from an unknown psalmist, but it sounds like something David would write and sing. In a way, it summarizes the whole purpose behind the Book of Psalms: "Let everything that has breath praise the LORD. Praise the LORD!" (Psalm 150:6).

Man of Faith

Besides being a man of mercy, worshiper, and writer of psalms, David was a person of great faith. In the Old Testament, faith often manifested itself through victories over one's enemies, and David's exploits of faith were no exception. Almost everyone knows the story of David's victory over Goliath. People have shared it countless times in songs, books, and films. Therefore, we will consider his story from Jonathan's point of view. What Jonathan, the son of King Saul, witnessed that day influenced him immensely. He acted in a way some might consider foolish for the heir apparent to the throne of Israel. "Then Jonathan and David made a covenant, because he loved him as his own soul. And Jonathan took off the robe that *was* on him and gave it to David, with his armor, even to his sword and his bow and his belt" (1 Samuel 18:3–4).

Word Picture: The Goliath Encounter

Oh my God! Did you see what happened? A young boy, someone who watches sheep, not a military leader, not a soldier—and he just slew a giant, the champion warrior of the Philistine army. *Unbelievable!* I've never seen or heard of anything like this in my life. Goliath must have been more than nine feet tall. This uncircumcised monster frightened every soldier in the army of Israel. Even my father, King Saul, who stood head and shoulders above every man in the realm, looked terrified. I felt the overwhelming terror as well.

Forty days this giant mocked and insulted our army, calling us cowards and blaspheming our God. None of us could face him. We all cowered in fear. *Lord, O Lord! A boy just killed a giant!* Did you see how little David charged toward him with just a stick and a handful of rocks for his sling? Never have I witnessed such faith.

David, here, please accept my robe, my armor, my sword, my bow — take my royal belt too. I lay it all at your feet. I feel unworthy to be heir to Israel's throne. You are the one, the Lord's champion. From this day forward, I pledge to serve you with all my heart. I don't care if my father, King Saul, agrees with me or not. You should be the one to lead Israel. *My God, my God! Did you see it? David slew Goliath!*

In the distance, three young men watched in awe. *Incredible! One shot! David really nailed him good!* Faith swelled in their hearts as they talked. After watching David's amazing victory, they felt different inside, fearless, strong — even mighty. Maybe someday they will test their courage on the battlefield too. When the time is right, why not offer to help David. Who knows, maybe one day he will be the king.

David's Three Mighty Men

David's faith rubbed off on others. All those who served under David's command were loyal and capable soldiers, but David had three men who were unlike any others. They were his three mighty men. One of them took on eight hundred enemy soldiers by himself. Another defeated an entire troop of advancing Philistines while defending a patch of peas. These three warriors were strong, fearless, anointed, and committed.

Mighty Man 1: "These are the names of the mighty men whom David had: Josheb-basshebeth a Tahchemonite, chief of the captains, he was called Adino the Eznite, because of eight hundred slain by him at one time" (2 Samuel 23:8 NASB).

Mighty Man 2: "And after him was Eleazar the son of Dodo the Ahohite, one of the three mighty men with David when they defied the Philistines who were gathered there to battle and the men of Israel had withdrawn. He arose and struck the Philistines until his hand was weary and clung to the sword, and the LORD brought about a great victory that day; and the people returned after him only to strip *the slain*" (2 Samuel 23:9–10 NASB).

Mighty Man 3: "Now after him was Shammah the son of Agee a Hararite. And the Philistines were gathered into a troop where there was a plot of ground full of lentils, and the people fled from the Philistines. But he took his stand in the midst of the plot, defended it and struck the Philistines; and the LORD brought about a great victory" (2 Samuel 23:11–12 NASB).

Getting Water

On another occasion, David, fatigued and battle worn, wished for a drink of cool water from the well in Bethlehem. It was more musing than anything else. Besides being impractical and somewhat foolish, an obstacle stood in the way: a garrison of enemy Philistines who occupied Bethlehem. "David had a craving and said, 'Oh that someone would give me water to drink from the well of Bethlehem which is by the gate!' So the three mighty men broke through the camp of the Philistines, and drew water from the well of Bethlehem which was by the gate, and took *it* and brought *it* to David. Nevertheless he would not drink it, but poured it out to the LORD" (2 Samuel 23:15–16 NASB).

The three mighty men overheard his comment and took it literally. They fought their way into town, filled a waterskin, and fought their way back out, just to give David a sip of water from his favorite well. No stealth was involved, nor were such military successes due to tactics alone. Instead, David and his men relied on God to deliver them and bring victory. We can summarize their mighty exploits with the following statement: "Saul has slain his thousands, and David his ten thousands" (1 Samuel 18:7).

As a man of faith, David inspired others to have faith, win battles, and accomplish mighty things in God's name. But where we find people of faith, we usually find something else—intercession.

Man of Intercession

David is remembered for his positive attributes and great accomplishments, but his role as a prayer intercessor probably tops the list. Even in the worst circumstances, his prayers revealed his desire to have a sincere heart. "Create in me a clean heart, O God, and renew a steadfast spirit within me. Do not cast me away from Your presence, and do not take Your Holy Spirit from me" (Psalm 51:10–11).

After King David sinned with Bathsheba and organized a murder plot against her husband, God sent Nathan to give David the "You *are* the man!" prophecy (see 2 Samuel 12:7). Although his reputation suffered, David didn't blame Bathsheba, the devil, or anyone else. He knew the offense was his alone. When the child from their infidelity became sick, David interceded with all his heart.

"David therefore pleaded with God for the child, and David fasted and went in and lay all night on the ground. So the elders of his house arose *and went* to him, to raise him up from the ground. But he would not, nor did he eat food with them" (2 Samuel 12:16–17). Although their child still died, a heartbreaking event for any parent, it never shook David's faith in God or stopped him from interceding on other occasions.

One day, David felt confident about things in the kingdom and wanted to see how many people his realm contained. Joab, a trusted general, advised David against taking a census, pointing out that the kingdom belonged to God, not him. David ignored the advice. Cunningly, Satan had tricked David to commit the sin of pride by trusting in his assets instead of God. By the time David realized the gravity of his sin, seventy thousand men in Israel had died and an angel stood over Jerusalem with orders to destroy it (1 Chronicles 21:14–15). David accepted the blame. However, only intercession could avert a further judgment.

> Then David lifted up his eyes and saw the angel of the LORD standing between earth and heaven, with his drawn sword in his hand stretched out over Jerusalem. Then David and the elders, covered with sackcloth, fell on their faces.

> Then David said to Ornan, "Give me the site of *this* threshing floor, that I may build on it an altar to the LORD; for the full price you shall give it to me, that the plague may be restrained from the people."

> Ornan said to David, "Take *it* for yourself; and let my lord the king do what is good in his sight. See, I will give the oxen for burnt offerings and the threshing sledges for wood and the wheat for the grain offering; I will give *it* all."

> But King David said to Ornan, "No, but I will surely buy *it* for the full price; for I will not take what is yours for the LORD, or offer a burnt offering which costs me nothing."

> So David gave Ornan 600 shekels of gold by weight for the site. Then David built an altar to the LORD there and offered burnt offerings and peace offerings. And he called to the LORD and He answered him with fire from heaven on the altar of burnt offering.

The LORD commanded the angel, and he put his sword back in its sheath. (1 Chronicles 21:16, 22–27 NASB)

David understood all too well the consequences of sin, but he also knew what effectual, fervent prayer could achieve. His intercession saved a kingdom. One day, intercession from another Son of David would accomplish even more.

The Greatest King of Israel

Abraham led the people to Canaan, the land of promise. Moses organized them into a holy nation and gave Israel the Ten Commandments and the Law. When Moses died, the Israelites followed Joshua who helped them conquer and settle Canaan. After that, the judges of Israel took over and ran things for a while. When Samuel, the last godly judge, reached retirement age, the people asked for a king so they could be like other nations. "But the thing displeased Samuel when they said, 'Give us a king to judge us.' So Samuel prayed to the LORD. And the LORD said to Samuel, 'Heed the voice of the people in all that they say to you; for they have not rejected you, but they have rejected Me, that I should not reign over them'" (1 Samuel 8:6–7).

Through Samuel's prophecy, God warned Israel about the consequences of having a sovereign other than Yahweh, but they did not listen (see 1 Samuel 8:9–22). Therefore, God allowed them to have a king. Their first one, Saul, failed early in his reign, so God chose a young shepherd to take his place. Maybe if the people had waited a while, He would have sent them David anyway. Nevertheless, God blessed David, and he became the greatest king ever to rule in Israel. More than his love for worship, his earnest prayers, and his mighty exploits of faith, David was a man after God's own heart who did *all of God's will*.

King David brought all the tribes of Israel under one rule. It was a golden age for God's chosen people. David was certainly a great patriarch, a leader like few others. However, not all Jewish leaders were patriarchs; some were matriarchs. In the next chapter, we will focus on these anointed women. Their godly faith and heroic deeds are inspiring.

CHAPTER *10*

GREATEST WOMEN OF THE OLD TESTAMENT

Greatness lies not in being strong, but in the right use of strength.
—Henry Ward Beecher

Among other important things, the Bible tracks the histories of certain key individuals. Some of these people influenced the lives of their families; others impacted nations. All too often, historians seem to favor the records of men. That will not be the case with this chapter because some of the greatest leaders in the Bible were matriarchs. Although a matriarch is normally considered the head of a family or tribe, she could also be any highly respected woman that people looked to for advice and leadership, especially in times of crisis. God anointed such women and gave them callings few others could match or fulfill. Indeed, they deserve all the honors due them.

Interestingly, when I ask my Bible scholar friends to name the most important individuals in the Old Testament, they often list Abraham, Moses, and David—the same ones I used in the last three chapters.

This list, however, is incomplete without including the women. Not all their names are recorded in the Bible but many of their heroic deeds were. They swayed history. Their lives and circumstances foreshadowed future events: Some were types and shadows of redemption; others facilitated greater moments. It seems only fitting this chapter highlights several of the greatest women from the Old Testament. We will start with Hannah.

Hannah: The Intercessor

> She, greatly distressed, prayed to the LORD and wept bitterly. She made a vow and said, "O LORD of hosts, if You will indeed look on the affliction of Your maidservant and remember me, and not forget Your maidservant, but will give Your maidservant a son, then I will give him to the LORD all the days of his life, and a razor shall never come on his head." Now it came about, as she continued praying before the LORD, that Eli was watching her mouth. As for Hannah, she was speaking in her heart, only her lips were moving, but her voice was not heard. So Eli thought she was drunk. (1 Samuel 1:10–13 NASB)

Hannah's prayer is a type of intercession, a desperate cry for help where mere words do not express one's feelings or needs. The Holy Spirit helps these prayers touch heaven. Apostle Paul explained it this way: "Likewise the Spirit also helps in our weaknesses. For we do not know what we should pray for as we ought, but the Spirit Himself makes intercession for us with groanings which cannot be uttered" (Romans 8:26). Paul's explanation typifies Hannah's prayer of intercession, and some believe it parallels praying in *unknown* tongues where understanding is unfruitful (see 1 Corinthians 14:14). The similarities are interesting. Hannah's intercessory prayer probably entailed words (her lips moved), but they were either silent or unrecognizable. Eli misjudged her, believing she was simply drunk and mumbling her words.

In response to Hannah's heartfelt intercession, God granted her the ability to have a son by healing her barren womb. "So it came to pass in the process of time that Hannah conceived and bore a son, and called his name Samuel, *saying,* 'Because I have asked for him from the LORD'" (1 Samuel 1:20).

After Hannah weaned Samuel (probably at three years old according to the custom of the day), she took him to the tabernacle of the Lord in Shiloh, along with an offering of flour, wine, and three bulls. She handed her son to Eli the priest and said, "For this child I prayed, and the LORD has granted me my petition which I asked of Him. Therefore I also have lent him to the LORD; as long as he lives he shall be lent to the LORD" (1 Samuel 1:27–28a). After worshiping, she returned home encouraged and full of faith. "So Samuel grew, and the LORD was with him and let none of his words fall to the ground" (1 Samuel 3:19).

Sometimes regular, routine prayer can seem ineffective, falling flat on the floor. When this happens, we should continue praying until we sense a breakthrough, pouring out our hearts to God in all sincerity — because "the prayer of a righteous person is powerful and effective" (James 5:16b NIV). If you need a real miracle, a healing, or a solution to an unsolvable problem, then pray as Hannah prayed. Intercession can open doors when nothing else will.

Hannah's name in Hebrew is *Channah,* which means grace.[41] It is a perfect description of her life. But more than exhibiting grace, Hannah was an intercessor.

Deborah: Prophet, Poet, and Warrior

"Now Deborah, a prophetess, the wife of Lapidoth, was judging Israel at that time. And she would sit under the palm tree of Deborah between Ramah and Bethel in the mountains of Ephraim. And the children of Israel came up to her for judgment" (Judges 4:4–5).

Deborah was a prophet, poet, and capable military leader. She is most famous for orchestrating a daring attack against a Canaanite army that fielded nine hundred ironclad chariots. King Jabin from Canaan and his senior commander, Sisera, had been conducting raids and oppressing the people of Israel for twenty years. One day, while Deborah sat under the palm tree, God gave her a prophetic message— it was time for Israel to fight back.

Along with Barak, her general, Deborah led an army of ten thousand Israelites into battle and routed the Canaanite solders. And it happened just the way Deborah prophesied it would (see Judges 4:6–7). "So on that day God subdued Jabin king of Canaan in the presence of the children of Israel. And the hand of the children of Israel grew stronger and stronger against Jabin king of Canaan, until they had destroyed Jabin king of Canaan" (Judges 4:23–24).

Deborah's deeds of bravery are immortalized in a poetic number she wrote in Judges 5. Below are seven stanzas from her thirty-verse song:

Song of Deborah and Barak

In the days of Shamgar the son of Anath,
In the days of Jael, the highways were deserted,
And travelers went by roundabout ways.

The peasantry ceased, they ceased in Israel,
Until I, Deborah, arose,
Until I arose, a mother in Israel.

New gods were chosen;
Then war *was* in the gates.
Not a shield or a spear was seen
Among forty thousand in Israel.

My heart *goes out* to the commanders of Israel,
The volunteers among the people;
Bless the LORD!

You who ride on white donkeys,
You who sit on *rich* carpets,
And you who travel on the road—sing!

At the sound of those who divide *flocks* among the watering places,
There they shall recount the righteous deeds of the LORD,
The righteous deeds for His peasantry in Israel.
Then the people of the LORD went down to the gates.

Awake, awake, Deborah;
Awake, awake, sing a song!
Arise, Barak, and take away your captives, O son of Abinoam.
—Judges 5:6–12 (NASB)

Considering the number of historical scrolls produced over the years, her poetic song would have hit gold long ago. Deborah's victory over the Canaanites brought forty years of peace to the twelve tribes. She became a respected judge in Israel at a time when women normally held subservient roles. Deborah in Hebrew means bee.[42] Her parents named her correctly, and the Canaanite soldiers may have concurred—for they experienced her wasp-like sting in battle and ran for their lives.

Rahab: Woman of Great Faith

"Now Joshua the son of Nun sent out two men from Acacia Grove to spy secretly, saying, 'Go, view the land, especially Jericho.' So they went, and came to the house of a harlot named Rahab, and lodged there" (Joshua 2:1).

Rahab the harlot lived in a house connected to the fortified wall of Jericho. Perhaps it provided a good location for attracting customers or contained a lavish apartment. Either way, it offered a good view. If she had looked out her window that evening, she may have seen two men approaching from the distance—scouts from Joshua's camp sent to spy out the land.

The scouts entered the city, seemingly unnoticed in the darkness; feeling drawn to one particular home, they knocked at Rahab's door. Unfortunately, several neighbors also noticed her two guests and reported it to the king. When the king's security squad arrived to investigate, Rahab hid the spies under stalks of flax on her roof. Then she made up a phony story and sent the king's men on a wild goose chase. Later, she helped the spies escape through her side window, using a rope to lower them off the wall.

Rahab, along with all the inhabitants of Jericho, had heard the stories of Yahweh: "I know that the LORD has given you the land, that the terror of you has fallen on us, and that all the inhabitants of the land are fainthearted because of you. For we have heard how the LORD dried up the water of the Red Sea for you when you came out of Egypt, and what you did to the two kings of the Amorites who *were* on the other side of the Jordan, Sihon and Og, whom you utterly destroyed" (Joshua 2:9*b*–10).

She knew that eventually Jericho would fall, so Rahab made an accord with the spies: their safety for her safety. She had risked her life by hiding them from the king of Jericho. In return, Rahab wanted her family spared and their possessions left alone when the Israelites stormed the city. The spies agreed but in good faith asked her to hang a crimson cord out the window. When they saw the sign, they would spare everyone in her house. The crimson cord is a clear picture of our redemption through the blood of Christ at Calvary.

Rahab who started with a shady past ended with a glorious heritage—only possible to someone with great faith: "By faith the harlot Rahab did not perish with those who did not believe, when she had received the spies with peace" (Hebrews 11:31). Rahab's name in Hebrew means grow wide or grow large,[43] and it's a perfect analogy of her life after Jericho. Rahab became the wife of Salmon and mother of Boaz, which placed her in the lineage of King David (see Matthew 1:5–6). Her family line continued on to Joseph who espoused Mary, the mother of Jesus.

Ruth: The Faithful Companion

Ruth lived in Moab with her husband and family. After ten years of marriage, her husband passed away leaving her with two choices: stay in Moab and remarry or move to Bethlehem with her mother-in-law, Naomi, who was also a widow. Out of love and commitment to Naomi, she decided to forsake her pagan gods in favor of Yahweh and the people of Israel.

Then she said, "Behold, your sister-in-law has gone
back to her people and her gods; return after your
sister-in-law."

But Ruth said, "Do not urge me to leave you *or* turn
back from following you; for where you go, I will go,
and where you lodge, I will lodge. Your people *shall be*
my people, and your God, my God."

So Naomi returned, and with her Ruth the Moabitess,
her daughter-in-law, who returned from the land of
Moab. And they came to Bethlehem at the beginning
of barley harvest. (Ruth 1:15–16, 22 NASB)

God's unseen hand of providence led Ruth to glean in the fields of
Boaz, a wealthy relative of Elimelech, Naomi's late husband. When
Boaz discovered that Ruth was related to Naomi, he allowed her to
glean during both the barley and wheat harvests. The Law of Moses
allowed gleaning (picking up the leftovers) after the reapers harvested
their fields. Field owners showed this act of kindness or benevolence to
orphans, widows, the poor, and strangers in the land (Leviticus 19:9–
10; Deuteronomy 24:19). After Ruth's first day of gathering grain,
Boaz offered her protection, encouragement, and a few suggestions:

"Let your eyes be on the field which they reap, and go
after them. Indeed, I have commanded the servants not
to touch you. When you are thirsty, go to the water jars
and drink from what the servants draw."

Then she fell on her face, bowing to the ground and
said to him, "Why have I found favor in your sight that
you should take notice of me, since I am a foreigner?"

> Boaz replied to her, "All that you have done for your
> mother-in-law after the death of your husband has
> been fully reported to me, and how you left your father
> and your mother and the land of your birth, and came
> to a people that you did not previously know." (Ruth
> 2:9–11 NASB)

Ruth grew up worshiping idols, not Yahweh. She didn't know about the covenant blessing given to Abraham and his descendants (Genesis 12:3). Yet Ruth had blessed Naomi through her dedication and faithfulness, and now this new God had returned the blessing. Little did she know that Yahweh had even greater plans for her.

After harvest season ended, the threshing season began. At Naomi's suggestion, Ruth went to the threshing floor one night, waited until Boaz fell asleep, and then lay down at his feet. Around midnight, Boaz woke up and noticed Ruth. Her virtue and humility were evident by her honorable actions. As he listened to Ruth share her heart, Boaz realized she wanted to marry him as her kinsman-redeemer (see Ruth 3:9). Boaz loved her, too, but Ruth had a nearer kinsman who had first option. Contemplating the possibilities, Ruth headed back home in the morning, her shawl overflowing with barley grain—a gift for Naomi.

Under the Law, the nearest blood relative (or kinsman) had the responsibility to redeem a family member in case of a loss. There were three situations where this law applied:

1. When the loss involved being sold into slavery because of a debt, the kinsman would buy back his relative's freedom.
2. If unpaid debt caused land to be forfeited, a kinsman could repurchase the property for his family member.
3. When a relative died without an heir, the kinsman would marry the widow and raise children to carry on the family line.[44] Naomi and Ruth faced the latter two circumstances.

The final episode played out at the city gate before ten elders, where the nearer kinsman renounced his claim. When he understood the situation not only involved redeeming Naomi's land but also marrying Ruth and having more children, he passed on the deal. Therefore, Boaz was free to marry Ruth. They named their first child, Obed, who became the grandfather of King David (see Matthew 1:5).

Ruth's name means companion or friendship.[45] She is a perfect example of the redeemed Church and typifies the relationship between the heavenly Bridegroom and His bride. Ruth's story also illustrates the three main requirements for a *go-el* or kinsman-redeemer.[46]

1. Must be a near kinsmen (Ruth 3:9).
2. Must be able to redeem (Ruth 2:1; 4:4, 6, 9).
3. Must be willing to redeem (Ruth 3:13).

Jesus Christ fulfilled all these qualifications. He became a relative of humanity through Mary who birthed Him. Moreover, because He lived a perfect life He was able to redeem us. Even though Jesus bore our sins (1 Peter 2:24; Isaiah 53:4–6), He was not a sinner so He never fell short of the glory of God. These first two things qualified Him as a kinsman-redeemer. Most of all, Jesus was willing to redeem, and He paid the ransom price in full at the Cross.

Three Great Moms

Biblical history includes many great women. It would take volumes of books to record their names and describe all their deeds. This little chapter cannot do justice. Three more women, though, are worthy of mention—all of them mothers.

Eve: Mother of Humanity

Eve was the first woman. We usually remember her for eating the forbidden fruit. However, we should not forget that her husband ate the fruit too. Their disobedience or rebellion, known as the original sin, continued down the line of humanity. "Therefore, just as through one man sin entered the world, and death through sin, and thus death spread to all men, because all sinned" (Romans 5:12). However, we often overlook Eve's main contribution to the world.

Through DNA studies, researchers believe they have traced human ancestry back to a single woman they refer to as Mitochondrial Eve. Although these suppositions are interesting, scientific studies can err and sometimes draw the wrong conclusions, but the Bible never errs. According to Genesis 3:20, Eve is the birth mother of the entire human race: "And Adam called his wife's name Eve, because she was the mother of all living." A great legacy indeed!

Sarah: Princess of Faith

"By faith Sarah herself also received strength to conceive seed, and she bore a child when she was past the age, because she judged Him faithful who had promised" (Hebrews 11:11).

According to Romans 9:8–9, Sarah became a mother of promise with the birth of her son Isaac. And since Sarah believed God, "she judged Him faithful," Yahweh would have accounted her faith for righteousness like He did for Abraham (see Genesis 15:6; Romans 4:19–22). Moreover, Isaiah 51:1–2 refers to both Sarah and Abraham as spiritual rocks. Therefore, if we call Abraham the father of faith, then we should equally call Sarah the mother of faith. Such faith in God still accounts for righteousness in believers today. "Now it was not written for his sake alone that it was imputed to him, but also for us. It shall be imputed to us who believe in Him who raised up Jesus our Lord from the dead" (Romans 4:23–24).

God also changed her name. She went from of Sarai (princess) to Sarah (noblewoman). She would become a mother of nations and through her lineage, kings and kingdoms would arise (Genesis 17:15–16). Sarah not only birthed nations, she influenced Judaism, Christianity, and in some aspects, Islam.[47] When Sarah suggested that her maidservant, Hagar, have a child with her husband, she never realized the impact Ishmael and his descendants would have on biblical events and world politics. Many women have helped to shape history; some were unknowns, others had nobility, but few were spiritual rocks with faith like Sarah.

Zipporah: The Small One

Zipporah lived with her six sisters in the desert regions of northwestern Arabia. She and her sisters worked as shepherdesses for their father, Reuel, known to the locals as Jethro the priest of Midian. Zipporah married Moses and helped him get started in her father's shepherding business. *Tsipporah,* her name in Hebrew, comes from the noun *tsippowr,* which means small bird.[48] Ironically, Zipporah's small contribution in Exodus 4:24–26, not only spared the life of Moses the deliverer, it saved the Hebrews in Goshen from endless years of bondage under the Egyptians.

Moses had neglected to circumcise his son, a procedure required under the covenant of Abraham. Therefore, the Lord caught up to their caravan and sought to kill Moses for his disobedience (v. 24). That would have permanently ended her husband's call to set the captives free. Zipporah acted quickly, circumcising their son right on the spot. Putting her rationale aside, her actions showed bravery and a deep-rooted faith.

Many women listed in this chapter exhibited faith and courage in dire situations, but one stands out as the most heroic of all. She saved an entire population of disbursed Jews in Persia from certain annihilation.

Esther: Bravest Star of All

> Then Mordecai told *them* to reply to Esther, "Do not imagine that you in the king's palace can escape any more than all the Jews. For if you remain silent at this time, relief and deliverance will arise for the Jews from another place and you and your father's house will perish. And who knows whether you have not attained royalty for such a time as this?"
>
> Then Esther told *them* to reply to Mordecai, "Go, assemble all the Jews who are found in Susa, and fast for me; do not eat or drink for three days, night or day. I and my maidens also will fast in the same way. And thus I will go in to the king, which is not according to the law; and if I perish, I perish." (Esther 4:13–16 NASB)

Along with other captives, Nebuchadnezzar captured Hadassah and her family, deporting them to Babylon after the fall of King Jeconiah of Judah. At some point in her childhood, Hadassah's parents passed away, and Mordecai, her cousin, adopted her.

Then one day, the ruling king issued a royal decree for a beauty pageant. The selection committee searched the kingdom for the most beautiful women, and then entered them into a non-optional contest. King Ahasuerus of Persia, also known as King Xerxes, had just gone through an unfortunate divorce with Queen Vashti and was looking for a new wife, someone worthy to be his queen. The committee picked

Hadassah as one of the contestants, whose Persian name is Esther, meaning *star*.[49]

It may have been coincidental, but Esther became the *star* of the king's beauty pageant, outscoring all other contestants. Perhaps her Persian name swayed the decision. More likely, though, it was providence at work. "The king loved Esther more than all the *other* women, and she obtained grace and favor in his sight more than all the virgins; so he set the royal crown upon her head and made her queen instead of Vashti" (Esther 2:17).

The happy couple had no secrets, well, except one—Esther was a Jew from the tribe of Benjamin. If her husband the king ever found out, he could have Esther exiled like Vashti or even worse—executed. However, this was not Esther's only concern. Someone in upper leadership had taken offense at her cousin Mordecai's lack of recognition protocols.

Haman, recently promoted to prime minister of the realm, felt slighted when Mordecai refused to bow down and pay him homage. In fact, he became so livid that he devised a plan to exterminate every Jew in the Persian Empire. He tricked King Ahasuerus into authorizing an execution decree, which according to the laws of the Medes and the Persians could not be revoked.

When Mordecai told Esther what Haman had done, she called for all the Jews in the land to fast three days. Esther knew only one way to save her people: she must approach the king without a summons (generally a death sentence) and try to expose Haman's evil plot.

On the third day, Queen Esther went before King Ahasuerus, uninvited, not knowing whether he would extend his golden scepter. If he did not, she would forfeit her life for the unannounced intrusion. Fortunately, she found favor with the king due to all the praying and fasting on her behalf. When he asked the reason for her visit, Esther told him she wanted to invite the king and Haman to a special banquet where she could honor them. Ahasuerus happily agreed and summoned Haman to go with him. During dinner, Esther invited them back for a second banquet on the next day:

> Now the king and Haman came to drink *wine* with Esther the queen. And the king said to Esther on the second day also as they drank their wine at the banquet, "What is your petition, Queen Esther? It shall be granted you. And what is your request? Even to half of the kingdom it shall be done."
>
> Then Queen Esther replied, "If I have found favor in your sight, O king, and if it pleases the king, let my life be given me as my petition, and my people as my request; for we have been sold, I and my people, to be destroyed, to be killed and to be annihilated. Now if we had only been sold as slaves, men and women, I would have remained silent, for the trouble would not be commensurate with the annoyance to the king."
>
> Then King Ahasuerus asked Queen Esther, "Who is he, and where is he, who would presume to do thus?"
>
> Esther said, "A foe and an enemy is this wicked Haman!" (Esther 7:1–6*a* NASB)

When King Ahasuerus heard the truth about Haman's plans, he ordered Haman hanged on the same gallows he had built for Mordecai. The rest of the story is well known and celebrated every year at the Feast of Purim (see Esther 9:17–32).

Esther put her life on the line to save her people from certain disaster at the hands of her enemy. Her life foreshadows another person, Jesus Christ, who also faced death to save others. Esther is one of the most revered individuals in the Bible, matriarch or patriarch. Her actions preserved the descendants of Israel and saved the lineage of the Jewish people. She was truly a great leader and possibly the bravest Israelite of all.

One individual, however, has not been named. This person is the greatest patriarch Israel has ever known.

CHAPTER *11*

THE GREATEST PATRIARCH OF ISRAEL

A great leader's courage to fulfill his vision comes
from passion, not position.
—John C. Maxwell

The last several chapters highlighted the lives of great leaders from the Old Testament, all recognized for their accomplishments, all patriarchs or matriarchs in their own right. Notwithstanding, Israel produced many godly leaders: prophets like Elijah and Elisha, warriors like Joshua and Caleb, seers like Joseph and Daniel, even a few builders like Noah and Nehemiah.

According to the writer of Hebrews, God raised up many such leaders. "And what more shall I say? For the time would fail me to tell of Gideon and Barak and Samson and Jephthah, also *of* David and Samuel and the prophets: who through faith subdued kingdoms, worked righteousness, obtained promises, stopped the mouths of lions, quenched the violence of fire, escaped the edge of the sword, out of weakness were made strong, became valiant in battle, turned to flight the armies of the aliens" (Hebrews 11:32–34). The passage concludes by saying the world was not worthy of these people (v. 38). Some of these faithful heroes were named patriarchs; others were not but should have been.

Who Are Patriarchs?

Bible scholars usually refer to Abraham, Isaac, and Jacob as the three patriarchs of the patriarchal period. If we include their wives— Sarah, Rebekah, Leah, and Rachel as matriarchs—then that totals seven.[50] However, in actuality, we can find many more. The Bible labels King David (Acts 2:29) and the twelve sons of Jacob (Acts 7:8–9) as patriarchs. If people like David and Joseph had this title, then Moses should too. We can equally add Adam, Seth, Enoch, Methuselah, Noah, and others who lived before the Flood to the list as well (see Genesis 5:1–32; Romans 9:5 NIV; John 7:22 NIV). All these individuals were patriarchal ancestors of humanity. Moreover, in early church history, the bishops of Rome, Constantinople, Jerusalem, Antioch, and Alexandria held the title of patriarch, including several Popes who used the designation, *Patriarch of the West*,[51] until the Vatican discontinued its use in 2006.

Dictionaries define a patriarch as a powerful, respected, older man who rules a family, clan, or tribe. Simply put, he was a wise, authoritative, esteemed leader in the community. We will use the latter definition, widening the category to include all patriarchs of the Old Testament and other "heroes of the faith," serving God under the Law of Moses. Jesus considered one of these individuals greater than all the rest.

None Greater than John

> As these men were going *away,* Jesus began to speak to the crowds about John, "What did you go out into the wilderness to see? A reed shaken by the wind?
>
> But what did you go out to see? A man dressed in soft *clothing?* Those who wear soft *clothing* are in kings' palaces!
>
> But what did you go out to see? A prophet? Yes, I tell you, and one who is more than a prophet. This is the one about whom it is written, 'BEHOLD, I SEND MY MES-SENGER AHEAD OF YOU, WHO WILL PREPARE YOUR WAY BEFORE YOU.'
>
> Truly I say to you, among those born of women there has not arisen *anyone* greater than John the Baptist! Yet the one who is least in the kingdom of heaven is greater than he." (Matthew 11:7–11 NASB)

The prophets Isaiah and Malachi foretold of John's arrival. Jesus called him the greatest leader ever born—prophet or otherwise. In fact, John was more than a prophet. Nicknamed *the Baptist,* John was a fiery preacher, an anointed teacher, and a spiritual mentor for many who lived in Israel. None were greater. He rose from relative obscurity to become the greatest patriarch to have ever lived. His messages, which challenged some people and angered others, centered on a common theme: "Repent, for the kingdom of heaven is at hand!" (Matthew 3:2).

An Impossibility Made Possible

The Bible tells us that Elizabeth, the mother who birthed John the Baptist, was elderly, barren, and therefore unable to have children. Her husband, Zacharias, had also reached advanced age. Their chances of conceiving a child were nearly impossible. Such limitations, however, are never a problem with God: "For with God nothing will be impossible" (Luke 1:37).

The story unfolds with Zacharias' division of priests, Abijah, ministering in the temple. King David had organized the priests into twenty-four divisions to allow for a fair and orderly system of service (1 Chronicles 24:7–19). With the large number of priests serving in the temple, the opportunity to burn incense at the altar rarely happened—traditionally, only once in a lifetime. The lot fell on Zacharias that day. He would be burning the daily incense at the altar of incense in the holy place, not in the Most Holy Place. Only the high priest could enter the Most Holy Place (also called the Holy of Holies), and this happened just once a year on the Day of Atonement (Hebrews 9:7).

It was probably a Sabbath day since a large crowd had gathered at the temple to pray. As Zacharias entered the holy place, an angel of the Lord appeared and stood by the right side of the altar. The unexpected visit from a heavenly messenger worried him. Some might think seeing a real angel would be the ultimate experience but a fearful response is more likely.

> But the angel said to him, "Do not be afraid, Zacharias, for your petition has been heard, and your wife Elizabeth will bear you a son, and you will give him the name John. You will have joy and gladness, and many will rejoice at his birth. For he will be great in the sight of the Lord; and he will drink no wine or liquor, and he will be filled with the Holy Spirit while yet in his mother's womb.
>
> And he will turn many of the sons of Israel back to the Lord their God. It is he who will go *as a forerunner*

before Him in the spirit and power of Elijah, TO TURN THE HEARTS OF THE FATHERS BACK TO THE CHILDREN, and the disobedient to the attitude of the righteous, so as to make ready a people prepared for the Lord." (Luke 1:13–17 NASB)

The experience left him speechless for about nine months. Amazingly, his barren wife conceived and bore a son just like the angel prophesied. Most people assumed the couple would name their newborn boy after his father. At the circumcision ceremony, however, a silent Zacharias surprised friends and relatives: first by writing his son's name is John, and second by speaking aloud. Soon afterward, he began praising God and prophesying about John's ministry.

John's Ministry Unparalleled

"The law and the prophets *were* until John. Since that time the kingdom of God has been preached, and everyone is pressing into it" (Luke 16:16).

At some point, John moved out of his parent's house and set up residence in the Judean wilderness. He wore hairy garments made of scratchy camel skins that he tied together with a leather belt. He lived off the land, existing on a diet of wild honey and flying locusts. Apparently, locusts, grasshoppers, and crickets were kosher foods under the Law of Moses (see Leviticus 11:22). Hoppers are not my idea of an appetizing meal, but maybe the honey helped with palatability.

John's ministry grew rapidly. Soon he had baptized countless converts in the Jordan River, asking them to repent from their sins and turn to God. The message below is indicative of one of John's hellfire and brimstone sermons:

But when he saw many of the Pharisees and Sadducees coming for baptism, he said to them, "You brood of vipers, who warned you to flee from the wrath to come? Therefore bear fruit in keeping with repentance; and do not suppose that you can say to yourselves, 'We have Abraham for our father'; for I say to you that from these stones God is able to raise up children to Abraham.

The axe is already laid at the root of the trees; therefore every tree that does not bear good fruit is cut down and thrown into the fire.

As for me, I baptize you with water for repentance, but He who is coming after me is mightier than I, and I am not fit to remove His sandals; He will baptize you with the Holy Spirit and fire. His winnowing fork is in His hand, and He will thoroughly clear His threshing floor; and He will gather His wheat into the barn, but He will burn up the chaff with unquenchable fire." (Matthew 3:7–12 NASB)

His messages stirred up revival fires in Jerusalem, Judea, and the areas surrounding Jordan (Matthew 3:5–6). While the populace flocked into wilderness to hear him preach, the religious elite in Jerusalem wondered about his real identity and the reason he never became a temple priest like his father. Who did this Baptist think he was anyway, the Messiah?

A Voice Crying in the Wilderness

This is the testimony of John, when the Jews sent to him priests and Levites from Jerusalem to ask him, "Who are you?"

And he confessed and did not deny, but confessed, "I am not the Christ."

They asked him, "What then? Are you Elijah?"

And he said, "I am not."

"Are you the Prophet?"

And he answered, "No."

Then they said to him, "Who are you, so that we may give an answer to those who sent us? What do you say about yourself?"

He said, "I am A VOICE OF ONE CRYING IN THE WILDERNESS, 'MAKE STRAIGHT THE WAY OF THE LORD,' as Isaiah the prophet said." (John 1:19–23 NASB)

This voice from the wilderness turned the children of Israel back to their God and hearts of the fathers toward their children. Not an ordinary voice but an anointed one—and it cried out for repentance and revival. The Holy Spirit filled John even before birth (Luke 1:15). All others, God anointed when He needed them to perform some duty or ministry, but with John, the Spirit remained every moment of every day. His anointing seemed so strong that some thought he might be the Anointed One (*Messiah* in Hebrew, *Christ* in Greek). If not Him, then maybe John was Elijah; many Jews believed Elijah's return would precede the Messiah's appearance. Others wondered if John could be the unnamed prophet mentioned by Moses: "The LORD your God will raise up for you a Prophet like me from your midst, from your brethren. Him you shall hear" (Deuteronomy 18:15).

No, John was not the Christ, Elijah returning from a heavenly chariot ride, or some unknown prophet. God sent John to clear away rocks and debris—to make a straight highway for the coming Messiah. This imagery comes from a day when established roads were a rarity, especially in desert wildernesses. If a king needed to travel, he sent a forerunner to build a new road or smooth out an existing one. Otherwise, his royal chariot might encounter delays, undergo endless detours, or bog down in the muck and mire. Herein is a perfect word picture of John's ministry as a forerunner for Messiah. God sent him to prepare the people for a divine king.

Forerunner for Messiah

Forerunners were people who blazed new trails or repaired old ones, setting the stage for those who followed them. They were anointed specialists, their contributions invaluable to the kingdom of God. One of the greatest was Moses. "But since then there has not arisen in Israel a prophet like Moses, whom the LORD knew face to face" (Deuteronomy 34:10). Then John arose as more than a prophet (Matthew 11:9) with a greater ministry. Jesus made that determination when He said, "Assuredly, I say to you, among those born of women there has not risen one greater than John the Baptist" (Matthew 11:11*a*).

John the Baptist became the last forerunner under the Old Covenant, a patriarch in his own right. However, John understood he must step aside when the Messiah arrived on the scene (John 3:30). This Messiah would introduce a New Covenant (see Jeremiah 31:31–34, Hebrews 12:24) and become the greatest messenger or deliverer ever sent to Israel:

- Greater than Jonah (Matthew 12:41)
- Greater than Solomon in all his glory (Matthew 12:42)
- Greater than Abraham, the father of faith (John 8:56–58)

In fact, He would be greater than all the patriarchs, prophets, and priests combined. The angels would call His name Immanuel.

PART FOUR:

MOMENTS FROM THE LIFE OF JESUS

CHAPTER 12

IMMANUEL COMES TO BETHLEHEM

As the centuries pass, the evidence is accumulating that,
measured by His effect on history,
Jesus is the most influential life ever lived on this planet.
—Historian Kenneth Scott Latourette

Mary and Joseph lived in Nazareth of Galilee. After their betrothal agreement, they spent more time with each other—under the watchful eye of relatives. Along with family members, they attended Sabbath services at the local synagogue and listened to elders read from the Torah. Mary wanted to have children, own a nice home, and help Joseph expand his carpentry business. With his skill in woodworking, they could make a decent wage and live happy, productive lives. Joseph figured if he watched his finances and put aside a few silver coins, then someday he could take Mary on a trip to the Mediterranean coast. He also knew of a few places in Egypt where Jewish families could safely visit. A scenic boat ride down the Nile after flood season might be nice as well. Although this word picture is speculative, their dreams were not unlike many betrothed couples of their day—or ours. Then one week, something happened that changed everything.

Word Picture: Mary

Mary, called *Miryam* in Hebrew, grew up in the city of Nazareth. Although her name meant rebellious and bitter,[52] her temperament never portrayed those traits. Mary was honest, meditative, and often kept her opinions to herself. Many believed she had royal blood in her family, possibly through King David and the tribe of Judah (Luke 3:23–33), but Mary seldom discussed this connection with others.[53]

Finances were limited for most Jewish families living in the province of Galilee—no thanks to the Romans and their taxes—so Mary probably stayed with her parents in a simple brick or stone dwelling. Her parents may have arranged her betrothal to Joseph, following the traditional customs of the day. She liked Joseph, and as time passed she fell in love with him. Mary stayed busy, helping with chores around the house and making plans for her upcoming marriage. Her life seemed fairly normal, that is, until someone named Gabriel knocked at her door. The angelic messenger told her to rejoice because God highly favored her. His salutation troubled her.

Mary's Angelic Visitation

> The angel said to her, "Do not be afraid, Mary; for you have found favor with God. And behold, you will conceive in your womb and bear a son, and you shall name Him Jesus.
>
> He will be great and will be called the Son of the Most High; and the Lord God will give Him the throne of His

father David; and He will reign over the house of Jacob forever, and His kingdom will have no end."

Mary said to the angel, "How can this be, since I am a virgin?"

The angel answered and said to her, "The Holy Spirit will come upon you, and the power of the Most High will overshadow you; and for that reason the holy Child shall be called the Son of God." (Luke 1:30–35 NASB)

Word Picture: Joseph

Joseph's name, *Yowceph* in Hebrew, meant Yahweh has added.[54] The name seemed to fit him since he liked counting his options or adding improvements to his woodwork. As a descendant of King David, he had royal lineage too (Matthew 1:16). He grew up in Bethlehem, his ancestral home, but now lived and worked in Nazareth. He learned carpentry from his father and enjoyed having a good reputation around town. One day, he would make a good father but not anytime soon, he hoped. He betrothed a lovely young girl named Mary and cared deeply for her. As their marriage day drew near, the wedding arrangements weighed heavy on his mind.

After work one day, Mary told him she was pregnant. The news broke his heart. In fact, it angered him a little. He knew the child couldn't be his because he had been faithful to his vows—but what about Mary. *Oh no, what would his neighbors and relatives think?* Maybe he should end the relationship now, discreetly, before the rumors circulated.

Had Mary taken up with some other fellow? She said there wasn't anyone else, but the facts seemed to speak for themselves. And where did she get these unorthodox stories about seeing an angel, being overshadowed by the Holy Spirit, and conceiving the Son of God? A certificate of divorce to end the betrothal might work best for both of them. He would sleep on it and make a final decision in the morning. If only God would tell him what to do.

Joseph's Angelic Visitation

> But when he had considered this, behold, an angel of the Lord appeared to him in a dream, saying, "Joseph, son of David, do not be afraid to take Mary as your wife; for the Child who has been conceived in her is of the Holy Spirit.
>
> She will bear a Son; and you shall call His name Jesus, for He will save His people from their sins."
>
> Now all this took place to fulfill what was spoken by the Lord through the prophet: "BEHOLD, THE VIRGIN SHALL BE WITH CHILD AND SHALL BEAR A SON, AND THEY SHALL CALL HIS NAME IMMANUEL," which translated means, "GOD WITH US." (Matthew 1:20–23 NASB)

The Sign of Immanuel

Did the angel say the baby's name would be Jesus or Immanuel? Actually, the angel used both names. Jesus is a Greek rendering of the name Joshua.[55] The Hebrew equivalent, *Yeshua (yēšûaʿ*, from *yᵉhôšuaʿ)*, means Yahweh is salvation.[56] By contrast, Immanuel translates as God with us. We find Immanuel mentioned twice in Isaiah (7:14; 8:8). If we count Isaiah 8:10, which only refers to the name, then it's three times. The names, Jesus and Immanuel, give us an undeniable word picture of who this Child is and what He will do: He will save people, in person, by drawing close to them—a perfect description of salvation in Christ.

145

Staying within the historical context, the sign of Immanuel concerned the birth of a child in Isaiah's day. His prophetic word came at a critical time when King Ahaz of Judah faced an overwhelming army from Syria. The prophecy described an unusual circumstance, not a normal pregnancy, because an ordinary conception would not have been noteworthy. Immanuel's birth became a defining moment for Judah, although short-lived (see Isaiah 7:16–17). Isaiah's prophecy about a virgin birthing a son pointed to another prophetic event, a more revered one. The chapters in this book are likewise leading to one esteemed event—the greatest moment of all.

Word Picture: Taxes and Mangers

"And it came to pass in those days *that* a decree went out from Caesar Augustus that all the world should be registered. This census first took place while Quirinius was governing Syria" (Luke 2:1–2).

The Romans liked to keep track of people. Therefore, taking a census made perfect sense to them, especially for taxation purposes, and the Romans had a tax for just about everything. All subjects living in their empire needed to return to their birthplace and register. After packing up, Joseph took his wife, who had reached full term in her pregnancy, and headed for his hometown of Bethlehem. Depending on the route they took, a trip from Nazareth to Bethlehem involved traveling eighty to ninety miles—and they walked it all. What about the donkey? The biblical account does not mention transportation helps. Besides, riding camels or using pack animals were luxuries—extras they probably could not afford.

Since Joseph had friends and family in Bethlehem, he undoubtedly checked with them first, but all the extra rooms and flat roof spaces were taken. One look at the caravansary told the story there. It was slammed, a madhouse—no place for a woman about to deliver a baby. Finally, a local herdsman pointed to a cave on the hill. It looked empty except for some animals milling about. Joseph wondered why nobody had taken it. After they ascended the hill, he discovered the reason. The place looked messy and it smelled—a typical animal stall. Thankfully, he found some clean straw and an empty feeding trough. They would have to do. None too soon, either, for Mary's labor contractions had begun. God willing, they would have the baby before morning.

"So it was, that while they were there, the days were completed for her to be delivered. And she brought forth her firstborn Son, and wrapped Him in swaddling cloths, and laid Him in a manger, because there was no room for them in the inn" (Luke 2:6–7).

Shepherd's Story

"Now there were in the same country shepherds living out in the fields, keeping watch over their flock by night" (Luke 2:8). Who were these shepherds? The Bible doesn't say. They could have been resident sheepherders, a band of vagabonds moving their sheep through the area, or shepherds who watched over the temple flock. This latter group took care of sheep destined for sacrifice at the temple in Jerusalem. Whoever these shepherds were, they camped near Bethlehem, had access to good pasture, and kept a nightly watch. Nighttime usually consisted of four watches, three hours each, starting at sundown.

What season of the year did these events take place? Again, no one really knows. Shepherds usually pastured their flocks in the open fields from spring to autumn. Temple sheep, however, remained in the fields throughout the year, even during winter. With mild winters and moderate rainfall, Bethlehem averaged slightly less than twenty-five inches of precipitation a year. Even with chilly winds, occasional hailstorms, and a few isolated snow showers—winter temperatures stayed around forty degrees at night. Regardless of climate conditions or time of year, shepherds who watched over the temple flock would have been on duty.[57] Therefore, if the angel of the Lord appeared to these shepherds, it is conceivable the first Christmas actually happened on Christmas.

Shepherd's Angelic Visitation

> And an angel of the Lord suddenly stood before them, and the glory of the Lord shone around them; and they were terribly frightened.
>
> But the angel said to them, "Do not be afraid; for behold, I bring you good news of great joy which will be for all the people; for today in the city of David there has been born for you a Savior, who is Christ the Lord.
>
> This *will be* a sign for you: you will find a baby wrapped in cloths and lying in a manger."
>
> And suddenly there appeared with the angel a multitude of the heavenly host praising God and saying, "Glory to God in the highest, and on earth peace among men with whom He is pleased." (Luke 2:9–14 NASB)

After their initial fears abated, they followed the angel's advice and rushed off to Bethlehem. Being responsible shepherds, they probably left at least one person behind to watch the flock. A group of exuberant shepherds running through town at night must have created quite a ruckus. Focused and determined, they searched until they found Mary, Joseph, and their baby wrapped in swaddling cloths and lying inside a feeding trough. The shepherds told everyone they met about the angel encounter and this newborn Savior. Bethlehem would never be the same again. "But you, Bethlehem Ephrathah, *though* you are little among the thousands of Judah, *yet* out of you shall come forth to Me the One to be Ruler in Israel, whose goings forth *are* from of old, from everlasting" (Micah 5:2).

Local Prophets Agree

The Bible establishes certain matters through agreement, often by twos and threes (Matthew 18:19–20; 1 John 5:7–8). When two or more prophets agreed, it gave validation to their prophecies: "Let two or three prophets speak, and let the others judge" (1 Corinthians 14:29). Detailed prophecies, which confirm Scripture and foretell events, are one reason our Bibles are different from other religious books.

Prophets gave spiritual direction, pointed out iniquity, and foretold future events. The Old Testament alone has more than three hundred messianic prophecies revealing Immanuel's identity, purpose, and ministry. We will consider only three—the biblical standard for establishing agreement—all from hometown prophets in Judea.

Elizabeth's Prophecy

After hearing that Elizabeth conceived a child in her old age, Mary decided to visit her in the hill country of Judea, probably the city of Hebron, and hear this miraculous story for herself. Mary and Elizabeth were relatives, possibly first cousins, but the Bible doesn't name the exact relationship (Luke 1:36). As soon as Mary stepped through the door and offered her greeting, the Holy Spirit anointed Elizabeth and she began prophesying over Mary.

And she cried out with a loud voice and said, "Blessed *are* you among women, and blessed *is* the fruit of your womb! And how has it *happened* to me, that the mother of my Lord would come to me? For behold, when the sound of your greeting reached my ears, the baby leaped in my womb for joy. And blessed *is* she who believed that there would be a fulfillment of what had been spoken to her by the Lord." (Luke 1:42–45 NASB)

Simeon's Prophecy

Simeon, a devout Jew, lived in Jerusalem. God had revealed to him that he would not die until he had seen God's anointed Messiah. The Spirit led him into the temple that day. Mary and Joseph came to the temple, too, along with other parents who brought their firstborn sons for the ritual presentation and redemption sacrifice required by the Law (Luke 2:22–24; Leviticus 12:2–8; Exodus 13:12–15). When Simeon picked up Jesus to bless Him, he felt unction from the Holy Spirit and offered this inspired prayer: "Lord, now You are letting Your servant depart in peace, according to Your word; for my eyes have seen Your salvation which You have prepared before the face of all peoples, a light to *bring* revelation to the Gentiles, and the glory of Your people Israel" (Luke 2:29–32).

Friends and family in attendance, not to mention other couples waiting in line, heard Simeon's words. Then, after blessing Jesus and the immediate family, Simeon gave Mary a personal prophetic word: "Behold, this *Child* is destined for the fall and rising of many in Israel, and for a sign which will be spoken against (yes, a sword will pierce through your own soul also), that the thoughts of many hearts may be revealed" (Luke 2:34*b*–35).

Anna's Prophecy

A respected prophetess also ministered in the temple. The Scriptures do not record her exact words, but they must have been memorable. "Now there was one, Anna, a prophetess, the daughter of Phanuel, of the tribe of Asher. She was of a great age, and had lived with a husband seven years from her virginity; and this woman *was* a widow of about eighty-four years, who did not depart from the temple, but served *God* with fastings and prayers night and day. And coming in that instant she gave thanks to the Lord, and spoke of Him to all those who looked for redemption in Jerusalem" (Luke 2:36–38).

A Divine Pattern

Prophets predicted the birth of Jesus and confirmed His identity. One of the most credible prophets, Isaiah, foretold of a time when God would draw close to His people through the sign of Immanuel, which means God with us.[58] And it happened about seven hundred years later, just the way Isaiah prophesied. Somehow, the Holy Spirit overshadowed a young maiden, a virgin, causing the impossible to become possible. God placed a divine but fully human presence inside her womb. This holy Advent was a type and shadow of things to come, when God would offer salvation by placing Christ in the believer. It would become the divine pattern for spiritual intimacy: God with us (Matthew 1:23), Christ in us (Colossians 1:27).

The birth of Immanuel was one of the greatest moments of God's redemptive plan. Everything thus far has led to this one extraordinary incident. According to a common catchphrase, the Nativity embraces *the greatest story ever told*. Although amazingly wonderful, His birth is not the greatest story or moment. Another event would bear that honor.

CHAPTER *13*

SEVEN SIGNS OF CHRIST

Miracles are a retelling in small letters of the very same story,
which is written across the whole world in letters too large
for some of us to see.
—C. S. Lewis

I n seminary, we studied the life of Jesus Christ using different
methods. One was to work in chronological order, examining
gospel events by date and occurrence. Another involved a comparative analysis, contrasting and comparing the narratives of each gospel
writer. A third option entailed following His teachings, parables, or
miracles in a topical study. In this chapter, we will employ the latter
method using His miracles, which in itself could be a daunting task
since Jesus performed many signs and wonders. "And there are also
many other things that Jesus did, which if they were written one by
one, I suppose that even the world itself could not contain the books
that would be written. Amen" (John 21:25).

In studying the life of Christ through His miracles, we'll examine
the ones Apostle John included in his gospel. For some reason, John

only recorded a few miraculous signs accomplished by Jesus. Was John running low on ink or writing an abridged account? Hardly, he had a different reason for his lack of inclusion. "And truly Jesus did many other signs in the presence of His disciples, which are not written in this book; but these are written that you may believe that Jesus is the Christ, the Son of God, and that believing you may have life in His name" (John 20:30–31).

John envisioned a threefold purpose for his readers: *signs* would lead to *belief,* and *belief* would lead to *life*. John picked seven key *signs*—each showing an aspect of *belief*—each revealing an application of *life*. The first sign impressed several guests at a town wedding reception.

First Sign (John 2:1–11)

"On the third day there was a wedding in Cana of Galilee, and the mother of Jesus was there. Now both Jesus and His disciples were invited to the wedding. And when they ran out of wine, the mother of Jesus said to Him, 'They have no wine.' Jesus said to her, 'Woman, what does your concern have to do with Me? My hour has not yet come'" (John 2:1–4).

"My hour has not yet come" seems like a strange response from Jesus. Mary was only asking for a little help. The wedding party had run out of wine, and they needed more to keep the celebration going. Following the instructions from Jesus, servants filled six pots with water, drew some out, and offered it to the master of the feast. And behold, they had wine. Therefore, I must ask the dreaded question. Did Jesus turn water into an alcoholic beverage for His first recorded miracle? The best way to determine that answer is by considering the passage context, the historical setting, and the word or words translated as wine.

The Greek word used throughout this passage is *oinos,* which is equivalent to the Hebrew word *yayin.*[59] Both are common names for wine and can refer to wine in any stage of fermentation. However, they usually indicate fermented wine. Another Hebrew word is *tîrôš,* also rendered as *tiyrosh,*[60] which sometimes translates as new or sweet wine. New wine came from the first drippings of juice in the wine-press, and since fermentation sets in rapidly, it would not remain unfermented for long. Moreover, for religious festivals and wedding feasts, people traditionally used fermented wine.[61] Some theologians believe Jesus made new wine for his mother's wedding guests. If so, then the wine was probably unfermented or in the early stages of fermentation—not enough for intoxication—and barely distinguishable from grape juice.[62] Alcoholic or otherwise, the master of the feast thanked the bridegroom for saving the best wine until last.

Any *sign* of Christ could have several *life* applications, but this one revealed something unique: the Lord can perform creative miracles—making one thing out of another—a type of supernatural metamorphosis. Not only are God's innovative miracles spectacular, they occasionally provide refreshments. John, however, may have another reason for including the winemaking sign as one of his seven. Serving new wine at a wedding celebration foreshadows a prophetic moment when the Lord God betroths a redeemed bride. On that day, new wine will flow in abundance and so will His mercy (see Hosea 2:19–23).

Believe that God has a greater moment in store for you.

Second Sign (John 4:46–54)

"So Jesus came again to Cana of Galilee where He had made the water wine. And there was a certain nobleman whose son was sick at Capernaum. When he heard that Jesus had come out of Judea into

Galilee, he went to Him and implored Him to come down and heal his son, for he was at the point of death" (John 4:46–47).

Have you ever known a loved one or family member who became deathly sick? Such situations are difficult enough, even more so if doctors can do nothing to help. The father from Capernaum felt the same way about his son. The boy was dying right before his eyes. In a final effort to save his son, he searched for Jesus in Galilee, hoping to convince Jesus to return home with him. Maybe the Rabbi could perform one of His miracles and heal his child.

"Jesus said to him, 'Go your way; your son lives.' So the man believed the word that Jesus spoke to him, and he went his way" (v. 50). At a distance of twenty or more miles away, the nobleman's child recovered. Jesus did not need to be there for the healing to occur; His spoken word carried the same weight. God's power does not lessen with distance nor are His miracles restricted by lack of visual presence. This revelation gives us hope that from the outskirts of heaven, God can change our situation when we believe His Word and act upon it.

More than anything else, this miracle was about outreach: a father reaching out to save his son and Jesus reaching through the distance to heal him.

Believe that God can reach you wherever you are.

Third Sign (John 5:1–15)

"Now there is in Jerusalem by the Sheep *Gate* a pool, which is called in Hebrew, Bethesda, having five porches. In these lay a great multitude of sick people, blind, lame, paralyzed, waiting for the moving of the water. For an angel went down at a certain time into the pool and stirred up the water; then whoever stepped in first, after the stirring of the water, was made well of whatever disease he had. Now a certain man was there who had an infirmity thirty-eight years" (John 5:2–5).

This man, possibly a paralytic, had suffered with the same condition for almost forty years. John does not name the infirmity so it could have been arthritic, causing the man severe pain and immobility. One day, Jesus walked by and inquired about his sickness. "The sick man answered Him, 'Sir, I have no man to put me into the pool when the water is stirred up; but while I am coming, another steps down before me'" (v. 7). Jesus told the man to fold up his bedroll and walk. When the man arose, he realized Jesus had healed him. No longer needing to wait for a pool of bubbling water, he headed home. Through it all, God had not forgotten him.

I call this third sign the *forget-me-not* miracle. God did not leave the Hebrew children enslaved in Egypt, nor will He abandon us, overlook our situation, or misfile our name in His address book. Perhaps you, like the paralytic, have waited long enough.

Believe that God has not forgotten you.

Fourth Sign (John 6:1–14)

"After these things Jesus went over the Sea of Galilee, which is *the Sea* of Tiberias. Then a great multitude followed Him, because they saw His signs which He performed on those who were diseased. And Jesus went up on the mountain, and there He sat with His disciples. Now the Passover, a feast of the Jews, was near. Then Jesus lifted up *His* eyes, and seeing a great multitude coming toward Him, He said to Philip, 'Where shall we buy bread, that these may eat?'" (John 6:1–5).

No one conducted an exact count, but the crowd numbered at least five thousand men. If the tally had included women and children, the total would have been even higher. After a full day of revival services, the multitude grew tired and hungry. Consequently, Jesus assigned Philip the responsibility of overseeing their mealtime needs. After Phillip calculated the cost to feed this hungry group, he felt overwhelmed, probably wondering why Jesus chose him. But thank God for small favors! Andrew located a boy in the crowd with a sack lunch who offered to share it—almost a miracle in itself.

Some miraculous signs materialize out of nowhere; others need a catalyst. In this case, God used a little boy with five loaves and two fish. "And Jesus took the loaves, and when He had given thanks He distributed *them* to the disciples, and the disciples to those sitting down; and likewise of the fish, as much as they wanted. So when they were filled, He said to His disciples, 'Gather up the fragments that remain, so that nothing is lost'" (John 6:11–12).

This sign shows us that God's miracle power contains unlimited provision, enough for everyone and every need. However, it also reveals something just as important: Jesus wants us involved in the solution. Some miracles not only require faith but action on our part. Maybe this action is stepping out of a boat to walk on water like Peter or facing down a giant with a sling and shepherd's staff like David. Even donating five crackers and two sardines in faith can facilitate a mighty miracle.

> *Believe that God can use your faithful actions*
> *to bring forth abundant miracles.*

Fifth Sign (John 6:15–21)

"Now when evening came, His disciples went down to the sea, got into the boat, and went over the sea toward Capernaum. And it was already dark, and Jesus had not come to them. Then the sea arose because a great wind was blowing. So when they had rowed about three or four miles, they saw Jesus walking on the sea and drawing near the boat; and they were afraid" (John 6:16–19).

For some reason, John did not include the second part of this story, but Matthew does (Matthew 14:28–32). According to Matthew, Peter decided to walk on water for himself, so he stepped out of the boat and tried to duplicate Jesus' amazing feat. Peter succeeded at first, but after doubt and stormy weather got the best of him, he began to sink. Jesus grabbed him before he went under and helped him back to the boat—not really the best application of faith. Still, none of the other disciples even attempted it.

Moreover, according to Mark, Jesus didn't plan on riding in the boat with the disciples, "and would have passed them by" (Mark 6:48); He only stopped when they cried out. At first, they wondered if this water-walker was a ghost; however, when Jesus spoke they recognized His voice. Had they not panicked, the disciples could have rowed across the lake to Bethsaida because Jesus had already commissioned them for a successful trip (Mark 6:45). Jesus told them not to be afraid and then stepped into the boat. "And immediately the boat was at the land where they were going" (John 6:21*b*).

Among other things, this sign teaches that the laws of physics do not limit or diminish the power of God. God's purposes will always find a way to reach their intended goals. Although God created the rules of nature, designed the laws of gravity, and established scientific precepts, He does not need to abide by them when circumstances warrant otherwise.

Believe that God's power is not hindered
by physical laws or circumstances.

Sixth Sign (John 9:1–41)

"Now as *Jesus* passed by, He saw a man who was blind from birth. And His disciples asked Him, saying, 'Rabbi, who sinned, this man or his parents, that he was born blind?'" (John 9:1–2).

There are several reasons for blindness: some physical (Mark 8:25) and some spiritual (Matthew 12:22–24). When people are born blind, they're not being punished for the deeds of their parents or anyone else. Nor are they blind because of some horrible sin. Instead, their condition creates an opportunity for God to reveal His works and show forth His glory (John 9:3). Of all the signs of Christ, this one really offended and outraged the religious leaders. They didn't like it when His signs and wonders manifested without their approval or blessing.

This particular sign may have been one of the Lord's most controversial miracles. Jesus spat on the ground, rolled it around a bit, and then made some questionable-looking clay. He applied this mixture to each of the blind man's eyes. Since the procedure created a mess, He suggested the man wash in the pool of Siloam. After rinsing his eyes, the man could see for the first time. He told everyone that a prophet named Jesus had healed him. It created quite a disturbance in Jerusalem, especially since it happened on the Sabbath. When the Pharisees discovered that Jesus performed the healing, they really lost it—spewing angry words everywhere. One would think the pious shepherds of Israel would be pleased because someone from their flock had experienced a real miracle. Instead, they censured him.

> So they said to him, "What did He do to you? How did He open your eyes?"

He answered them, "I told you already and you did not listen; why do you want to hear *it* again? You do not want to become His disciples too, do you?"

They reviled him and said, "You are His disciple, but we are disciples of Moses.

We know that God has spoken to Moses, but as for this man, we do not know where He is from."

The man answered and said to them, "Well, here is an amazing thing, that you do not know where He is from, and *yet* He opened my eyes. We know that God does not hear sinners; but if anyone is God-fearing and does His will, He hears him. Since the beginning of time it has never been heard that anyone opened the eyes of a person born blind. If this man were not from God, He could do nothing."

They answered him, "You were born entirely in sins, and are you teaching us?" So they put him out. (John 9:26–34 NASB)

Helping individuals who are suffering because of unfortunate situations is high on God's list of priorities. This sixth sign shows God's compassion toward those who are broken, hurting, and in need of healing.

> *Believe that God cares about your life and*
> *wants to heal whatever is broken.*

Seventh Sign (John 11:1–45)

"Now a certain *man* was sick, Lazarus of Bethany, the town of Mary and her sister Martha. It was *that* Mary who anointed the Lord with fragrant oil and wiped His feet with her hair, whose brother Lazarus was sick. Therefore the sisters sent to Him, saying, 'Lord, behold, he whom You love is sick'" (John 11:1–3).

When Jesus heard His friend had taken a turn for the worse, He stayed put in Perea (an area beyond Jordon) for two more days instead of rushing to Bethany. By the time He arrived, Lazarus had been dead four days, his body already sealed in a tomb. Jesus met the sisters outside of town before heading to the gravesite. Once there, He asked some grieving bystanders to remove the stone in front of the burial cave. At first, they were unwilling, fearful of the smell from Lazarus' decomposing body. However, when Jesus told Martha she would see the glory of God, some of the mourners overheard and gladly complied. Shortly thereafter, the entire crowd witnessed a glorious miracle—a dead man coming back to life.

Besides demonstrating His power over death and the grave, this final sign revealed a deeper truth about Jesus. He not only had resurrection power, He was in fact, the Resurrection Himself. "Jesus said to her, 'Your brother will rise again.' Martha said to Him, 'I know that he will rise again in the resurrection at the last day.' Jesus said to her, 'I am the resurrection and the life. He who believes in Me, though he may die, he shall live. And whoever lives and believes in Me shall never die. Do you believe this?'" (vv. 23–26).

If Jesus had so desired, He could have resurrected every dead saint right then and there. However, that was not God's plan, at least not yet. One day, those who believe Jesus is the resurrection and the life will see even greater signs—and moments.

Believe that death is not the end but the beginning.

A Greater Sign Coming

These seven miraculous signs were astonishing, even motivating, but God had greater ones pending. The next two would arrive three days apart, and when completed, would accomplish more than all the other signs and wonders combined. The first one involved destroying a temple.

> So the Jews answered and said to Him, "What sign do You show to us, since You do these things?"
>
> Jesus answered and said to them, "Destroy this temple, and in three days I will raise it up."
>
> Then the Jews said, "It has taken forty-six years to build this temple, and will You raise it up in three days?"
>
> But He was speaking of the temple of His body. (John 2:18–21)

Destroying the temple of Christ at Calvary became one of humanity's cruelest deeds. The Cross held sorrow, suffering, and death for Jesus. Ironically, it would hold life too.

Chapter 14

LIFE IN THE CROSS

All God's plans have the mark of the cross on them.
—E. M. Bounds

We can find life in unlikely places. A good example is Death Valley, California—one of the most barren locations on this planet. Even the name suggests an inhospitable environment, a place devoid of life. However, some things are seldom what they seem. Beneath this hot, parched, moisture-deprived valley lies a huge underground system of water.

The deepest point in Death Valley is Badwater Basin. At minus 282 feet, this arid salt flat holds the record for being the lowest elevation in North America. The main attraction is a small pool of alkaline water fed by an underground spring. An early surveyor to the area marked his map, "bad water," because his mule wouldn't drink it.[63] Although the water is undrinkable and the desert heat deadly, life still exists there if one knows where to look. In a seemingly lifeless pool, visitors can find pickleweed, aquatic insects, and a tiny mollusk known as the Badwater snail, one of the area's rarest animals.[64]

Ironically, life flourishes within the boundaries of Death Valley. A closer look at Golgotha will reveal something similar: life in a place normally associated with death.

The Ninth Hour

Now from the sixth hour darkness fell upon all the land until the ninth hour.

About the ninth hour Jesus cried out with a loud voice, saying, "ELI, ELI, LAMA SABACHTHANI?" that is, "MY GOD, MY GOD, WHY HAVE YOU FORSAKEN ME?"

And some of those who were standing there, when they heard it, *began* saying, "This man is calling for Elijah." Immediately one of them ran, and taking a sponge, he filled it with sour wine and put it on a reed, and gave Him a drink.

But the rest *of them* said, "Let us see whether Elijah will come to save Him."

And Jesus cried out again with a loud voice, and yielded up His spirit.

And behold, the veil of the temple was torn in two from top to bottom; and the earth shook and the rocks were split.

The tombs were opened, and many bodies of the saints who had fallen asleep were raised; and coming out of the tombs after His resurrection they entered the holy city and appeared to many. (Matthew 27:45–53 NASB)

Sleeping Saints Raised

The death of Jesus released some aspect of life. When Jesus took His last breath, cried out, and yielded up His spirit, the saints who had fallen asleep (previously died) awoke. The above passage seems clear enough: "The tombs were opened, and many bodies of the saints who had fallen asleep were raised" (v. 52).

Although the saints did not come out of their graves until after the resurrection of Jesus three days later (v. 53), something powerful happened at the Cross. A rising occurred in some fashion. Perhaps these Old Testament saints sat up in their burial tombs and shouted *chayah* (alive, we live)![65] I can only speculate in awe. Nonetheless, a powerful, life-stirring event transpired at the exact moment Jesus died. Calvary would reveal other such moments.

Locked Doors Opened

The Cross released life into the temple as well. At the same moment Jesus expired on the cross, the temple veil tore in two, letting light shine into the Most Holy Place (v. 51). The Ark of the Covenant and the glory of the Lord—only seen by the high priest once a year—were now available for all to view.

Any priests who ministered in the temple would have felt the earthquake and seen the veil ripped open from top to bottom. This heavy, thick curtain had separated the holy place from the Most Holy Place for generations. Now, light rushed in and filled every corner. A new era had begun. The ministry of the Spirit (life) replaced the ministry of condemnation (death). Old Testament mercy became New Testament grace. With no barrier, a greater glory came forth. The New Covenant had arrived, one that superseded traditions, rituals, and religion. "But if the ministry of death, written *and* engraved on stones, was glorious, so that the children of Israel could not look steadily at the face of Moses because of the glory of his countenance, which *glory* was passing away, how will the ministry of the Spirit not be more glorious? For if the ministry of condemnation *had* glory, the ministry of righteousness exceeds much more in glory" (2 Corinthians 3:7–9).

Like the veil covering the face of Moses, the temple curtain concealed the glory of God, but the Cross tore this barrier apart and allowed entrance. Mysteries hidden for centuries were now unveiled in exceeding glory. The Cross contained even more secrets—the shed blood of Jesus held life too.

Life in the Blood

"For the life of the flesh *is* in the blood, and I have given it to you upon the altar to make atonement for your souls; for it *is* the blood *that* makes atonement for the soul" (Leviticus 17:11).

Thankfully, God did not require an individual's own blood, only the blood of an innocent animal as a substitute sacrifice. Such sacrifices were God's solution for the penalty of sin because "the soul who sins shall die" (Ezekiel 18:20). The penalty also involved spiritual death (separation from God). However, when a person atoned for sin, God granted a temporary reprieve. If that individual sinned again, then God required another blood sacrifice.

According to Leviticus, the blood represents life; in fact, our blood is our life. It is the most important component in our bodies. Without blood, we would die within minutes. Because of what blood symbolized, it became the atoning element for remission. When the blood of an animal (sacrificial lamb or other accepted animal) was sprinkled upon an altar, God accepted the life of the sacrifice instead of taking the life of the sinner, thereby remitting his or her sins. Remission is the cancelling of a debt or penalty. "And according to the law almost all things are purified with blood, and without shedding of blood there is no remission" (Hebrews 9:22). The Greek word translated remission in this verse is *aphesis*. It means forgiveness, pardon, or release from bondage.[66]

"But now in Christ Jesus you who once were far off have been brought near by the blood of Christ" (Ephesians 2:13). The blood of Christ was untainted by sin and therefore the only perfect and permanent solution for pardoning sin. "Much more then, having now been justified by His blood, we shall be saved from wrath through Him" (Romans 5:9). Salvation depended on the shed blood of Jesus Christ. As the unblemished sacrificial lamb sent from God, His death atoned for the penalty of sin, brought forth remission, and opened the door for eternal life. Yes, the Cross imparted death—but life for us.

Life Giving Flow

Lewis E. Jones wrote the gospel hymn, "There Is Power in the Blood." He penned those words during a camp meeting at Mountain Lake Park, Maryland. He believed the shed blood of Jesus created a powerful "life giving flow." To show relevance, I only listed a few stanzas from his song, but you can find all the verses in almost any Christian hymnal or in the public domain.

> Would you be free from the burden of sin?
> There's power in the blood, power in the blood;
> Would you o'er evil a victory win?
> There's wonderful power in the blood.
> There is power, power, wonder-working power
> In the precious blood of the Lamb.

Come for a cleansing to Calvary's tide;

There's wonderful power in the blood.

Would you be whiter, much whiter than snow?

There's power in the blood, power in the blood;

Sin stains are lost in its life giving flow;

There's wonderful power in the blood.

—Lewis E. Jones

In one powerful moment, the shed blood of Christ provided cleansing, victory, and life. Repetitive blood sacrifices were no longer required. A person only needed to believe in Jesus and His finished work at Calvary (Acts 16:31).

That day, a condemned criminal, who hung on a nearby cross, became one of the first individuals to receive eternal life through faith— no animal sacrifice made for his redemption—only the shed blood of Jesus. For him, it was a quick trip to Abraham's bosom (also called Paradise) and back out (Luke 23:42–43). Three days later, this former criminal, now a redeemed saint, was likely released into the streets of Jerusalem right out of the grave (see Matthew 27:52–53). Imagine the confusion for those who had just buried him.

The blood of Christ is indeed powerful. It not only cleanses us from sin, it contains a life giving flow that leads to eternal life.

Saved by His Life

"But God demonstrates His own love toward us, in that while we were still sinners, Christ died for us. Much more then, having now been justified by His blood, we shall be saved from wrath through Him. For if when we were enemies we were reconciled to God through the death

168

of His Son, much more, having been reconciled, we shall be saved by His life" (Romans 5:8–10).

Although His blood imparted justification (just as if we had never sinned) and His death brought reconciliation (restoring our broken relationship with God)—it was His life that saved us (v.10). Salvation is not just something *Jesus offers;* it is something *Jesus is.* He is our salvation (Isaiah 12:2). Even the name of Jesus, *Yeshua* in Hebrew, means Yahweh is salvation. For Christians, salvation is the divine life of Christ who resides in them: "Christ in you, the hope of glory" (Colossians 1:27*b*). The Cross delivered more than death; it also dispersed life, hope, and salvation.

My God, Why Have You Forsaken Me?

Did God really forsake His Son on the cross at the ultimate moment of His obedience? Is it possible the heavenly Father wasn't watching as one the greatest moments in history played out? It would seem so, unless of course, Jesus was quoting a prophetic psalm that paralleled the events at Golgotha. When Jesus said, *My God, My God, why have you forsaken Me?*—He may have been reciting or praying the verses of Psalm 22—not actually asking why God had forsaken Him. Perhaps a closer look at the verses will bring insight. Below are eleven passages from Psalm 22, followed by their corresponding New Testament fulfillments as read from the New American Standard Bible (NASB).

1. *My God, My God, why have You forsaken Me?—Psalm 22:1*
"About the ninth hour Jesus cried out with a loud voice, saying, 'ELI, ELI, LAMA SABACHTHANI?' that is, 'MY GOD, MY GOD, WHY HAVE YOU FORSAKEN ME?'" (Matthew 27:46).

2. *But I am a worm and not a man, a reproach of men and despised by the people. All who see me sneer at me; they separate with the lip, they wag the head.—Psalm 22:6–7*

"And those passing by were hurling abuse at Him, wagging their heads" (Matthew 27:39).

3. *Let Him deliver him; Let Him rescue him, because He delights in him.—Psalm 22:8*

"HE TRUSTS IN GOD; LET GOD RESCUE *Him* now, IF HE DELIGHTS IN HIM" (Matthew 27:43).

4. *Many bulls have surrounded me; strong bulls of Bashan have encircled me. They open wide their mouth at me, as a ravening and a roaring lion.—Psalm 22:12–13*

"In the same way the chief priests also, along with the scribes and elders, were mocking *Him* and saying, 'He saved others; He cannot save Himself.' The robbers who had been crucified with Him were also insulting Him with the same words" (Matthew 27:41–42*a*, 44).

5. *I am poured out like water.—Psalm 22:14*

"But one of the soldiers pierced His side with a spear, and immediately blood and water came out" (John 19:34).

6. *And my tongue cleaves to my jaws.—Psalm 22:15*

"After this, Jesus, knowing that all things had already been accomplished, to fulfill the Scripture, said, 'I am thirsty'" (John 19:28).

7. *For dogs have surrounded me; a band of evildoers has encompassed me.—Psalm 22:16*

"And the people stood by, looking on. And even the rulers were sneering at Him, saying, 'He saved others; let Him save Himself if this is the Christ of God, His Chosen One.' The soldiers also mocked Him" (Luke 23:35–36a).

8. *They pierced my hands and my feet.—Psalm 22:16*
"When they came to the place called The Skull, there they crucified Him" (Luke 23:33a).
"Then He said to Thomas, 'Reach here with your finger, and see My hands; and reach here your hand and put it into My side; and do not be unbelieving, but believing'" (John 20:27).

9. *I can count all my bones.—Psalm 22:17*
"But coming to Jesus, when they saw that He was already dead, they did not break His legs" (John 19:33).

10. *They divide my garments among them, and for my clothing they cast lots.—Psalm 22:18*
"Then the soldiers, when they had crucified Jesus, took His outer garments and made four parts, a part to every soldier and *also* the tunic; now the tunic was seamless, woven in one piece. So they said to one another, 'Let us not tear it, but cast lots for it, *to decide* whose it shall be'" (John 19:23–24a).

11. *For He has not despised nor abhorred the affliction of the afflicted; nor has He hidden His face from him; but when he cried to Him for help, He heard.—Psalm 22:24*
"I knew that You always hear Me" (John 11:42a).

Number 11 is my favorite. If the other ten passages paralleled events at Calvary, then so does this one. According to Psalm 22:24 and John 11:42, God did not hide His face from His Son or turn a deaf ear. The Father heard and watched everything unfold on that difficult but glorious day at Golgotha. Some people believe a holy God cannot look at sin, and since Jesus bore our sins on the cross, God had to look away (forsake His Son). Actually, God has been looking at sin and its damage for a long, long time. That's why He devised a repair plan called redemption.

Crucify Him, Crucify Him

"But they shouted, saying, 'Crucify *Him,* crucify Him!' But they were insistent, demanding with loud voices that He be crucified. And the voices of these men and of the chief priests prevailed. So Pilate gave sentence that it should be as they requested" (Luke 23:21, 23–24).

Pilate wanted to release Jesus. He didn't see any merit in accusations coming from the Jewish council, so he decided to scourge Jesus and look for some way to release Him. The ancient world had many types of scourges. Jews usually limited their floggings to forty lashes less one (2 Corinthians 11:24). Romans had no such limit. Their scourge, called flagellation, was the worst of all. It involved beating someone on the back with whips containing three or more leather cords, each knotted with pieces of metal or bone. These whipping clubs could have up to twelve separate cords. The procedure often killed the recipient before the flogging ended.[67] The Jewish rulers, however, were not satisfied with the results since Jesus somehow survived. They wanted Him crucified.

Pilate had hoped that punishing Jesus before discharging Him would appease the crowds. Besides, releasing a prisoner at Passover might show Rome's goodwill. Roman rulers had granted similar pardons, but a majority of the people, stirred up by Jewish leadership, called for the release of Barabbas instead. To save face, Pilate gave the order to crucify Jesus and then symbolically washed his hands to disown the matter.

Crucifixion is a horrible, painful death. Only individuals full of hate and jealously would wish it upon one of their own people. Ironically, the crowds had made the right request but for the wrong reason. They didn't understand that Jesus wanted to offer His life freely as ransom for many. Without His sacrificial death at Calvary, humanity had no hope for a true and lasting forgiveness. Jesus was the only person who could pay the penalty for sin and provide redemption for the world.

When Apostle Paul wrote in Galatians 3:13: "Christ has redeemed us from the curse of the law, having become a curse for us (for it is written, '*Cursed* is *everyone who hangs on a tree*')," he had taken a passage from the Law and applied it to Jesus on the cross. Calvary's tree carried a curse but released a blessing—represented death but facilitated life—displayed jealousy and hatred but revealed forgiveness and love. The Cross was truly a great moment, one of the greatest in the life of Jesus. Even so, the disciples and followers of Jesus were not celebrating. They would need to wait three more days for a greater moment to arise.

CHAPTER 15

THE GREATEST MOMENT FOR
JESUS OF NAZARETH

The entire plan for the future has its key in the resurrection.[68]

—Rev. Billy Graham

By the time Apollo 13 launched, two other Apollo missions had already landed on the moon and returned. Moon shots had grown routine. Many of us who watched our television sets nonstop for the first two missions had lost interest for the third one. However, what happened on the evening of April 13, 1970, drew us back with concerned hearts. Three days into the mission, something had gone horribly wrong. The clock read 55:55:20 G.E.T (Ground Elapsed Time) when Mission Control in Houston received a disturbing transmission:

> John Swigert: "Okay, Houston, we've had a problem here."

> Jack Lousma: "This is Houston. Say again, please."

> Jim Lovell: "Houston, we've had a problem. We've had a Main B bus undervolt."[69]

An oxygen tank explosion in the service module had crippled the spacecraft en route to the moon. Apollo 13 was 200,000 miles from Earth, losing fuel cells and venting oxygen into space. Things looked grim for astronauts James A. Lovell, John L. Swigert, and Fred W. Haise. Mission Control had no choice but to abort the lunar landing. However, returning the spacecraft to Earth would be challenging, dangerous, and maybe even impossible. But NASA pulled it off. With ingenuity and determination, they overcame every difficulty and brought the crew home for a successful splashdown in the Pacific Ocean near Samoa. On the afternoon of April 17, 1970, three worn-out astronauts boarded the USS Iwo Jima safe and sound.[70]

After the explosion damaged the craft, I stayed glued to my television set, listening to updates, pondering the analysis of experts, and praying for divine intervention. Over the years, I have heard various comments about the mission: Most people thought it was a series of mishaps and unfortunate events. Some saw the hand of providence at work—saving the lives of astronauts otherwise stranded. Jim Lovell referred to the flight as a successful failure. A few considered it a horrible catastrophe and faulted the space program, but I believe the Apollo 13 mission was a crowning accomplishment for NASA and its flight crew.

Interestingly, a comparable tragedy played out in the first century. What looked like a worst-case scenario for Jesus and His ministry ultimately became His finest hour.

His Finest Hour

Much had transpired since the birth of Jesus in Bethlehem. Local shepherds ran amuck through the countryside, claiming to have seen an angel. Then, a few years later, kings from the East arrived in Jerusalem. The Magi were following a star they believed signaled the arrival of a divine king. This miraculous sign led them to the house of Mary and Joseph where they dropped off elaborate gifts for the toddler. After the kings left town, Joseph and Mary departed for Egypt to escape a jealous King Herod who wanted their son killed. When the threat subsided, they returned to Israel and settled in Nazareth, where Joseph opened a woodworking shop and taught young Jesus the carpentry trade.

Jesus served as an apprentice in His dad's shop for a while. After John baptized Him in the Jordan River, Jesus launched a traveling ministry, enlisting a few disciples along the way. Actually, Jesus became quite popular, astonishing the crowds with His teachings and miracles. Some believed He might be the promised Messiah. Others hoped He would lead a revolt to free Israel from Roman oppression. Instead, they crucified Him. He now lay dead, sealed inside a tomb.

Then, the third day after Golgotha, it happened, possibly a miracle. If true, it would be the greatest thing Jesus had ever done. The news filtered in slowly at first, the reports confusing. Two people traveling down the road to Emmaus were trying to sort it all out.

The Road to Emmaus (Luke 24:13–32)

According to Luke, Emmaus was about seven miles from Jerusalem. Josephus, a Jewish historian, also mentioned a village called Emmaus at the same distance. The actual site, however, remains unidentified. Emmaus means *warm baths,* so the settlement probably had hot springs nearby.[71] As Cleopas and his companion traveled the Emmaus road, a stranger caught up with them and joined their conversation. The man seemed unaware of recent events in Jerusalem. Maybe he had been out of town for the last three days. Still, he was a pleasant fellow, easy to talk with, and he knew the Scriptures well.

For some reason, these two disciples did not recognize their Redeemer. Perhaps they were too preoccupied with their own circumstances. More likely, though, Jesus restrained their perception until He could set the stage for a greater reveal. Ironically, they did not see the solution for their sorrows walking right beside them. Discouraged and bewildered from reports in Jerusalem, they rehashed everything, looking for answers. Sadness filled their hearts.

> And [Jesus] said to them, "What are these words that you are exchanging with one another as you are walking?" And they stood still, looking sad.
>
> One *of them*, named Cleopas, answered and said to Him, "Are You the only one visiting Jerusalem and unaware of the things which have happened here in these days?"
>
> And He said to them, "What things?" (Luke 24:17–19a NASB)

Word Picture: What Things?

Where have you been? How could you not know about Jesus of Nazareth? We believed Him to be a great prophet. He performed miracles, one after the other, like they were easy. No one could heal people the way He did, and I mean nobody. It didn't matter if they were blind, sick, or dead. His miracles were the most incredible feats I've ever seen. Some of us wondered if He were Moses or Elijah who had come back from the grave. Others believed Him to be the promised Messiah.

We listened to His insightful teachings and witnessed His miraculous signs. Then those fools trumped up some charges against Him and convinced Pilate to crucify Him. Jesus was a good man, even a righteous man. I apologize for my frustration, but the people who did this to Jesus are a bunch of idiots. They tormented Him, mocked Him, and nailed Him to a cross. We watched Him suffer and die during the Festival. Then they placed His body in a new tomb and sealed the entry with a large stone. And that was that. Now, three days later, His body is gone. Several women who had followed Him said they encountered angels near His empty tomb; they are spreading rumors that Jesus is somehow still alive.

Emmaus Conversation Continues

> And He said to them, "O foolish men and slow of heart to believe in all that the prophets have spoken! Was it not necessary for the Christ to suffer these things and to enter into His glory?" Then beginning with Moses and with all the prophets, He explained to them the things concerning Himself in all the Scriptures.
>
> And they approached the village where they were going, and He acted as though He were going farther.
>
> But they urged Him, saying, "Stay with us, for it is *getting* toward evening, and the day is now nearly over." So He went in to stay with them.
>
> When He had reclined *at the table* with them, He took the bread and blessed *it,* and breaking *it,* He *began* giving *it* to them. Then their eyes were opened and they recognized Him; and He vanished from their sight.

They said to one another, "Were not our hearts burning within us while He was speaking to us on the road, while He was explaining the Scriptures to us?" (Luke 24:25–32 NASB)

Abide with Us

With evening coming on, they asked the stranger to lodge with them at the next inn. After settling into their rooms, they all sat down for dinner. What happened next was surreal. The stranger blessed the bread, broke it, and handed them each a piece. Immediately, their spiritual eyes were opened, and they recognized the stranger as Jesus. Before they could say anything else, He disappeared right in front of their eyes. They looked at each other in amazement, their hearts aflame, their souls stirred with passion.

Where did Jesus go that evening? He may have simply vanished. Yet at no other time did Jesus vanish unexpectedly, let alone in the middle of giving out a blessing (see the Gospel narratives).[72] On the other hand, Jesus had appeared on several occasions, seemingly out of nowhere: walking through closed doors, appearing at the empty tomb, and showing up at Peter's fishing spot. Before leaving, however, He always engaged in conversation, gave out instructions, spoke encouragement, shared a meal, or offered a farewell message. Could it be this time was different because a new dispensation had begun? Maybe, just maybe, Jesus did exactly what these two disciples asked, "Stay with us" (v. 29). The Greek word for stay is *meno,* which can also translate as abide, reside, or dwell.[73] When we become Christians, Jesus does not stay, reside, dwell, or abide with us physically; rather, He lives in our spiritual hearts and souls. The miracle of being born again, salvation, is an inward experience, not an outward one.

179

I believe Jesus could have entered the hearts of these two individuals, just as He does in all true believers today. He was no longer Jesus of Nazareth but the risen Christ, the hope of glory (2 Corinthians 5:16–17; Colossians 1:27). Moreover, the resurrected Christ was and is omnipresent: able to be in all places at all times. He can live in the heart of each saint on earth, sit at the right hand of the Father in heaven, and visit an individual personally—all during the same moment. If nothing else, the disciples' encounter with the resurrected Christ is a type and shadow of the New Testament salvation experience. If you need or want Jesus to abide with you, then the *Selah* below is for you.

Selah: Abide with Me

The exact meaning of the *Selah* is unknown. Scholars believe it may be a musical term meaning to pause and reflect. With that thought in mind, please take this *Selah* moment and consider the following appeal from Jesus: "Behold, I stand at the door and knock; if anyone hears My voice and opens the door, I will come in to him and will dine with him, and he with Me" (Revelation 3:20 NASB). When Jesus knocks at our heart's door, we must first recognize Him (hear His voice) before we open the door and invite Him to abide with us. We do this through faith (Ephesians 2:8).

This could be your first time asking. Perhaps you asked before but became discouraged and drifted away. Maybe you are looking for spiritual answers like the two who traveled the road to Emmaus. Either way, the prayer is the same: *Abide with me.* If you feel the Spirit of God tugging on your heart, then pray the words below, inviting Jesus to reside with you anew:

Dear Jesus, I need you. Please abide with me. Forgive me for anything I've done that displeased You. I regret every mistake, every shortcoming, and every sin. Take them out of my life forever. From this day forward, I will follow You as my Lord and Savior. Thank you for coming into my heart. In Your name, I pray. Amen.

Firstfruits of the Resurrection

With their minds enlightened, Cleopas and his companion understood the reason Jesus sacrificed His life. The Law and the Prophets even foretold it. The first two biblical festivals, Passover and Unleavened Bread, found fulfillment at the Cross as well. "For Christ, our Passover lamb, has been sacrificed. Therefore let us keep the Festival, not with the old bread leavened with malice and wickedness, but with the unleavened bread of sincerity and truth" (1 Corinthians 5:7*b*–8 NIV). If Jesus was the sacrificial lamb for Passover, then He must be the offering for Firstfruits, too. It all made sense now! The two travelers gathered their belongings and rushed back to Jerusalem. They must tell the disciples what happened on the road to Emmaus—and how they met the living Christ. "But now Christ is risen from the dead, *and* has become the firstfruits of those who have fallen asleep" (1 Corinthians 15:20).

The Festival of Firstfruits described in Leviticus 23:9–14, marked the beginning of the harvest season. The first barley grains usually ripened by the middle of April. These grain stalks were laid lengthways, tied together in bundles (called sheaves), and given to the priests to wave before the Lord as a firstfruits offering. With this act of obedience, the Jews thanked the Lord ahead of time for a bountiful final harvest.

Jesus Christ became the firstfruits for a spiritual harvest. His resurrection is our promise that the final harvest of souls will take place—and that all true believers who have died will rise from their graves to inherit eternal life. "For as in Adam all die, even so in Christ all shall be made alive. But each one in his own order: Christ the firstfruits, afterward those *who are* Christ's at His coming" (1 Corinthians 15:22–23).

The Holy Spirit also guarantees we will rise on Resurrection Day, for He placed a seal upon us when we first believed. His seal is the tangible assurance of our salvation. "In Him you also *trusted,* after you heard the word of truth, the gospel of your salvation; in whom also, having believed, you were sealed with the Holy Spirit of promise, who is the guarantee of our inheritance until the redemption of the purchased possession, to the praise of His glory" (Ephesians 1:13–14).

First Son-Rise Service

Now after the Sabbath, as it began to dawn toward the first *day* of the week, Mary Magdalene and the other Mary came to look at the grave.

And behold, a severe earthquake had occurred, for an angel of the Lord descended from heaven and came and rolled away the stone and sat upon it. And his appearance was like lightning, and his clothing as white as snow.

The guards shook for fear of him and became like dead men.

The angel said to the women, "Do not be afraid; for I know that you are looking for Jesus who has been crucified. He is not here, for He has risen, just as He said. Come, see the place where He was lying." (Matthew 28:1–6 NASB)

Greatest Moment for Jesus of Nazareth

The birth of Immanuel was a great event. His life and ministry were even greater since they included the purpose He came into this world. "And the Word became flesh and dwelt among us, and we beheld His glory, the glory as of the only begotten of the Father, full of grace and truth" (John 1:14). Likewise, His death was greater still because it further established God's redemption plan. However, His birth, sinless life, ministry of miracles, and sacrificial death on the cross would have accomplished little if He had not risen from the grave too. His resurrection on that Sunday morning fulfilled all of what God planned for Jesus of Nazareth. Here we see The Rule of the Greatest applied. When something is the greatest, it embraces everything preceding it. Although the resurrection of Christ was the greatest moment in the life of Jesus, it is still not the greatest moment. For that advent, the saints would need to come home.

PART FIVE:

MOMENTS OF GREAT EXPECTATION

Chapter 16

A Midnight Summons

When the Son of Man shall come in His glory to take the saints on high,
What a shouting in the skies from the multitudes that rise,
The trumpet shall sound, the dead shall be raised,
Changed in the twinkling of an eye.
—Frances Jane Crosby "In the Twinkling of an Eye" (1898)

We lived in Dayton, Oregon, when it happened. It began as a normal weekday evening for us: eat dinner, wash the dishes, tuck our daughters into their beds, and watch a program or two on television. I decided to stay up for the late news. When it ended, around 11:35 p.m., I headed for our bedroom. My wife lay curled up on her side of the bed, already sound asleep. Normally, I stay awake for a while, but I must have been extremely tired and within minutes, I drifted off to sleep.

Suddenly, out of nowhere, I heard Laura screaming. The noise jarred me awake. When my eyes finally focused, I rolled over and saw my wife sitting up in bed with her arms raised, yelling at the top of her lungs, "Hallelujah, Hallelujah! There He is! He's coming back!" Her eyes stared at the ceiling as if she could see right through it. She had this huge smile on her face. I remember asking, "Laura, are you all right? What's going on?"

Laura didn't respond to my questions; she just kept shouting her Hallelujahs. She appeared disoriented, unable to determine her own whereabouts. Maybe Laura was having a dream or vision. I hesitated a moment before I reached over and touched her shoulder. She stared back at me, her smile already fading away. After she gained her composure, I heard the details:

"I saw Jesus returning from heaven. My body began to float through the air toward Him. No words could express my joy, so I kept shouting, 'Hallelujah!' I heard you talking to me, asking questions, but since I could still see Jesus and feel an indescribable force lifting me upward, I ignored your inquiries. For a few moments, there were two separate realities: here and heaven. The urgency in your voice brought me back to this one. I'm not exactly sad, just disappointed."

As for me, I didn't see or hear anything. Apparently, my wife was going up in the Rapture, and I had missed it. I'm glad it turned out to be a dream. Being left behind is not a pleasant thought, especially when you're the lead pastor at a church. When I glanced at our digital clock, it read a few minutes past midnight. I don't think I slept the rest of the night.

Our Gathering Together

"Now, brethren, concerning the coming of our Lord Jesus Christ and our gathering together to Him, we ask you, not to be soon shaken in mind or troubled, either by spirit or by word or by letter, as if from us, as though the day of Christ had come. Let no one deceive you by any means; for *that Day will not come* unless the falling away comes first, and the man of sin is revealed, the son of perdition" (2 Thessalonians 2:1–3).

The words "falling away" in the previous passage can also be translated "departing." The Authorized Version says this gathering is "unto Him" (v. 1). The terms, departing and unto Him, sound more like a rapture event than anything else. Moreover, the phrase, *"that Day will not come,"* relates to our gathering together on the day Christ returns. When these words are kept in context, the meaning becomes much clearer. To me, the passage indicates the actual Rapture. Although you will not find the word *rapture* in the Bible, most Christians understand the event, even though they disagree on when it occurs.

Rapture Events Happened Before

When Enoch turned 365 years old, he went on a hike with the Lord and never returned (Genesis 5:23–24). God took him to heaven with no explanation offered other than Enoch delighted Him. "By faith Enoch was taken away so that he did not see death, *'and was not found, because God had taken him'*; for before he was taken, he had this testimony, that he pleased God" (Hebrews 11:5).

In a similar incident, a horse-drawn chariot of fire within a whirlwind transported Elijah into heaven. After the wind subsided, the only thing left behind was his coat. "Then it happened, as they continued on and talked, that suddenly a chariot of fire *appeared* with horses of fire, and separated the two of them; and Elijah went up by a whirlwind into heaven. And Elisha saw *it,* and he cried out, 'My father, my father, the chariot of Israel and its horsemen!' So he saw him no more" (2 Kings 2:11–12*a*). The difference between these two translations: Elijah had a ride; Enoch simply disappeared. However, neither of these saints died before entering eternity.

God used rapture events in the past, and since He often repeats His methods, we can expect others. His next rapture will occur on a grander scale. The Lord plans to take a large group of redeemed believers to His heavenly home, simultaneously.

Escape Plans

While some of God's methods involve supernatural raptures, others are just well-organized escape plans: Noah's ark and the Hebrew exodus from Egypt are prime examples of the latter. In another getaway scenario, two angels helped Lot and his family flee the coming judgment in Sodom. Seemingly, God finds nothing wrong with divine escape plans to avoid end-time disasters, nationwide destruction, or worldwide turmoil. Jesus even told the church in Philadelphia that He would save them from a season of tribulation coming upon the world. "Because you have kept My command to persevere, I also will keep you from the hour of trial which shall come upon the whole world, to test those who dwell on the earth" (Revelation 3:10). This statement points to evading or avoiding a last day judgment. Some believe it refers to a rapture event for Christian "Philadelphian" believers in today's Church.

In 1 Thessalonians 5, Paul said, "For God did not appoint us to wrath, but to obtain salvation through our Lord Jesus Christ" (v. 9). He made this comment "concerning the times and the seasons" prior to "the day of the Lord" (vv. 1–2) when Jesus comes back as a thief in the night. Paul encouraged the followers of Jesus to watch and be ready as children of the light, so that day would not overtake them like a thief or find them asleep (vv. 4–6).

An Imminent Return

"Watch therefore, for you do not know what hour your Lord is coming. But know this, that if the master of the house had known what hour the thief would come, he would have watched and not allowed his house to be broken into. Therefore you also be ready, for the Son of Man is coming at an hour you do not expect" (Matthew 24:42–44). The Bible contains many passages about the imminent return of Christ:

→ Watch every hour, every day (Matthew 25:13).

→ Take heed, keep alert; the timing is unknown (Mark 13:33).

→ Be ready, the Son of Man will arrive at an unexpected hour (Luke 12:40).

→ Discern the signs with expectation (Luke 21:25–28).

→ Stay awake and live uprightly (Revelation 16:15).

→ Realize the day of the Lord comes like a thief in the night (2 Peter 3:10).

All these Scriptures, and others like them, describe the Lord's return as imminent. Dictionaries define imminent as liable to happen, occurring soon, impending. This soon-to-occur return is biblical and confirmed by New Testament writers. Even Jesus prophesied He would come back. "In My Father's house are many mansions; if *it were* not *so,* I would have told you. I go to prepare a place for you. And if I go and prepare a place for you, I will come again and receive you to Myself; that where I am, *there* you may be also" (John 14:2–3). Simply put, Jesus wanted believers to be ready for this event whenever it happened.

The Departure

"Let no man deceive you by any means, for the Lord cometh not, except there come a departing first, and that that sinful man be opened, the son of perdition" (2 Thessalonians 2:3 Tyndale New Testament).[74] "Departing" is an interesting translation of the Greek word *apostasia*. The root verb *aphistemi* from which *apostasia* is derived means to depart from.[75] William Tyndale, one of the first to translate the Bible into English, rendered *apostasia* as departing (v. 3). The Coverdale Bible and other early translations did, as well.[76] Some Bibles translate the word as rebellion, and rebellion does occur during times of anarchy, but departure seems more in context with the entire passage (see 2 Thessalonians 2:1–4). Either way, a departure of some type must come first before the sinful man of perdition is revealed (v. 3).

According to the apostle Paul, Satan and his plan of worldwide iniquity will be hindered until something or someone is taken out of the way: "For the mystery of lawlessness is already at work; only He who now restrains *will do so* until He is taken out of the way. And then the lawless one will be revealed" (2 Thessalonians 2:7–8*a*). If this hindering force is the Holy Spirit, then that explains why the lawless one cannot work until the Spirit is taken out of the way. However, if Paul meant an entity indwelt by the Holy Spirit, then we can reasonably assume this verse refers to the Church. Therefore, believers are the ones removed, along with the Holy Spirit. Regardless of interpretation, a rapturous departure seems imminent.

Meeting in the Sky

> But we do not want you to be uninformed, brethren, about those who are asleep, so that you will not grieve as do the rest who have no hope.
>
> For if we believe that Jesus died and rose again, even so God will bring with Him those who have fallen asleep in Jesus.

191

> For this we say to you by the word of the Lord, that we who are alive and remain until the coming of the Lord, will not precede those who have fallen asleep.
>
> For the Lord Himself will descend from heaven with a shout, with the voice of *the* archangel and with the trumpet of God, and the dead in Christ will rise first.
>
> Then we who are alive and remain will be caught up together with them in the clouds to meet the Lord in the air, and so we shall always be with the Lord. (1 Thessalonians 4:13–17 NASB)

Jimmy, my neighbor, enjoyed discussing the second coming of Christ with anyone who would listen. For the most part, he witnessed to his co-workers at the cemetery. Since the work crew took their lunch breaks together outside among the gravestones, Jimmy used the setting to his advantage. His graveyard musings bothered most of his coworkers—but two of them listened with conviction and intrigue—imagining what it would be like to see the dead in Christ arise during one of their shifts. No doubt, they wouldn't have much time to observe it, if any, because in a twinkling of an eye, the three of them would be next.

Whether someone could actually see the dead in Christ rise from their graves during the Rapture is academic. All true believers will be gone. However, those left behind might see something. After Jesus rose from the grave on the third day, many residents reported seeing Old Testament saints walking around the streets of Jerusalem (see Matthew 27:52–53).

The Trump of God

"It shall come to pass, when they make a long *blast* with the ram's horn, *and* when you hear the sound of the trumpet, that all the people shall shout with a great shout; then the wall of the city will fall down flat. And the people shall go up every man straight before him" (Joshua 6:5).

The above passage concerns the fall of Jericho. It describes God's people going up in victory after the trumpet sounded, which could be a type and shadow of the Rapture. When we read about trumpets in the Old Testament, they were shofars. Shofars are one of the oldest known wind instruments. They were usually made from a ram's horn, but the horn of any kosher, male animal would suffice. Israel blew shofars on Rosh Hashanah and at other times.[77] When Gideon defeated the Midianite army, he did so with three hundred Israelites blowing their shofars in unity (Judges 7:16–21). Shofar trumpeters used four main sounds.

1. *Tekiah (long single blast)* sounded bright and piercing.
2. *Shevarim (three short wail-like blasts)* sounded like someone crying.
3. *Teruah (nine or more short blasts)* raised an alarm; trumpeters used all three sounds during Rosh Hashanah, including this fourth one.
4. *Tekiah hagadol (great long blast)* sounded similar to the first, except a trumpeter blew it until he ran out of breath.[78]

I believe this fourth blast is the last trump described by the apostle Paul: "Behold, I tell you a mystery: We shall not all sleep, but we shall all be changed—in a moment, in the twinkling of an eye, at the last trumpet. For the trumpet will sound, and the dead will be raised incorruptible, and we shall be changed" (1 Corinthians 15:51–52).

One day, a shofar will sound one long blast—the last trump—and like God's people in Joshua 6:5, the faithful will "go up" in victory. The Lord will descend from heaven and call forth His saints for a meeting in the sky. When Jesus arrives, three manifestations occur: a shout (battle cry), the voice of an archangel (probably Michael, see Daniel 12:1 and Jude 9), and the trumpet of God (shofar blast). These three manifestations may be one and the same or refer to three separate but simultaneous announcements. Either way, all true believers will be translated and meet the Lord in the air. "And thus we shall always be with the Lord. Therefore comfort one another with these words" (1 Thessalonians 4:17*b*–18).

The Midnight Shout

> But at midnight there was a shout, "Behold, the bridegroom! Come out to meet *him*." Then all those virgins rose and trimmed their lamps.
>
> The foolish said to the prudent, "Give us some of your oil, for our lamps are going out."
>
> But the prudent answered, "No, there will not be enough for us and you *too;* go instead to the dealers and buy *some* for yourselves."
>
> And while they were going away to make the purchase, the bridegroom came, and those who were ready went in with him to the wedding feast; and the door was shut.
>
> Later the other virgins also came, saying, "Lord, lord, open up for us."
>
> But he answered, "Truly I say to you, I do not know you."
>
> Be on the alert then, for you do not know the day nor the hour. (Matthew 25:6–13 NASB)

The above verses are from the *Parable of Ten Virgins*. They refer to the second coming of Christ—one of many last-day events leading to and including the resurrection of the saints. However, the return of Christ comes in two parts: the Rapture first, and then a later return that ushers in the prophetic day of the Lord. The midnight shout given to the ten virgins concerns the bridegroom's midnight approach. This shout is undoubtedly the same voice of an archangel mentioned in 1 Thessalonians 4:16. Some believe this parable refers to the Rapture, where a divine Bridegroom comes as a thief at midnight to steal away His betrothed bride. Others see a later fulfillment or one that applies only to Jewish people. Regardless of interpretation, the Bridegroom will return when all things in His Father's house are prepared (John 14:2–3). In the meantime, Jesus told us to watch, pray, and study His parables. When we consider all the signs of the times, His return seems imminent, certain, even at the door. I hope and pray we are all ready.

Paul Believed in the Rapture

In his two epistles to the Thessalonians, Apostle Paul wrote about the Rapture. He even encouraged Titus, one of his trusted associates, to look forward to this blessed event. "Looking for the blessed hope and glorious appearing of our great God and Savior Jesus Christ, who gave Himself for us, that He might redeem us from every lawless deed and purify for Himself *His* own special people, zealous for good works" (Titus 2:13–14).

Although the return of Christ will come like a thief in the night, Christians are children of the light and do not live in darkness. As believers, we will sense when this event is getting close, even see certain signs. We may not know the day or hour, but we can know the season. Therefore, Paul wanted believers to continue watching, meeting together, and uplifting one another. "And let us consider one another in order to stir up love and good works, not forsaking the assembling of ourselves together, as *is* the manner of some, but exhorting *one another,* and so much the more as you see the Day approaching" (Hebrews 10:24–25).

One day soon, a departure will take place and the saints will gather together unto Him. Prophetically, the stage is set, the season approaching. The Rapture will be one of the greatest days for the Church and for heaven. However, it is still not the greatest moment. Several other moments must occur first. The next one will be both great and terrible.

CHAPTER 17

DAY OF ACCOUNTING

At the Day of Judgment, we shall not be asked
what we have read, but what we have done.
—Thomas à Kempis

E very year on the second Sunday of February, our church conducted their annual business meeting required by the constitution and bylaws. The pastor would account for his ministry before the congregation. The board secretary read the minutes and financial reports. Various department heads gave their reports as well: youth, Sunday school, benevolence, and each outreach ministry. The membership scrutinized every little thing. If members liked what they heard, they retained the pastor. If not, they called for a vote of confidence. The pastor could be out the door in less than two weeks. Being the lead pastor in question, I approached this time of accounting with great anticipation—and some anxiety.

According to several Old Testament prophets, another day of accounting is coming when angelic scribes open up the archives in heaven. God will hear a report, consider the record, and render His judgment for every person who has ever lived (Revelation 20:12–13). Every jot and tittle will be scrutinized (Matthew 5:18–19). The Bible calls it a great and terrible day. It may be just a coincidence, but there are two distinct judgments in heaven: one is great, the other terrible. The *great* one occurs at the judgment seat of Christ after the Rapture. The *terrible* one takes place in front of the white throne of God, a thousand years later.

Great and Terrible

"Behold, I am going to send you Elijah the prophet before the coming of the great and terrible day of the LORD. He will restore the hearts of the fathers to *their* children and the hearts of the children to their fathers, so that I will not come and smite the land with a curse" (Malachi 4:5–6 NASB).

"I will show portents in the heavens and on the earth, blood and fire and columns of smoke. The sun shall be turned to darkness, and the moon to blood, before the great and terrible day of the LORD comes. Then everyone who calls on the name of the LORD shall be saved" (Joel 2:30–32*a* NRSV).

In Hebrew, God's judgments were often referred to as great *(gadowl)* and terrible *(yare')*.[79] English versions also translate *yare'* as awesome or dreadful. Regardless of the translation, *gadowl* and *yare'* create an interesting yet contrasting word picture. One writer, an unknown psalmist, combined great and terrible to describe God's name. "The LORD *is* great in Zion; and he *is* high above all the people. Let them praise thy great and terrible name; *for* it *is* holy" (Psalm 99:2–3 KJV). Nehemiah blended the same words in a prayer: "I beseech thee, O LORD God of heaven, the great and terrible God" (Nehemiah 1:5*a*

KJV). Malachi and Joel often paired these words together to describe the day of the Lord.

Day of the Lord

"For the day of the LORD *is* great and very terrible; who can endure it?" (Joel 2:11*b*). The phrase, "day of the Lord," is found over twenty times in the Bible. Isaiah, Jeremiah, Ezekiel, Joel, Amos, Obadiah, Zephaniah, Zechariah, and Malachi used this term in their prophetic words. Paul and Peter wrote about *that day* in letters to the Church (1 Thessalonians 5:2, 4; 2 Peter 3:10, 12). Revelation alludes to it as well (see Revelation 6:17; 16:14).

The day of the Lord is associated with a time of judgment or accounting, but it is also used in connection with the second coming of Christ, the Rapture (1 Thessalonians 4:13–5:11), and with the Sabbath holy day (Isaiah 58:13). Some passages denote times when God showed forth His strong hand of justice and righteousness. Such judgments might come through an enemy attack or through a natural disaster, like the plague of locusts mentioned in Joel. However, most "day of the Lord" passages point to a future time of reckoning and retribution. All of us will face a day of accounting. We will stand either before God's white throne or before Christ's judgment seat.

Judgment Seat of Christ

"For we shall all stand before the judgment seat of Christ. For it is written: '*As I live, says the LORD, every knee shall bow to Me, and every tongue shall confess to God.*' So then each of us shall give account of himself to God" (Romans 14:10*b*–12*a*).

Judgment seats were places where magistrates made decisions and handed out judgments. Pontius Pilate sat on such a bench while hearing accusations against Jesus (Matthew 27:19). An angry crowd hauled Paul before one in Corinth (Acts 18:12). People often think of judgment seats only in the negative sense, but the one Christ sits upon is different. It has a positive connotation for Christians. Although believers account to Jesus concerning their works, they are also rewarded for their faithfulness. "For we must all appear before the judgment seat of Christ, that each one may receive the things *done* in the body, according to what he has done, whether good or bad" (2 Corinthians 5:10).

Word Picture: Judgment Seat

I knew Lee from a local Bible study group. He had already suffered three strokes, and then a fourth one struck—this one severe. When the paramedics arrived on the scene, they diagnosed his situation and called Life Flight to transport him to Oregon Health & Science University in Portland, Oregon. Being in critical condition, they placed Lee in ICU where he struggled to stay alive. He had lost eighty percent of his vision. While he lay in his bed unresponsive and unconscious, Lee had a dream.

In the dream, Lee saw himself still on the hospital bed; in front of him were all the works he had accomplished through his ministry. They looked like presents, stacked in huge piles. He thought, "Wow! Look at all the treasures I've laid up for myself in heaven."

Then the Lord came into his room and said, "Lee, let us test these treasures of yours and see how they stand up to judgment." Then poof! Most of them went up in smoke. Ashes lay everywhere. After the smoke cleared, only a couple small piles of silver and gold remained.

Lee looked at the Lord with a sad frown and asked, "What happened to all my works, my programs, my ministries?" God answered him with a passage from 1 Corinthians:

> For no man can lay a foundation other than the one which is laid, which is Jesus Christ. Now if any man builds on the foundation with gold, silver, precious stones, wood, hay, straw, each man's work will become evident; for the day will show it because it is *to be* revealed with fire, and the fire itself will test the quality of each man's work. If any man's work which he has built on it remains, he will receive a reward. If any man's work is burned up, he will suffer loss; but he himself will be saved, yet so as through fire. (1 Corinthians 3:11–15 NASB)

Then the Lord replied, "Lee, please don't frown; I'm going to help you store treasures in heaven that really matter. I will teach you what is most important to Me, not what people think is important." After the dream ended, Lee awoke. Four days had passed; it was early Wednesday morning. To the utter amazement of everyone on the medical staff, his condition had improved.

Our treasures are those things we do in life: our efforts, ministries, acts of obedience or disobedience. In essence, they are our works, whether good or bad. Jesus told His followers to lay up for themselves treasures in heaven (see Matthew 6:20–21). At the judgment seat, Jesus will test these treasures, and we will find out which works hold up to divine scrutiny. Even though we may lose a few worthless ones, no punishments are handed out, nor is our salvation ever in jeopardy.

Pastors Take Note

Ministers, preachers, Bible teachers, and all those who are spiritual shepherds will not only answer for their personal works, they will also account for their oversight of souls: "Obey those who rule over you, and be submissive, for they watch out for your souls, as those who must give account. Let them do so with joy and not with grief, for that would be unprofitable for you" (Hebrews 13:17).

As a pastor for over thirty years, this next passage has drawn my attention on many occasions, putting the fear (respect and reverence) of God in proper perspective: "Not everyone who says to Me, 'Lord, Lord,' shall enter the kingdom of heaven, but he who does the will of My Father in heaven. Many will say to Me in that day, 'Lord, Lord, have we not prophesied in Your name, cast out demons in Your name, and done many wonders in Your name?' And then I will declare to them, 'I never knew you; depart from Me, you who practice lawlessness!'" (Matthew 7:21–23). On that day, only those who did the will of God can enter the kingdom of heaven and receive His eternal rewards.

Four Imperishable Crowns

In addition to other honors given to believers, there are four specific awards mentioned in the New Testament. God gives these for faithful service.

1. *Crown of Life:* All believers love God, but the crown of life is given to those who have stood the test of temptation and persevered. "Blessed *is* the man who endures temptation; for when he has been approved, he will receive the crown of life which the Lord has promised to those who love Him" (James 1:12).

2. *Crown of Rejoicing:* This triumphant crown will go to missionaries and those like the apostle Paul who have discipled and evangelized others. "For what *is* our hope, or joy, or crown of rejoicing? *Is it* not even you in the presence of our Lord Jesus Christ at His coming? For you are our glory and joy" (1 Thessalonians 2:19–20).

3. ***Crown of Glory:*** Some people call this the preacher's crown. It is awarded to all those who faithfully shepherd the body of Christ. Someday, every pastor, elder, deacon, teacher, prophet, minister, or overseer of the flock will humbly wear one.

> Therefore, I exhort the elders among you, as *your* fellow elder and witness of the sufferings of Christ, and a partaker also of the glory that is to be revealed, shepherd the flock of God among you, exercising oversight not under compulsion, but voluntarily, according to *the will of* God; and not for sordid gain, but with eagerness; nor yet as lording it over those allotted to your charge, but proving to be examples to the flock. And when the Chief Shepherd appears, you will receive the unfading crown of glory. (1 Peter 5:1–4 NASB)

4. ***Crown of Righteousness:*** Devoted followers should be looking for Jesus to return someday, but those who love His appearing are doing more than just watching, they are serving God with all their hearts, while falling more in love with Him each day. They desire the return of Jesus more than life itself. "Finally, there is laid up for me the crown of righteousness, which the Lord, the righteous Judge, will give to me on that Day, and not to me only but also to all who have loved His appearing" (2 Timothy 4:8).

Separating Sheep from Goats

"When the Son of Man comes in His glory, and all the holy angels with Him, then He will sit on the throne of His glory. All the nations will be gathered before Him, and He will separate them one from another, as a shepherd divides *his* sheep from the goats. And He will set the sheep on His right hand, but the goats on the left" (Matthew 25:31–33).

Bible land shepherds often tended combined flocks, but during certain daytime periods, it became necessary to separate the sheep from the goats. Sheep and goats did not graze well together. The goats were headstrong, rambunctious, and preferred grazing the rocky foothills throughout the day. The sheep, however, needed specific times for rest and favored feeding in the grassy pastures.[80]

Right Hand

Using a five to six-foot long staff, shepherds divided their flocks by tapping their sheep on the right side and their goats on the left. Sheep would gather around the shepherd's right hand while goats moved to the left. The sheep found food and relaxation, but the goats continued to clamber around restlessly.[81]

> Then the King will say to those on His right, "Come, you who are blessed of My Father, inherit the kingdom prepared for you from the foundation of the world.
>
> For I was hungry, and you gave Me *something* to eat; I was thirsty, and you gave Me *something* to drink; I was a stranger, and you invited Me in; naked, and you clothed Me; I was sick, and you visited Me; I was in prison, and you came to Me."
>
> Then the righteous will answer Him, "Lord, when did we see You hungry, and feed You, or thirsty, and give You *something* to drink? And when did we see You a stranger, and invite You in, or naked, and clothe You? When did we see You sick, or in prison, and come to You?"

The King will answer and say to them, "Truly I say to you, to the extent that you did it to one of these brothers of Mine, *even* the least *of them,* you did it to Me." (Matthew 25:34–40 NASB)

Left Hand

With this word picture, Jesus portrays a scene from the final judgment. The righteous inherit a kingdom filled with eternal rest, blessed by the right hand of promise. Since the left hand carries no such promise or blessing, the unrighteous depart to a kingdom of everlasting turmoil without rest.

> Then He will also say to those on His left, "Depart from Me, accursed ones, into the eternal fire which has been prepared for the devil and his angels;
>
> for I was hungry, and you gave Me *nothing* to eat; I was thirsty, and you gave Me nothing to drink; I was a stranger, and you did not invite Me in; naked, and you did not clothe Me; sick, and in prison, and you did not visit Me."
>
> Then they themselves also will answer, "Lord, when did we see You hungry, or thirsty, or a stranger, or naked, or sick, or in prison, and did not take care of You?"
>
> Then He will answer them, "Truly I say to you, to the extent that you did not do it to one of the least of these, you did not do it to Me." (Matthew 25:41–45 NASB)

Sometimes, it is not what people say or do, it is what they don't say or do that speaks against them on Judgment Day.

White Throne Judgment

If the judgment seat of Christ is the great part on the day of accounting, then the white throne judgment is the terrible part.

> Then I saw a great white throne and Him who sat upon it, from whose presence earth and heaven fled away, and no place was found for them.
>
> And I saw the dead, the great and the small, standing before the throne, and books were opened; and another book was opened, which is *the book* of life; and the dead were judged from the things which were written in the books, according to their deeds.
>
> And the sea gave up the dead which were in it, and death and Hades gave up the dead which were in them; and they were judged, every one *of them* according to their deeds.
>
> Then death and Hades were thrown into the lake of fire. This is the second death, the lake of fire.
>
> And if anyone's name was not found written in the book of life, he was thrown into the lake of fire. (Revelation 20:11–15 NASB)

All those who did not believe in Him for salvation will stand before God's white throne—and none will earn eternal life through their works. "He who believes in Him is not condemned; but he who does not believe is condemned already, because he has not believed in the name of the only begotten Son of God" (John 3:18). Instead of more commentary, maybe a word picture will help us understand this sad but awesome moment.

Word Picture: White Throne

"And it shall come to pass afterward that I will pour out My Spirit on all flesh; your sons and your daughters shall prophesy, your old men shall dream dreams, your young men shall see visions" (Joel 2:28). In the latter days, young men will see visions, and old men will dream dreams about God. I guess this means I'm no longer a young man because I only have dreams now. Most are nonsense—a combination of watching late night television and devouring spicy pizza. I seldom remember the details, and if I do, it's only just bits and pieces. Sometimes though, I have one of those dreams Joel prophesied about—a spiritual one. Such is the case with the dream below. Years later, I still remember every word and every detail. All I ask is for you to consider the message and any truth found therein.

One night, I dreamed of a huge amphitheater built entirely from polished white marble. It looked somewhat like an ancient Roman colosseum but with incredible height, towering into the heavens. The middle of the amphitheater contained a stage area with two tables: one large, the other small. Each table had a stool, but no one sat on it. The large table held stacks of scrolls in various sizes. One angel stood by the small table; another angel stood behind the large table but off to the side. Other angels entered and exited on a regular basis.

Jesus sat behind the stage area on a giant white bench. I took this to be the white throne judgment seat. Jesus looked just like I expected, except His shoulder-length hair appeared white instead of dark brown. He wore a long, white robe that almost covered His sandals. His face revealed a deep sadness. From time to time, He nodded His head and spoke to a person sitting next to Him: Jesus was on the right, a father-looking figure on the left. Although silhouetted, the father figure radiated a brilliant, almost blinding, white glow.

The light from various lampstands reflected everywhere. Saints from all the ages filled the amphitheater's seating area. A long line of people formed at the steps leading up to the stage area. One person stood before the small table. One by one, an angel called each individual to come forward.

The accounting process was tedious. Each person spoke their piece and answered questions. The angel behind the large table opened scroll after scroll as the interview proceeded. He checked every person's reply against the official records. After reading each entry, the angel would slowly shake his head saying, "No," and then ask, "Anything else?" The review continued until an individual had nothing else to add. Then the angel behind the little table opened a large single scroll and searched for that person's name and place of birthing. Interview after interview, this angel unrolled the large scroll and searched for names, but never found them. He would say, "I'm sorry, so very sorry, but you are not listed in the *Scroll of Life*."

When an interview ended, a group of angels escorted that person off the stage and down the hall to a portal of some type. Somehow, I knew this portal led to the lake of fire. Some people screamed in horror, their bodies trembling uncontrollably; others walked away in silence, their heads lowered in shame. Many just shook their heads in disgust—knowing they had failed—all their good works had missed the mark of holiness and righteousness. *They wondered how they could have been so wrong*. The interviews seemed to go on forever, but none of those standing in line were deemed worthy to stay in heaven.

After each case history, Jesus looked at some particular saint (we were all sitting around the throne behind Him) and said, "I was not willing this person should perish." Then, someone I recognized walked up the steps. It was Tony. He was my next-door neighbor in Dayton,

Oregon. I talked with him all the time. Tony's interview proceeded as usual, but like all the others, he ended up going to hell. Then Jesus looked in my direction; His eyes seemed to look right through me. Then He said, "I was not willing this person should perish" (see 2 Peter 3:9). Immediately, I broke down in tears, the sobs heavy in my chest. I had never cried so hard in my life. At that moment, I realized I had been the unwilling one. Maybe there were others, but I had no excuse. Tony only lived two houses away, and I never once told him about eternal life or invited him to church—and I was the pastor. Tony was the first one I knew personally—others followed—and each time Jesus would look at me. Emotionally I fell apart. *Oh God, if I had only known Judgment Day would be like this!*

By the time all accounting and judgments ended, tears flowed everywhere as the saints wept uncontrollably. I hurt so much inside; never have I experienced such sorrow. Then, Jesus stood, walked among us, and dried our eyes—just like the verse in Revelation 21:4 says He will: "And God will wipe away every tear from their eyes; there shall be no more death, nor sorrow, nor crying. There shall be no more pain, for the former things have passed away."

I have often wondered why the saints would need their tears wiped away. This is heaven after all, a joyful place. Now I know. It's because of what they will witness. Watching most of humanity being cast into the lake of fire will surely evoke a profound emotional response from anyone who observes it. "For the gate is small and the way is narrow that leads to life, and there are few who find it" (Matthew 7:14 NASB).

Great and Terrible Day

Judgment Day will no doubt entail great and terrible moments, and as redeemed saints, we will see them all. However, we are more than spectators; we also participate. Although the Bible does not elaborate, it does give us a few hints. "Or do you not know that the Lord's people will judge the world? And if you are to judge the world, are you not competent to judge trivial cases? Do you not know that we will judge angels? How much more the things of this life!" (1 Corinthians 6:2–3 NIV). Since God is the only righteous judge, our role at the white throne is probably more of a judge pro tem. For additional hints about our involvement as judges in eternity see Revelation 3:21, Matthew 19:28, and Jude 6, 14–15.

Although I discussed both judgments in this chapter, believers only face the judgment seat of Christ, not God's white throne judgment. Christ's judgment seat will not be terrible if you are born again. In fact, you should look forward to it. As Christians, we all get crowns. We all receive rewards. We all rejoice together. Sure, a few of our treasures are burnt up, but we really didn't need those anyway. After all the decisions from the judgment seat of Christ are rendered, our focus will change. Other matters are pressing. We have a reception dinner to attend.

Yes, heaven's day of accounting will be an awesome event, but it's still not the greatest moment. A greater one is waiting at the wedding chapel.

Chapter 18

Invitation to a Reception Dinner

The King bids you come and partake of the feast,
For all there is room even unto the least,
But if you would enter the palace so fair,
The pure wedding garment you surely must wear.
—Harriet E. Jones "Have You the Garment of White?" (1894)

They called me in the morning so I had no time to prepare or to conduct my normal counseling interview. Later that afternoon, with my wedding folder of notes and ceremonies in hand, I left for Vancouver, Washington. A couple from my church wanted me to officiate over the renewal of their wedding vows. Since they were from the Fiji Islands, they had planned a Fijian-style ceremony similar to the one they participated in twenty-five years earlier.

Expecting to be the person in charge, I was surprised when they asked me to take a seat and wait until they called me forward. After I voiced my concerns of being "ill-prepared" and "that's not the way I usually do it," I reluctantly took my seat—and just in time. The lights in the room had already dimmed, except the ones highlighting the center aisle where the bridal party waited for the procession to begin.

The best man entered the hall first, followed by the faithful husband who wore a stylish tuxedo with a white cummerbund. The husband smiled and nodded at everyone as he walked down the rows. The best man then began a lengthy tribute about his honorable friend, naming all his accomplishments to date. After each comment, the guests clapped and shouted their approval. After passing the last row, he took his place at the front, surrounded by family and friends who were given the privilege of standing next to him.

The lovely bride, the wife of the faithful husband, entered last. Her white garments dazzled under the bright lights, reflecting her beauty and purity. Two sons escorted her down the center aisle, one on the right and the other on the left. The best man spoke about her faithfulness, love, and commitment to her husband and their family. Standing to their feet, the guests shouted their approval. Caught up in the moment, I stood too. Even though I hardly knew the bride and groom, I could sense their love and commitment to one another.

A family member interrupted my joyful clapping to tell me the time had come for restating vows. I grabbed my wedding material and rushed forward, but I never had a chance to use it. Instead, I listened to the bride and groom share their own unique vows—the same ones they had spoken on their wedding day. Their words held depth and meaning, much better than the canned presentation my notes would have offered. Never have I witnessed a more thoughtful renewal service. As for my officiating, I only shared a couple Scriptures and prayed a closing benediction.

After the ceremony, we gathered for a lavish reception dinner. Relatives had prepared a special menu in honor of the bride and groom. A dozen tables featured huge platters and bowls of delicious entrées. They were all Fijian foods; several of the dishes held symbolic meaning. Before a serving platter emptied, someone filled it again with more food. Everything tasted fantastic. During the meal, festive music began to play, and then the dancing broke out. Joy and laughter filled the hall. All the Fijian women wore brightly colored outfits trimmed with shiny sequins. The men dressed in their Sunday best. It was a marriage ceremony and supper to remember.

Marriage Supper of the Lamb

> And a voice came from the throne, saying, "Give praise to our God, all you His bond-servants, you who fear Him, the small and the great."
>
> Then I heard *something* like the voice of a great multitude and like the sound of many waters and like the sound of mighty peals of thunder, saying, "Hallelujah! For the Lord our God, the Almighty, reigns. Let us rejoice and be glad and give the glory to Him, for the marriage of the Lamb has come and His bride has made herself ready."
>
> It was given to her to clothe herself in fine linen, bright *and* clean; for the fine linen is the righteous acts of the saints.
>
> Then he said to me, "Write, 'Blessed are those who are invited to the marriage supper of the Lamb.'" And he said to me, "These are true words of God." (Revelation 19:5–9 NASB)

God is planning an elaborate reception dinner in heaven. The Scriptures call it the marriage supper of the Lamb. This gathering takes place sometime after the judgment seat of Christ but before the white throne judgment. The passage calls it a *marriage,* not a *wedding,* which may only be a matter of semantics. Even more interesting, though, is the phrase, "and His bride has made herself ready" (v. 7). The Authorized Version, Young's Literal Translation, the Darby Bible, and Zondervan's Greek Interlinear translate γυνή *(gune)* as wife, not bride.[82] Several other Bible versions do the same. Since *gune* (pronounced goo-nay) can refer to a woman of any age, a wife, or a betrothed bride,[83] we should consider the marriage customs of the day and context of the passage for clarification. This would point to an earlier ceremony where the bride and bridegroom already exchanged vows, a betrothal perhaps.

The Betrothal

According to *The Jewish Encyclopedia,* the rabbinical term used for betrothal is *kiddushin.*[84] Family members or people appointed as their deputies usually worked out the arrangements for a betrothed couple. The final agreement, however, required the consent of the prospective bride if she was of age. The passages below highlight the negotiation efforts and other details involved in arranging betrothals in the Bible.[85]

→ Seeking a bride for Isaac (Genesis 24:1–67)

→ Jacob's bridal negotiations (Genesis 29:18–28)

→ Brothers of the Shulamite (Song of Solomon 8:8–9)

→ Acquiring a Philistine bride for Samson (Judges 14:2–10)

An important part of these negotiations involved *mohar* or bride price that the groom paid in cash or rendered service.[86] The betrothal covenant was binding upon both the groom and bride who were

214

regarded as husband and wife in all legal and religious aspects, except for actual cohabitation.[87]

In 2 Samuel 3:14, David called his betrothed bride a wife: "Give *me* my wife Michal, whom I betrothed to myself." The Law of Moses also regarded betrothed women as wives (see Deuteronomy 22: 23–24). Rabbinical law declared that betrothals were equivalent to actual marriages and should only be dissolved by a bill of divorce,[88] which is what Joseph had considered for Mary when she became pregnant before their marriage (Matthew 1:19).

During the betrothal ceremony, parties agreed to terms, Scriptures were recited, promises exchanged, and the bridegroom gave his bride a ring or other object of value. Betrothed men also handed out additional gifts (called *mattan* in Hebrew). Some of these were token presents; others met upcoming needs. Male friends of the bridegroom would also send friendship gifts to help defray wedding costs.[89]

Jesus likewise offered *mattan* to His betrothed bride.[90] Apostle Paul called them spiritual gifts (see 1 Corinthians 12:1–11). Jesus imparted these wonderful giftings through the Holy Spirit to sustain the Church until the day He returns to take her home. Although precious and necessary during the betrothal-waiting period, these gifts will not be needed after the home-taking, having already accomplished their intended purpose (1 Corinthians 13:8–10).

Home-Taking

After the agreed waiting period, sometimes up to twelve months, the bridegroom stole his betrothed wife for the formal home-taking *(nissuin).*[91] Accompanied by his friends and dressed in festive attire, the bridegroom went to the bride's residence. He then led her back to either his house or his parent's home. She would be dressed in bridal garments, veiled, and accompanied by her companions. The bridal party celebrated, danced, and sang joyful songs of praise in honor of the couple. If the procession took place in the evening, torches or oil lamps illuminated the path. After the wedding nuptials, the wedding supper began. The festivities often continued for a week.[92]

An Anticipated Event

The Lamb's marriage supper may be the official wedding reception that God postponed until all His guests could arrive in heaven. When my wife and I were married, we had a small reception dinner following our ceremony with our immediate family. Later, when all the relatives could gather, we organized another reception—a much larger affair with all the pomp and circumstance we missed with the first one. It was just like our wedding day and in some ways, better. Perhaps this dinner is a homecoming anniversary celebration for the saints. Either way, the marriage supper of the Lamb (Revelation 19:9) is a blessed event that no one should miss. To make it even more memorable, God has arranged for a special guest, a good friend of the Bridegroom, to oversee the festivities.

John: Friend of the Bridegroom

At most Christian weddings today, the groom asks a close friend or relative to be his best man. Along with other groomsmen, the best man stands by the groom during the wedding ceremony. At the reception, he presents the first toast, which is usually a short speech or charge to the guests and newly married couple. These are only some of his duties; tradition reveals many others: The best man would assist the groom with all wedding duties and festivities. He helped with travel plans and honeymoon accommodations, attended to garment-related needs, and kept the groom company while waiting for the bride's grand entrance. In some weddings, the best man served as the host or master of ceremonies.

The friend of the bridegroom performed a similar role for Jewish weddings. He made preliminary marriage arrangements and helped with wedding festivities. As a trusted liaison, he served the couple and attended to their bridal chamber needs. Sometimes, there were two friends: one for the groom and one for the bride. At the wedding in Cana of Galilee, the master of the feast may have been a friend of the bridegroom (John 2:9). After the wedding ceremony, the friend of the bridegroom stood outside the bridal chamber and rejoiced when the groom told him the marriage was consummated (John 3:29). This word picture is the same one John the Baptist painted for himself.

During a water baptism service near Salim in the land of Judea, some questions arose concerning ceremonial washing and John's real identity. John told his disciples he was not the Christ—only a joyful friend of the bridegroom. God had sent him to Israel to help prepare her for an upcoming wedding. "You yourselves bear me witness, that I said, 'I am not the Christ,' but, 'I have been sent before Him.' He who has the bride is the bridegroom; but the friend of the bridegroom, who stands and hears him, rejoices greatly because of the bridegroom's voice. Therefore this joy of mine is fulfilled" (John 3:28–29).

More Friends of the Bridegroom

In Exodus 19:17, Moses led the Israelites out of the camp to the foot of Mount Sinai so they could meet with God. Here, Moses assumed the role of friend of the bridegroom. He introduced Israel to Yahweh, handled covenant arrangements under the Law, and served as an intermediary between bride and bridegroom. This marriage-like relationship held new hope and understanding for Israel: "And *as* the bridegroom rejoices over the bride, *so* shall your God rejoice over you" (Isaiah 62:5*b*).

In 2 Corinthians 11:2, Apostle Paul said, "For I am jealous for you with godly jealousy. For I have betrothed you to one husband, that I may present *you as* a chaste virgin to Christ." In this verse, Paul referred to his own role as friend of the bridegroom. Moses held this position for Israel, and Paul embraced it for the Church. Paul helped with betrothal arrangements and led believers to the hope of glory, which is Christ in them (Colossians 1:27). He will have the honor of presenting the virtuous bride before Christ. In the meantime, his epistles will teach the bride about her heavenly Bridegroom, help her develop an intimate relationship, and prepare her for His return.

One day soon, the friends of the Bridegroom will gather in heaven. One of them will present the bride and be the main speaker at the marriage supper of the Lamb. Maybe it will be John the Baptist, Moses the Lawgiver, or Paul the Apostle. Perhaps all three will give their charges. But why stop with just three "friends" when many others shared this role, too, including judges, prophets, priests, and kings. Since time is no longer an issue in eternity, the saints and invited guests may hear speeches from all of them. Then, after the presentations and testimonials end, everyone will sit down for the long-awaited wedding feast.

The Dinner Menu

Instead of an elaborate dinner filled with delicious entrées, I wonder if this reception meal will be a simpler affair—unleavened bread with a cup of wine—the fulfillment of a Passover dinner Jesus cut short the night Judas betrayed Him. The traditional Passover meal used four cups of wine (listed below) to symbolize the four redemptions promised by

God to the Hebrews enslaved in Egypt.[93] Their corresponding promises are found in Exodus 6:6–7.

Cup of Sanctification
"I will bring you out [of Egypt]" (v. 6).

Cup of Judgment (also called Cup of Deliverance)
"I will rescue you from their bondage" (v. 6).

Cup of Redemption
"I will redeem you with an outstretched arm and great judgments" (v. 6).

Cup of Praise (also called Cup of Restoration)
"I will take you as My people, and I will be your God" (v. 7).

Although the Bible does not go into detail, we can assume Jesus shared the first three cups with His disciples and partook of them Himself. "Then He said to them, 'With *fervent* desire I have desired to eat this Passover with you before I suffer; for I say to you, I will no longer eat of it until it is fulfilled in the kingdom of God.' Then He took the cup, and gave thanks, and said, 'Take this and divide *it* among yourselves; for I say to you, I will not drink of the fruit of the vine until the kingdom of God comes'" (Luke 22:15–18).

Jesus passed on the fourth cup and is waiting for the right moment to share it with His bride in God's heavenly kingdom. Perhaps it will happen at the marriage supper of the Lamb.

Word Picture: The Question

No doubt, the redeemed saints will have many questions on their minds. What does the future hold, where will they live, and what will they do throughout eternity? If He allows me to pose a question, I might ask, "Lord, tell us about Calvary?" I have no idea what Jesus

219

would actually say or if He will take questions at the reception dinner, so the following word picture is for reflective consideration only. Still, I wonder if His reply might be, *Dear Beloved, the Cross was like this… would you pass the bread please?* As He breaks the unleavened bread and passes it around, our eyes become misty. Swallowing becomes difficult, but somehow we consume every broken piece. He then adds… *will you pass the wine too?* After receiving the cup, He blesses it, takes a sip Himself, and then offers it to us. With tears streaming down our cheeks, we drink from the fourth Passover cup, every precious drop. All other questions seem trivial at this point. Our tears keep us company until Jesus wipes them away, but that doesn't occur until after the white throne judgments are complete (see Revelation 21:4).

Word Picture: Wedding Party Enters

Similar to the Fijian wedding ceremony described earlier in this chapter, our heavenly wedding day will entail much pomp and circumstance—but from a divine perspective. It will be filled with holiness, righteousness, and overshadowed by glory.

One night, I dreamed a dream about a celestial wedding day. An angelic announcer introduced a heavenly Bridegroom who entered an endless hall, escorted by Moses on the right and Elijah on the left. Both these saints previously stood at His side on the Mount of Transfiguration, where they met together to discuss upcoming events that likely included Calvary, redemption, and the greatest moment (see Matthew 17:1–9; Luke 9:30–31).

The procession continued with thousands upon thousands of angels—some seraphim, others cherubim—all led by Michael, the archangel of victory. Four living creatures joined the ranks and cried out repetitively, "Holy, holy, holy, Lord God Almighty, who was and is and is to come!" (Revelation 4:8*b*). The wedding party encountered many delays because every few steps, twenty-four elders bowed down with their faces to the ground and said, "You are worthy, O Lord, to receive glory and honor and power; for You created all things, and by Your will they exist and were created" (Revelation 4:11).

The bride entered next, adorned in a glorious gown and escorted by the Holy Spirit Himself. The announcer for the entire procession was the angelic prince Gabriel, faithful messenger of God. The Lord selected Gabriel because he has been a presenter of good news for centuries. Gabriel described in detail the exploits of every angel and servant of God, which further added to the prestige of the Groom and His redeemed bride. Since the halls of heaven are quite extensive, it took a while for everyone in the wedding party to enter the ceremonial area where the marriage vows would be renewed.

Renewal of Vows

During a renewal ceremony, couples usually reaffirm their wedding vows or pledges. Traditional ones have changed little over the centuries. If you were a bride, then yours may have sounded something like the one below, adapted from the *Book of Common Prayer*.[94]

I take you to be my wedded husband, to have and to hold from this day forward. I promise to love and cherish you and be your faithful, loving wife; for better or for worse, for richer or poorer, in sickness or in health; and to leave all others and cleave only unto you as long as we both shall live.

The day we accept Jesus as our Savior, He not only becomes our Lord, He becomes our Bridegroom and we, His betrothed bride. If we stay within the betrothal-salvation context, then our salvation prayer contains our betrothal pledge and vow. After asking Jesus to forgive us for our sins (being unfaithful), we invite Him into our hearts as Savior. We are then saved (born again). Somewhere during this prayer, we pledge to love Him with all our hearts and to follow Him faithfully.

Although individual salvation prayers vary, in essence you promise to "love the LORD your God with all your heart, with all your soul, with all your mind, and with all your strength" (Mark 12:30*b*). This all-encompassing promise is our betrothal pledge. If the Lord has a marriage or renewal ceremony in heaven for His bride, and it appears He will, then our betrothal pledge will become our marriage or renewal vow. The Holy Spirit, acting as our advocate, will probably reaffirm that vow. For the Spirit of truth was present the day we accepted Jesus as Lord—and He can bear witness to the integrity of our words.

After being born again, we only know Jesus as our Lord and Master, but in heaven, we will call Him our Husband: "And it shall be, in that day," says the LORD, "*that* you will call Me 'My Husband,' and no longer call Me 'My Master'" (see Hosea 2:16).

The Bride

"Then one of the seven angels who had the seven bowls filled with the seven last plagues came to me and talked with me, saying, 'Come, I will show you the bride, the Lamb's wife'" (Revelation 21:9).

Most brides spend hours getting ready for their weddings. They usually purchase white wedding dresses and garments to accentuate their beauty. They adorn their hair with ivory-toned ornamental bows and ribbons and cover their faces with veils of transparent white tulle. They desire to be beautiful for their future husbands. The bride of Christ is no different, except her beauty is inward not outward, and her elegant wedding garments are handwoven.

"And to her it was granted to be arrayed in fine linen, clean and bright, for the fine linen is the righteous acts of the saints" (Revelation 19:8). In heaven, our garments emulate our good works.

The Groom

Like brides, most grooms put on their best clothes, usually the finest pressed suit or tuxedo they can afford. Our heavenly Bridegroom is no exception. He dresses in the finest garments that heaven has to offer. He wears a crimson red robe with a divine insignia or logo that says King of Kings and Lord of Lords. The same words are written on His thigh.[95] His head holds many crowns or other kingly headdresses. One of those probably contains a name no one has ever seen or heard. Only Jesus knows this name and its meaning. No doubt, the Lord has other names He has yet to reveal. Maybe at His marriage supper He will share one with us.

> And I saw heaven opened, and behold, a white horse, and He who sat on it *is* called Faithful and True, and in righteousness He judges and wages war.
>
> His eyes *are* a flame of fire, and on His head *are* many diadems; and He has a name written *on Him* which no one knows except Himself.
>
> *He is* clothed with a robe dipped in blood, and His name is called The Word of God. And the armies which are in heaven, clothed in fine linen, white *and* clean, were following Him on white horses.
>
> From His mouth comes a sharp sword, so that with it He may strike down the nations, and He will rule them with a rod of iron; and He treads the wine press of the fierce wrath of God, the Almighty.

And on His robe and on His thigh He has a name written, "KING OF KINGS, AND LORD OF LORDS." (Revelation 19:11–16 NASB)

One Great Moment Still Awaits

The marriage supper of the Lamb, including all the festivities, will be one of the great moments in the Bible. But it's still not the greatest. Our heavenly Father has one moment planned that tops them all. It occurs sometime after the saints arrive in heaven. Like the Rapture, the Lamb's marriage supper, the Second Coming, and other prophetic incidents, the exact timing for this event is not mentioned. No doubt, God has reasons for keeping the unveiling of His greatest moment a surprise. Although biblical time frames are essential, even intriguing, they're not as important as scriptural content and context. For that, we will continue following Isaiah's precept-building approach: word by word, verse by verse (Isaiah 28:10).

The greatest word is next, followed by the greatest Scripture. They will help lead us to the greatest moment of all.

Part Six:

The Greatest Moment
in the Bible

CHAPTER *19*

GREATEST WORD

We have too many high sounding words,
and too few actions that correspond with them.
—Abigail Adams

As a teenager, I enjoyed watching game shows on television. One of my favorites was *Password,* which originally aired during the 1960s. For someone who didn't like English class or memorizing spelling words, my parents thought it odd that I liked this program. With Allen Ludden as host, two teams competed to guess the featured word. Each team had one contestant and one celebrity. Teammates would give each other one-word clues in hopes of discovering the all-important password before the round ended or the rival team won.

The Bible has important passwords too. Several are spiritual pass-keys that open or close doors. They bind and loose real situations in heaven and on earth (Matthew 16:19) and when used in agreement, bring answers to prayer and cause miracles to manifest (Matthew 18:18–19). Other words share encouragement, show compassion, and release the fruits of the Spirit (Galatians 5:22–23). The greatest words, however, are the ones that describe the nature of God and reveal His worthy attributes. One of them is greater than all the rest.

Three Great Words

"And now abide faith, hope, love, these three; but the greatest of these *is* love" (1 Corinthians 13:13). In this verse, Paul lists three great words. One of them is greater than the other two; however, the reasons for that distinction are not given. A closer look at their biblical meanings may reveal Paul's rationale.

Faith

Faith and belief are synonymous: believing is the action; faith is the result. "But without faith *it is* impossible to please *Him,* for he who comes to God must believe that He is, and *that* He is a rewarder of those who diligently seek Him" (Hebrews 11:6). Through faith, we please God and receive spiritual and physical rewards, including the most important one: our salvation. "For by grace you have been saved through faith, and that not of yourselves; *it is* the gift of God, not of works, lest anyone should boast" (Ephesians 2:8–9).

Ironically, although faith, not works, saves us—works are motivated by faith. "And these signs will follow those who believe: In My name they will cast out demons; they will speak with new tongues; they will take up serpents; and if they drink anything deadly, it will by no means hurt them; they will lay hands on the sick, and they will recover" (Mark 16:17–18).

Faith is a great word, especially when that faith rests in Christ. Faith is one of the passkeys that opens or closes kingdom doors. No wonder Paul included it in his top three. But faith needs the right substance to operate. "Now faith is the substance of things hoped for, the evidence of things not seen" (Hebrews 11:1). A substance is what something is made from, its properties, what it consists of. Since faith gets its substance from hope, a closer look at hope will help us understand more about faith.

Hope

Simply put, hope is a feeling of expectation, a strong desire to have something happen. The biblical usage, however, is even more inclusive:

→ Hope is an anchor of the soul (Hebrews 6:18–19).

→ Hope purifies (1 John 3:3).

→ Hope is life (1 Peter 1:3).

→ Hope never disappoints (Romans 5:5).

→ The New Covenant brings a better hope (Hebrews 7:19).

→ God's appearing is the blessed hope (Titus 2:13).

→ Jesus Christ is our hope (1 Timothy 1:1).

Hope and faith also have an interesting association. When we find faith, hope is usually nearby. The Bible tells us that we are saved in hope (Romans 8:24) and through hope we believe (Romans 4:17–18). No wonder hope adds substance to faith. Hope is the passkey that opens the door to faith. When we hope (desire and expect) to know God as our Savior, it leads us to belief. If we hope (desire and expect) to see our sick children healed in the name of Jesus, will not hope give substance to our faith and bring results? The Bible says it will.

In essence, hope is greater than faith. The passion and desire found in hope is what energizes faith. If Paul listed these two words in order of importance or greatness, then hope is above faith for obvious reasons.

Nevertheless, both faith and hope are dependent upon something even greater: *Love*.

Love

The Bible tells us that faith works through love (Galatians 5:6). Therefore, love is greater. In fact, love includes faith, and since faith uses hope to believe (Romans 4:18), then love includes hope as well. According to The Rule of the Greatest from chapter 2, when something is the greatest, it incorporates what is great, greater, plus more. Such is the case with love. If we believe on the Lord Jesus Christ, the Bible says we will be saved (Acts 16:31). However, if we love God with all our heart, mind, soul, and strength, we can inherit eternal life (Luke 10:25–28), which is another term for salvation. Is love that powerful? Yes, love is higher, greater, and encompasses both faith and hope. Moreover, whoever abides in love abides in God, and God in them (see 1 John 4:16).

Love is a divine word. It originates from the heart of God, "for God is love" (1 John 4:8). The word John uses in this verse is *agape,* the Greek word for love.[96] In Romans, Apostle Paul expounds on God's *agape* love, describing it as compassionate, powerful, unlimited, unceasing, and inexhaustible. "For I am persuaded that neither death nor life, nor angels nor principalities nor powers, nor things present nor things to come, nor height nor depth, nor any other created thing, shall be able to separate us from the love of God which is in Christ Jesus our Lord" (Romans 8:38–39).

His revelations about "the love of God" *(agape)* were more than doctrinal; they were personal. He sensed God's wondrous love at work in his own life, even when he considered himself the worst sinner of all. Through all his trials, mistakes, and shortcomings, God's love never abandoned him. This type of unconditional love influenced Paul's life and ministry. His views concerning it were a direct result of experiencing it firsthand. Paul recorded his teachings on the supremacy of love in 1 Corinthians 13, commonly known as *The Love Chapter*:

> If I speak with the tongues of men and of angels, but do not have love, I have become a noisy gong or a clanging cymbal.
>
> If I have *the gift of* prophecy, and know all mysteries and all knowledge; and if I have all faith, so as to remove mountains, but do not have love, I am nothing.
>
> And if I give all my possessions to feed *the poor,* and if I surrender my body to be burned, but do not have love, it profits me nothing.
>
> Love is patient, love is kind *and* is not jealous; love does not brag *and* is not arrogant, does not act unbecomingly; it does not seek its own, is not provoked, does not take into account a wrong *suffered,* does not rejoice in unrighteousness, but rejoices with the truth; bears all things, believes all things, hopes all things, endures all things. Love never fails;
>
> But now faith, hope, love, abide these three; but the greatest of these is love. (1 Corinthians 13:1–8*a,* 13 NASB)

Love is certainly a great word, but other words in the Bible are just as great. Some are even greater. The next three rank higher than many others do. They are lofty, matchless, deserving words that need mentioning before we discover the greatest word of all. *Holy* is one of them.

Holy

Holiness describes God's absolute excellence. God is holy—little else can be added to improve this highly merited word, unless of course, it is doubled or tripled in succession. One day, the prophet Isaiah heard such a phrase.

"In the year that King Uzziah died, I saw the Lord sitting on a throne, high and lifted up, and the train of His *robe* filled the temple. Above it stood seraphim; each one had six wings: with two he covered his face, with two he covered his feet, and with two he flew. And one cried to another and said: 'Holy, holy, holy *is* the LORD of hosts; the whole earth *is* full of His glory!'" (Isaiah 6:1–3). The Hebrew word Isaiah used for holy is *qadowsh*. It can translate as holy, sacred, Holy One, or set apart.[97] Certain angels have spoken this triple-worded phrase, day and night, nonstop, since eternity began (see Revelation 4:8).

When the Bible repeats a word or phrase, it is noteworthy. When this repetition occurs three times, it becomes even more significant. In the Hebrew language, repeating a word gave it special emphasis, like quotation marks or exclamation marks do in the English language.

Holy is the only attribute of God the Bible duplicates three times. God isn't just holy—He is holy, holy, holy!

Lovingkindness

"How precious *is* Your lovingkindness, O God!" (Psalm 36:7a). Lovingkindness, *checed* in Hebrew, translates as mercy, kindness, or goodness.[98] The closest equivalent in the New Testament is the word grace, *charis* in Greek.[99] To further emphasize the priceless value of lovingkindness, the psalmist added the adjective *yaqar,* a Hebrew word that means precious, costly, or excellent.[100]

In lovingkindness, God's great love and His great kindness are combined into one word. According to The Rule of the Greatest, this combined word is greater because it comprises both meanings. Without God's lovingkindness, we would truly be lost with no hope for eternal salvation.

"Whoever *is* wise will observe these *things,* and they will understand the lovingkindness of the LORD" (Psalm 107:43). We can find either this word or its concept in every book of the Bible. Regardless of language or translation, lovingkindness is God's mercy manifested. It is truly an unparalleled word. The next word, however, ranks even higher.

Peace

Shalom, the Hebrew word for peace is greater than all the words previously introduced in this chapter. It is one of the most powerful, all-inclusive words in the Bible. You may have heard the phrases "peace and quiet" or "peace of mind," but these expressions offer only a limited view of peace. *Shalom* encompasses so much more. It also conveys completeness, soundness, safety, welfare, health, tranquility, contentment, prosperity, and friendship.[101]

In a biblical sense, peace *(shalom)* can be interpreted as *all that ought to be there.* That might explain how Jesus Christ became our peace: "But now in Christ Jesus you who once were far off have been brought near by the blood of Christ. For He Himself is our peace, who has made both one, and has broken down the middle wall of separation, having abolished in His flesh the enmity, *that is,* the law of commandments *contained* in ordinances, so as to create in Himself one new man *from* the two, *thus* making peace" (Ephesians 2:13–15). Here we see Christ, our *shalom,* making peace with the Law and its commandments and regulations. Therefore, when we have Christ, we have reconciliation and redemption.

In Psalm 35:27, it says that the Lord has pleasure in the prosperity of His servant. The word translated as prosperity in this verse is *shalom*. For some in Christianity, the concept of prosperity has negative overtones. However, if we look at prosperity as part of God's provision for peace, we might be less critical of those believers who are trusting God for all His promises and benefits.

"And the peace of God, which surpasses all understanding, will guard your hearts and minds through Christ Jesus" (Philippians 4:7). Some say knowledge is the key to success, but in God's kingdom, *shalom* is more essential. It guards our physical and spiritual well-being and enriches our minds. When we have the peace of God, we have everything we need *(all that ought to be there)*.

Peace, as revealed in the Scriptures, is truly an amazing word. It is in a league of its own, seemingly unsurpassed. In fact, it might be the greatest word in the Bible—were it not for another one that expresses even more.

Glory: All That God Is

Glory is the most majestic, awe-inspiring, revered word of all. It is unparalleled in the Scriptures. Glory came from God, belonged to God, and existed before the foundation of the world. "And now, Father, glorify me in your presence with the glory I had with you before the world began" (John 17:5 NIV). Jesus first revealed God's glory in Cana of Galilee where He turned water into wine. "This beginning of signs Jesus did in Cana of Galilee, and manifested His glory; and His disciples believed in Him" (John 2:11). Even Moses, who already knew God personally, wanted to see His glory manifested: "And he said, 'Please, show me Your glory'" (Exodus 33:18).

Moreover, through glory, our inward salvation and unity in Christ become a reality. In other words, we are saved because of God's glory. "And the glory which You gave Me I have given them, that they may be one just as We are one: I in them, and You in Me; that they may be made perfect in one" (John 17:22–23*a*).

The Bible tells us that God is rich, but His wealth is based entirely on His glory (see Philippians 4:19; Romans 9:23). Over the years, I have heard several definitions for God's glory, but my favorite one defines it as *all that God is*. One of the root meanings for glory further illustrates this concept of richness.

The primary Hebrew word for glory is *kabowd*.[102] It conveys the idea of inexhaustible riches or an unlimited treasure, and since biblical wealth was measured by weight, it carries the connotation of being heavy or weighty.[103] "For our light affliction, which is but for a moment, is working for us a far more exceeding *and* eternal weight of glory" (2 Corinthians 4:17). Glory is not only weighty; it is eternal. One of my favorite songs, "Let the Weight of Your Glory Fall" written by Steve Merkel, embodies this idea. You can find his lyrics in the *Jerusalem Arise!* songbooks and worship albums through Integrity's Hosanna! Music.

Since weight represents the immensity of the treasure, it bestows a corresponding degree of honor. Therefore, God's glory manifests itself as a weighty treasure of infinite riches that brings tremendous honor. No wonder His glory encompasses everything He is.

We can find an excellent example of God's glory at the resurrection of Lazarus in the Gospel of John. When Jesus arrived on the scene, He asked certain individuals in the crowd to remove the stone sealing

Lazarus' tomb. At first they hesitated, worried about the smell from a decomposing body. However, when Jesus told Martha she would see the glory of God, her reluctant helpers overheard. Like Moses on Mount Sinai, they knew what seeing the glory meant, and they wanted to witness it. Immediately, they unsealed the tomb. The anticipation must have been incredible. Then Jesus spoke, God's glory entered the tomb, and a man who had been dead four days walked out. When the people saw the glory manifested, they believed (see John 11:39–45). Experiencing God's glory will stir our faith as well.

Besides *kabowd*, the Bible contains other words that either translate as or denote glory. Glory or a variation of the word is found at least four hundred times in the Scriptures. If we include all inferred references, the count would climb even higher. The next eight Scriptures are just a few of the many verses revealing the majesty of God's glory:

→ *The city had no need of the sun or of the moon to shine in it, for the glory of God illuminated it.—Revelation 21:23*

→ *For it is the God who commanded light to shine out of darkness, who has shone in our hearts to give the light of the knowledge of the glory of God in the face of Jesus Christ.—2 Corinthians 4:6*

→ *The temple was filled with smoke from the glory of God and from His power, and no one was able to enter the temple till the seven plagues of the seven angels were completed.— Revelation 15:8*

→ *The heavens declare the glory of God.—Psalm 19:1*

→ *But [Stephen], being full of the Holy Spirit, gazed into heaven and saw the glory of God, and Jesus standing at the right hand of God.—Acts 7:55*

→ *For all the promises of God in Him are Yes, and in Him Amen, to the glory of God through us.—2 Corinthians 1:20*

→ *The light of the gospel of the glory of Christ.—2 Corinthians 4:4*

→ *Glory to God in the highest, and on earth peace, goodwill toward men!—Luke 2:14*

An angelic host spoke this last verse. After Jesus was born to Mary in Bethlehem, the angels used one main word to describe this blessed Advent: *Glory!* No other word describes God or expresses His majesty like glory does. Glory is God's compassion, love, hope, peace, and lovingkindness—all wrapped together into one word. No single term is richer or weightier.

"And the Word became flesh and dwelt among us, and we beheld His glory, the glory as of the only begotten of the Father, full of grace and truth" (John 1:14). When Jesus came to earth as our kinsmen-redeemer, He revealed God's glory in the highest possible degree. God blessed the heavens and the earth that day. "Glory to God in the highest heaven, and on earth peace to those on whom his favor rests" (Luke 2:14 NIV). The heavens would see glory *(all that God is)* and the earth would have peace *(all that ought to be there)*.

One final thought to consider: Our ultimate purpose in life is not just to reach heaven; it's to embrace the glory of God (Romans 3:23). When Adam and Eve first sinned, they fell short of God's glory, and as humanity, we have been falling short ever since. Therefore, God needed a plan to bring us back into His glory. In fact, He needed several plans, each one built upon the other, all leading to one glorious moment.

Two Thoughtful Questions

Contemplation often illuminates our minds and opens our hearts. Such is the case with the two questions below. They are thought-provoking questions that can lead us to a greater revelation of God's purpose.

> What if God, although choosing to show his wrath and make his power known, bore with great patience the objects of his wrath—prepared for destruction?

> What if he did this to make the riches of his glory known to the objects of his mercy, whom he prepared in advance for glory—even us, whom he also called, not only from the Jews but also from the Gentiles? (Romans 9:22–24 NIV)

The next chapter has answers for those questions, including why the riches of His glory are so important for eternity. The chapter will also reveal ten of the most profound, comprehensive verses in the Bible, ending with what may be the greatest Scripture of all. Apostle Paul penned that verse in his epistle to the Ephesians. This amazing Scripture and other enlightening revelations are highlighted in the pages ahead.

CHAPTER *20*

GREATEST SCRIPTURE

All Scripture *is* given by inspiration of God, and *is* profitable for doctrine, for reproof, for correction, for instruction in righteousness.

—2 Timothy 3:16

W hen the lesson ended, I expected some kind of test. I hoped it would be an open Bible exam or short essay question. Instead, the pastor gave our ministerial class a weekend assignment: we were to find the greatest Scripture in the Bible, write it down, and bring it to the next session. He told us not to compare answers with other students in the class. However, we could use any Bible version or commentary, talk to ministers, Bible scholars, school librarians, or anyone we believed was an authority on the Bible. Right about then, someone in the back of the chapel whispered an inaudible comment, followed by a few snickers. Not derailed by the distraction, the pastor continued, "This assignment is more important than you realize. Take it seriously." After a few more comments, he dismissed the class with his usual blessing and a short prayer for success.

The following week when our class met, we all expected to see a common choice for the greatest Scripture, but instead everyone had picked a different verse. When the pastor questioned us about our decisions, we discovered our choices were generally based on what we liked, not on the scope or greatness of the verse. Fortunately, he also brought a Scripture to class, which he later expounded upon during his Sunday evening sermon. His verse came from the first chapter of Ephesians, and after we heard the truths it encompassed, we could see why this one particular verse was greater than the rest.

What Makes Something the Greatest of All?

As presented in the opening chapters, greatest is an absolute. Dictionaries define absolute as something perfect or complete, total, not diminished in any way, free from imperfection. Greatest is also a superlative: an adjective or adverb used to indicate the best, highest, or greatest within a certain context. For something to be considered the greatest, it needs to include what is great, greater, greater yet, plus more. When it incorporates all that is great within a specified category, it becomes the greatest of all. Therefore, to regard a Scripture, a moment in time, or a single word as the absolute greatest, we must look to see if it comprises the highest degree of greatness (completeness) in what it conveys. Guidelines or rules are helpful, but we must remember God does not view greatness the way humanity does. In His kingdom, the least can end up being the greatest.

Furthermore, since greatest is an absolute, the Bible probably has one book greater than all the rest. In the Old Testament, the prophetic book of Isaiah is unlike any other. It has numerous prophetic words about Christ and describes them in undeniable detail. When Isaiah speaks about Christ, he sounds more like a New Testament writer.

Many Christians consider Isaiah to be one of the greatest prophetic books in the Bible.

Likewise, Paul's Epistle to the Ephesians as an entire volume is overflowing with revelation and truth. It is also a great book, possibly even the greatest in the New Testament. However, we are searching for a single Scripture revealing as much as possible about God's plan and purpose for everything: Creation, redemption, eternal life. Can such a verse be found? Yes, according to the Bible, it can. "Ask, and it will be given to you; seek, and you will find; knock, and it will be opened to you. For everyone who asks receives, and he who seeks finds, and to him who knocks it will be opened" (Matthew 7:7–8).

Obviously, anyone can combine several verses and come up with an enormous, all-inclusive passage. But to find one distinct verse greater than all the others is not only feasible, it's a welcomed dilemma. God's greatness and other divine truths about His kingdom, though sometimes hidden, are not forbidden knowledge. In fact, God wants us to discover them. "*It is* the glory of God to conceal a matter, but the glory of kings *is* to search out a matter" (Proverbs 25:2).

The Greatest Scriptures

The Scriptures below are the most revealing, comprehensive, preeminent verses in the Bible. After forty years of theological study, not to mention a divinity degree or two, these are the greatest Scriptures I've ever encountered. They are not based on personal preference but on God's divine purpose and eternal plan for humanity. I listed only ten, but the Bible holds many more. The ones highlighted below cover themes about redemption, the riches of His glory, and Christ in us. Their scope alone makes them excellent choices for the greatest Scripture.

Top Ten List

1. Isaiah 9:6: "For unto us a Child is born, unto us a Son is given; and the government will be upon His shoulder. And His name will be called Wonderful, Counselor, Mighty God, Everlasting Father, Prince of Peace."

2. Jeremiah 31:33: "But this *is* the covenant that I will make with the house of Israel after those days, says the LORD: I will put My law in their minds, and write it on their hearts; and I will be their God, and they shall be My people."

3. Ephesians 1:10: "That in the dispensation of the fullness of the times He might gather together in one all things in Christ, both which are in heaven and which are on earth—in Him."

4. Romans 5:10: "For if when we were enemies we were reconciled to God through the death of His Son, much more, having been reconciled, we shall be saved by His life."

5. Colossians 1:27: "To them God willed to make known what are the riches of the glory of this mystery among the Gentiles: which is Christ in you, the hope of glory."

6. 1 John 3:2: "Beloved, now we are children of God; and it has not yet been revealed what we shall be, but we know that when He is revealed, we shall be like Him, for we shall see Him as He is."

7. Ephesians 2:7: "That in the ages to come He might show the exceeding riches of His grace in His kindness toward us in Christ Jesus."

8. Ephesians 4:13: "Till we all come to the unity of the faith and of the knowledge of the Son of God, to a perfect man, to the measure of the stature of the fullness of Christ."

9. Romans 9:23: "And that He might make known the riches of His glory on the vessels of mercy, which He had prepared beforehand for glory."
10. John 3:16: "For God so loved the world that He gave His only begotten Son, that whoever believes in Him should not perish but have everlasting life."

The last two Scriptures on this list were used in preceding chapters. Romans 9:23 was part of the "Two Thoughtful Questions" in the last section of chapter 19, and John 3:16 helped illustrate The Rule of the Greatest in chapter 2. Both are great passages and highly merited. My favorite verse is John 3:16, but it is not the greatest Scripture. The Bible holds one lofty, awe-inspiring verse that surpasses all others.

The Greatest Scripture of All

Ephesians is one of the richest, most relevant books in the Bible, especially for Christian believers. It contains a wealth of captivating truths, doctrines, and revelations about Jesus Christ and the Church. Therefore, it is not surprising to find the greatest Scripture in this epistle.

The eyes of your understanding being enlightened;
that you may know what is the hope of His calling,
what are the riches of the glory of His inheritance in the saints.
—Ephesians 1:18

So what makes this one Scripture so great? There are many reasons, but we will start with understanding and enlightenment.

The eyes of your understanding being enlightened...

To know the ways of God, we need understanding—not the secular kind gained from study and experience—but the divine kind received through the Spirit of God. When the Holy Spirit opens our spiritual eyes, we are able to comprehend the deep and treasured things of God. "But God has revealed *them* to us through His Spirit. For the Spirit searches all things, yes, the deep things of God" (1 Corinthians 2:10).

Right at the start of Ephesians 1:18, Paul beckons us to get ready—a valuable truth is forthcoming. Unless our understanding is increased, enhanced, or fine-tuned, we might miss something important. According to his previous verses (vv. 16, 17), he has been praying for the Church to receive this needful enlightenment.

That you may know...

"For what man knows the things of a man except the spirit of the man which is in him? Even so no one knows the things of God except the Spirit of God. Now we have received, not the spirit of the world, but the Spirit who is from God, that we might know the things that have been freely given to us by God" (1 Corinthians 2:11–12).

After praying for our understanding to increase, Paul says there is something we need to know. His introduction sounds important, even urgent. Perhaps a problem has arisen in the Church that warrants notification. Maybe he needs to introduce a new guideline for successful Christian living. No, Paul has a different concern, and it comes from the very heart of God. He must tell believers about the hope of His calling.

What is the hope of His calling...

Before determining *the hope of His calling,* we need to distinguish whose calling it is. Is Paul referring to Jesus Christ, the Holy Spirit, or

God the Father? As usual, the passages before and after a Scripture are the best places to decide context. For Ephesians 1:18, the prior verse states, "That the God of our Lord Jesus Christ, the Father of glory, may give to you the spirit of wisdom and revelation in the knowledge of Him" (v. 17). The context reveals two things: One we already know—that wisdom, revelation, and knowledge from God are necessary for enlightenment. The other tells us something more vital—that this calling belongs to the Father of glory. It is His call.

Because Paul is writing about callings, we should identify what they are. Most would say a calling is our profession or vocation. I have often heard the comment, "These people are doctors and nurses; that's their calling." If so, then a calling is what we do with our lives, who we are, what gives us hope or purpose. However, if the calling comes from God, then it is more than a profession or choice of career, it is a ministry. The Father's calling is His ministry, and it's higher than any call we have because His call holds eternal consequences—not just for a certain church, city, or a nation—but for the entire universe. So what is the hope of the Father's calling? At this point in the passage, Paul does not tell us. We only know it is the Father's greatest desire.

What are the riches of the glory...

Since glory is the greatest word in the Bible, it is not surprising to find it included in this majestic Scripture verse. According to the previous chapter, glory can be summarized as *all that God is*. So what are the riches of the glory? They are the value of *all that God has*. We can find this term many times in the Bible. The wording can vary—the riches of His glory, the riches of His grace, mercy, or goodness, even the unsearchable riches of Christ. The Father's glory comprises all these riches and more. Two verses from Colossians describe this treasure in even greater detail: "That their hearts may be encouraged, being knit together in love, and *attaining* to all riches of the full assurance of understanding, to the knowledge of the mystery of God, both of the Father and of Christ, in whom are hidden all the treasures of wisdom and knowledge" (Colossians 2:2–3).

Paul often wrote about the richness of God's glory. Here are just a few examples:

→ "That He would grant you, according to the riches of His glory, to be strengthened with might through His Spirit in the inner man" (Ephesians 3:16).

→ "To me, who am less than the least of all the saints, this grace was given, that I should preach among the Gentiles the unsearchable riches of Christ, and to make all see what *is* the fellowship of the mystery, which from the beginning of the ages has been hidden in God who created all things through Jesus Christ" (Ephesians 3:8–9).

→ "In Him we have redemption through His blood, the forgiveness of sins, according to the riches of His grace" (Ephesians 1:7).

→ "But God, who is rich in mercy, because of His great love with which He loved us" (Ephesians 2:4).

→ "Or do you despise the riches of His goodness, forbearance, and longsuffering, not knowing that the goodness of God leads you to repentance?" (Romans 2:4).

Obviously, God is rich in all aspects of glory, but is there a more significant connection?

Of His inheritance in the saints

Sometimes we overlook small, seemingly unimportant words in a sentence. In this case, we see the preposition "of" linking "the riches of the glory" to something greater, "His inheritance." And that inheritance is us—the saints. Here we see the Bible's greatest word, glory, connected to the Father's inheritance and the hope of His calling. God is rich in His saints, which is His greatest, most glorious treasure of all. God has invested His entire, divine bankroll in the saints. To Him, they are like a rare pearl of great price or a hidden treasure in a field (Matthew 13:44–46) that enriches heaven and eternity itself. No wonder He put everything on the line to get them back, including sacrificing His only Son.

Some verses touch on parts of this glorious truth, but none say it like this: "The eyes of your understanding being enlightened; that you may know what is the hope of His calling, what are the riches of the glory of His inheritance in the saints" (Ephesians 1:18).

God's hope, His calling, His glory, His riches, His inheritance—are all tied up in one passion—His saints. Everything God has done or will do involves getting the saints back to His house. All His plans evolve around this one goal, and it has been that way since the foundation of the world. Herein is the hope of His calling.

The world was created, the garden planted, patriarchs called, judges appointed, laws given, kingdoms established, prophets sent—all for one reason. Jesus came to earth, lived among us, died on the cross, and rose again—all for one reason. The Rapture, the betrothal, the wedding supper—all of it is for us. We are the reason. All His efforts have been leading to one final, anticipated, exalted moment planned before anything existed. This moment will be greater than all the rest. The following chapter will attempt to describe this wondrous, almost indescribable event, but first we should consider the post-context for Ephesians 1:18.

He Who Fills All in All

The next five verses add perspective to our Scripture: they tell us about the Father's great power and His eternal plan for the saints.

> And what *is* the exceeding greatness of His power toward us who believe, according to the working of His mighty power which He worked in Christ when He raised Him from the dead and seated *Him* at His right hand in the heavenly *places,* far above all principality and power and might and dominion, and every name that is named, not only in this age but also in that which is to come. And He put all *things* under His feet, and gave Him *to be* head over all *things* to the church, which is His body, the fullness of Him who fills all in all. (Ephesians 1:19–23)

Ironically, God, who can fill everything and every place, decided to share His majesty with us lowly saints. Although Bible commentaries try their best to explain it, no one but God fully comprehends this mystery. Somehow, the Church has become the body of Christ and the fullness of Him who fills all in all. "For now we see in a mirror, dimly, but then face to face. Now I know in part, but then I shall know just as I also am known" (1 Corinthians 13:12).

Word Picture: An Enlightening Story

Once upon a time, a father and his son decided to build a model boat. After much planning, they agreed upon the perfect design. With loving care, they glued their little boat together, piece by piece. The father's expert craftsmanship could be seen in every detail of its creation. The son and his father enjoyed working on the project together. Finally, after six days, it was finished. After giving it several coats of red paint, they walked over to the river, which flowed deep and wide through the kingdom, and launched their boat into the current. A gentle wind blowing overhead seemed to guide the boat along the shoreline.

The son tied a crimson cord to the craft so he could pull it back and forth in the water. Father and son had so much fun with their boat. Then somehow, the cord detached and the little red boat slowly floated away. He and his father were heartbroken. What they had worked so hard to create had been lost. Search as they may, they could not find it. It seemed like their boat would be gone forever.

Then one day, the son made a trip to the village and walked down the main street, looking in store windows. And there it was—in the display window of the novelty shop—the little red boat he and his father had built.

After waiting for the paying customers to finish at the counter, he asked Mr. Devilyn, the assistant manager, to return his boat. The cunning assistant, however, was less than sympathetic. "No, no! Nothing is free in this shop. Besides, how do I know it's really yours?" Then in a mocking tone he added, "Ha, ha! If you want it back, you must pay the full price like everyone else."

The son looked at the price tag; it would be costly. Nevertheless, he hurried home, sad but not deterred. Finding his dad in his workshop, he asked if he could break open his treasure box, which held all the money he had ever earned, and use it to buy back their little red boat.

The father said, "Well, son, that's a lot of money, but it's your choice…" Before the father could finish, his son grabbed the treasure box, tucked it under his arm, and ran out the door, heading back to the village. The father watched him disappear down the road, and then he walked back to his workbench, concerned but with a smile upon his face.

Mr. Devilyn counted it out three times, hoping the rightful owner was a penny short, but the payment was correct, the exact amount needed to redeem the boat. Reluctantly, he handed it back. As the son rushed back home, he said to himself, "You are twice mine: my dad and I made you, we lost you, and now we have you back again. You are mine, you are mine, and I will never lose you again."

The son could hardly wait to show his father the little red boat. He found his dad waiting at the door. It was a great moment. In fact, his father could think of none that were greater or more glorious.

This story illustrates the truth, richness, and glory behind the greatest moment. Here we see the greatest Scripture connected to the greatest word, revealing the foremost event in the Bible. As mentioned in the *Introduction,* no other moment is greater, more revered, or significant to humanity. And now, *The Greatest Moment of All.*

CHAPTER *21*

THE GREATEST MOMENT OF ALL

Having made known to us the mystery of His will,
according to His good pleasure which He purposed in Himself.
—Ephesians 1:9

Their battle cries echoed in the background, sounding like lions hungering for a victory feast. Elephants, under control earlier, stampeded on the left flank, blasting their trumpets in piercing harmony. On the right, a cavalry unit formed ranks and prepared to make its final charge. Camouflaged infantry taunted us as they pushed a large cannon into range. Generals wearing full dress uniforms shouted their orders in every direction.

Aerial surveillance soared overhead, keeping us pinned down, watching our every move. Fortunately, our position was well fortified. Our unit occupied the high ground, and we carried extra rations; I figured we could hold out until the new recruits arrived. When their combined forces deployed to the center staging area, I sensed the end approaching, a finale of sorts. We all felt the suspense, especially my children who enjoyed every moment—and so did I. We were at the circus, the greatest show on earth.

A few weeks later, a volunteer solicitor for the city fire department called. She was happy to inform me that for a certain contribution, my children could receive free passes to see the greatest show on earth. After listening to her presentation, I realized she was talking about a different circus, not the one we attended earlier. This made me wonder: "How can two different productions be 'the greatest show on earth,' when only one is truly the greatest?" Likewise, only one moment in the Bible is the greatest. Before trying to describe this awe-inspiring event, let us review our journey thus far.

A Moment for Review

If you flipped to this chapter before reading the rest of the book, that's exactly what I would have done. Who wouldn't want to know the greatest moment in the Bible or at least what the author believed was the greatest. Although insight is helpful, it is not what I think that matters, only what God's Word says. Therefore, if you haven't already, I hope you will read chapter 2 on The Rule of the Greatest and the two previous chapters about heaven's greatest word and the Bible's greatest Scripture.

Throughout this book, we have taken the greatest words, Scriptures, and moments in the Bible and layered them upon each other. We followed Isaiah's pattern for establishing truth: precept upon precept, line upon line, a little here, a little there (see Isaiah 28:9–10). We also learned why the word *greatest* is an absolute and reviewed eight biblical guidelines, which help determine, validate, and distinguish greatness in the kingdom of God.

When something is the greatest, it does not obtain this ranking independently but is composed of all the parts preceding it. Only then can we call it the greatest of all. Determining this point of greatness has set the stage and focus for this book. Now, after putting all these pieces together, moment by moment, chapter by chapter, we have arrived at the single greatest moment in the Bible. Following the trail of redemption has led us back to the Father's house.

The Father's House

In the *Parable of the Lost Son,* Jesus tells a story about a generous father who loved his two sons. The younger son unwisely decided to leave his father's house and live life his own way. He withdrew everything from his inheritance account and wasted it on prodigal living. He committed every sin in the book. When the money ran out, he found himself lost, alone, and starving—not just for food—but for true companionship.

He had made a grave error, and it was probably too late to do anything about it. Still, if he could somehow return to his father's house, maybe he could apply for an entry-level position. Even working as a servant would be an improvement. He no longer considered himself a son, assuming his father had disowned him long ago.

> So he got up and went to his father. But while he was still a long way off, his father saw him and was filled with compassion for him; he ran to his son, threw his arms around him and kissed him.
>
> The son said to him, "Father, I have sinned against heaven and against you. I am no longer worthy to be called your son."

> But the father said to his servants, "Quick! Bring the best robe and put it on him. Put a ring on his finger and sandals on his feet. Bring the fattened calf and kill it. Let's have a feast and celebrate. For this son of mine was dead and is alive again; he was lost and is found." So they began to celebrate.
>
> Meanwhile, the older son was in the field. When he came near the house, he heard music and dancing.
>
> So he called one of the servants and asked him what was going on.
>
> "Your brother has come," he replied, "and your father has killed the fattened calf because he has him back safe and sound." (Luke 15:20–27 NIV)

When the father saw his prodigal son coming home, he could hardly wait to shower him with kisses of affection. A celebration followed with joyful music, dancing, and steak dinners for everyone. Our homecoming in heaven will also echo with festivity. Our rejoicing and celebrating, however, will be modest compared to that of the heavenly Father. His exuberant praises will fill the heavens. Like the parable, God's sons and daughters were also lost, without hope, separated from Him by their sins and trespasses—but they are coming home, and the Father is getting His dancing shoes ready.

A Lost Humanity

Long ago, God made humanity in His own image and likeness. In a garden east of Eden, He gave the first humans a living soul. His stamp of approval was upon them. They had high value, but then they sinned and fell short of the glory of God (Romans 3:23), and humanity has continued down this same path. The Bible tells us that the soul who sins will surely die (Genesis 2:17; Ezekiel 18:20). Because of sin, we died spiritually and drifted away from God.

As a result of this separation, our relationship with God wavered and then failed. In fact, both God and humanity were impacted: He experienced a heartbreaking loss, and we forgot our created purpose and true value. God had made us to be His glorious treasure. To Him, we were the hope of His calling, the riches of His glory, and His prized inheritance. Sin had separated us from Him, and no matter the cost, He would get us back.

A Glorious Treasure

"Again, the kingdom of heaven is like treasure hidden in a field, which a man found and hid; and for joy over it he goes and sells all that he has and buys that field. Again, the kingdom of heaven is like a merchant seeking beautiful pearls, who, when he had found one pearl of great price, went and sold all that he had and bought it" (Matthew 13:44–46).

In the passage above, Jesus shares two parables with a similar ending. One is about a man who finds a great treasure in a field; the other concerns a merchant looking for a pearl of great price. In each case, the men find what they are searching for and immediately sell all they have to purchase their rare finds. Most Christian commentaries compare these two parables to the joy of finding Jesus, and they are correct. Eternal life, like a pearl of great value, is a precious find, and we are willing to give up everything, including our lives to gain it.

The pearl analogy also represents a truth about God. He found a great pearl too—and was willing to sacrifice everything, including His only Son to redeem it. God's pearl of great price are His people. According to Ephesians 1:18, the saints are God's greatest joy and most priceless treasure. Moses said the same thing concerning saints living under the Old Covenant: "The LORD your God has chosen you out of all the peoples on the face of the earth to be his people, his treasured possession" (Deuteronomy 7:6*b* NIV).

The ransom was high, almost too high, but the Son redeemed this hidden treasure for His Father. The Holy Spirit played His role as well, comforting, helping, guiding, and watching over this rare gem (John 14:16–17, 26; 16:8, 13).[104] The saints, regardless of age or dispensation, are the Father's cherished possession. And like the son who presented the lost boat to his father, so Jesus will present a lost but redeemed inheritance back to His Father. Though it's been a long time coming, all moments have led to this one.

The Moment of All Moments

I'm not sure when this moment of moments will occur. The Bible only hints at its timing. Maybe it will happen immediately after the Rapture. However, some of God's inheritance would be missing: Saints from the great tribulation have not yet joined the redeemed. They are still waiting to wash their robes white in the blood of the Lamb (Revelation 7:13–17). Perhaps the greatest moment will occur during the marriage supper of the Lamb. That, however, would leave out the saints living on the Earth during the thousand-year millennial reign (Revelation 20:4–5). So not everyone is present and accounted for yet.

Surely this epic moment will wait until after the white throne judgment to assure every name has been crosschecked with the Lamb's Book of Life (Revelation 20:12, 15). Maybe the event will occur during the dispensation of the fullness of the times when all things are gathered in Christ (see Ephesians 1:10). Notwithstanding, God's plans are always perfect, so whenever the time is right, the greatest moment will begin. Besides, surprises are more glorious. One thing is certain—the heavenly Father will have His inheritance returned, thanks to His Son's atonement at Calvary. I can only wonder what this awesome encounter will entail.

The Greatest Moment

I've heard it said that the heavenly Father has only seen us through the blood of Christ. Like a filter, the blood covered or hid our sins, making us acceptable to God. However, after we arrive in heaven, the blood will no longer be needed, having accomplished its redemptive purpose. At the perfect moment, with nothing else to distract, the divine Bridegroom will take us by the hand, lead us to His Father, and then step aside.

After an eternity of waiting, do you know what the Father sees? He sees humanity—just the way we looked, long, long ago—perfect, virtuous, and worthy of adoption.

Like the lost boat illustration from the previous chapter, we are twice His. God has a double claim on us. He made us, lost us to sin, and then redeemed us back again. The hope of His calling, the riches of His glory, the glory of His inheritance have finally come home. The greatest moment is when the Son returns God's cherished treasure, something created long ago with some dirt and the breath of life.

The Father's house will no longer be the same because His Son has a bride now, and she will live in the Father's home, loved and honored throughout eternity. In fact, this was the plan from the very beginning. It's a mystery of enormous magnitude; the majesty of it overwhelms me.

The Mystery of His Will

"Having made known to us the mystery of His will, according to His good pleasure which He purposed in Himself, that in the dispensation of the fullness of the times He might gather together in one all things in Christ, both which are in heaven and which are on earth—in Him" (Ephesians 1:9–10).

The saints from every dispensation have tremendous value to God. He was more than willing to pay the redemption price. One day, when the dispensation of the fullness of times comes, God will take all true believers, all redeemed saints from every tribe and nation, and bring them together in Christ. However, the verse indicates that "all things" are gathered together in heaven as well. Was Paul suggesting the angels would also find unity in Christ? *Perhaps*. Are there other created things or beings from ages long ago, and if so, are they included? *Unknown*. Eternity has much to reveal about this gathering and being "in Him" (v. 10).

In John 17, Jesus asked the Father to share their special oneness with the saints. After the Father gets His inheritance back, He will fully answer His Son's prayer and incorporate the redeemed into His family. We will be one with the Father just as Jesus is one. The Father will share His glory with us and love us the same way He loves His only Son. This great mystery is hard to fathom, yet it appears to be true. One day, the Trinity may well include the Father, the Son (along with His bride), and the Holy Spirit. Here is what Jesus prayed:

> I do not pray for these alone, but also for those who will believe in Me through their word; that they all may be one, as You, Father, *are* in Me, and I in You; that they also may be one in Us, that the world may believe that You sent Me.

257

> And the glory which You gave Me I have given them,
> that they may be one just as We are one: I in them, and
> You in Me; that they may be made perfect in one, and
> that the world may know that You have sent Me, and
> have loved them as You have loved Me. (John 17:20–23)

With Greatness Comes Responsibility

Winston Churchill, a respected world leader, gifted orator, and notable writer once said, "The price of greatness is responsibility." The apostle Paul would have concurred. When Paul understood the importance of God's greatest moment and all the implications, he realized why a higher calling was necessary. Seeing this moment from a divine perspective changed his life and impacted his ministry. For him, things would never be the same again.

The final two chapters may be the most important ones in this book, not just for you and me, but also for those who are lost and in need of salvation. *The High Call of God* is next, followed by *The Greatest Work*. Both will influence the outcome at the greatest moment.

PART SEVEN:

THE MISSION

CHAPTER 22

THE HIGH CALL OF GOD

There is no higher calling, no loftier dream, and no greater goal
than to live, breathe, and be poured out for Jesus Christ.
—Brother Andrew (Open Doors USA)

Over the years, I have talked to many people who said they had
a calling from God. Most of their callings seemed biblical:
individuals called to preach, pray, lead worship, prophesy, or serve
as deacons. Others felt drawn to departmental ministries in their local
churches. A few were led to build buildings, make movies, or write
books. Missionaries laboring in foreign lands and street preachers
called to inner cities touched my heart the most.

Some callings, however, I have questioned. One person told me her
call was to bring division to our church by praying for a membership
split. Another said God called him to cast demons out of the church
staff. Several individuals told me they were called only to observe from
the pew, so don't ask them to get involved or help with ministry needs.
All these people believed their calling came from God. Only one such
call alarmed me: the person who believed God wanted him to serve

as a messenger of judgment. No wonder I have doubts about certain callings circulating in the Church today.

Before becoming an apostle, Paul felt called of God to imprison Christians and to see them executed if necessary (see Acts 7:58; 8:1–3; 9:1–2). Unfortunately, for Christians like Stephen, Paul excelled in this task. At some point, though, Paul (also called Saul) became disillusioned with his glorious mission. Maybe we all need a Damascus Road experience to point us back to the real thing—a calling not from men or through men—but from God.

> As he journeyed he came near Damascus, and suddenly a light shone around him from heaven. Then he fell to the ground, and heard a voice saying to him, "Saul, Saul, why are you persecuting Me?"
>
> And he said, "Who are You, Lord?"
>
> Then the Lord said, "I am Jesus, whom you are persecuting. It *is* hard for you to kick against the goads."
>
> So he, trembling and astonished, said, "Lord, what do You want me to do?"
>
> Then the Lord *said* to him, "Arise and go into the city, and you will be told what you must do." (Acts 9:3–6)

Calling Defined

"And we know that all things work together for good to those who love God, to those who are the called according to *His* purpose" (Romans 8:28). "Called" in this passage comes from the Greek word *kletos,* usually translated as invited or called. In Scripture, *kletos* has

261

three basic meanings: invited to attend some function, called to discharge certain duties, or selected for a specific ministry position.[105]

Another Greek word for called is *kaleo*. It means to call, invite, bid, or name.[106] We see *kaleo* used in 2 Timothy 1:9. "Who has saved us and called *us* with a holy calling, not according to our works, but according to His own purpose and grace which was given to us in Christ Jesus before time began."

Calling All Saints

"To the church of God which is at Corinth, to those who are sanctified in Christ Jesus, called *to be* saints, with all who in every place call on the name of Jesus Christ our Lord, both theirs and ours" (1 Corinthians 1:2). The saints (*ḥᵃsîdîm* and *qᵉḏôšîm* in Hebrew, *hagios* in Greek) are faithful and devout ones, those set apart to God, holy ones, usually translated as saints in English. These terms are used for the people of God.[107] This description would include Old Testament saints, New Testament Christians, and one day, saints from the Millennium. God's call "to be saints" has gone out to all His children in every generation. "Behold what manner of love the Father has bestowed on us, that we should be called children of God!" (1 John 3:1*a*).

The invitation to believe in God is all-inclusive. "*There is* one body and one Spirit, just as you were called in one hope of your calling; one Lord, one faith, one baptism; one God and Father of all, who *is* above all, and through all, and in you all" (Ephesians 4:4–6). The Father has called every person to belief. This is the first calling. At His discretion, God gave certain individuals administrative callings. The Old Testament reveals three of these leadership categories: prophet, priest, and king.

The Prophet

"I will raise up for them a Prophet like you from among their brethren, and will put My words in His mouth, and He shall speak to them all that I command Him" (Deuteronomy 18:18). Actually, this verse refers to the Messiah but is indicative of all prophets. Prophets and prophetesses were God's spokespersons. They received their messages from God through dreams, visions, and sometimes by direct visitations from angels. The prophetic calling was threefold: to point out sin; to warn of coming judgments; and to exhort individuals, groups, or nations to repent. Prophets like Samuel, Isaiah, Elijah, Daniel, Ezekiel, and Deborah are well known, but the Bible names many. Some remain unnamed, mentioned only by their deeds.

The Priest

Priests ministered as God's representatives. They were intercessors who mediated between God and the people with prayers, offerings, and sacrifices. During the patriarchal age, the clan or group leader usually performed the duties of a priest for the family. Therefore, Abraham, Isaac, and Jacob were priests. Moses served as a priest too. He often interceded for his young Hebrew nation who always seemed to be backsliding. "Now it came to pass on the next day that Moses said to the people, 'You have committed a great sin. So now I will go up to the LORD; perhaps I can make atonement for your sin'" (Exodus 32:30). Priests also taught the commandments and ordinances of God.

The King

God called kings to serve in a judicial or executive position. As leaders, the judges of Israel ministered within this same calling. Throughout the Old Testament, God anointed sovereigns to rule and reign over His people. "Samuel also said to Saul, 'The LORD sent me to anoint you king over His people, over Israel. Now therefore, heed the voice of the words of the LORD'" (1 Samuel 15:1). Like prophets and priests, kings represented a higher authority, Yahweh, the King of heaven. Sadly, most of them abused their callings. First and 2 Kings and 1 and 2 Chronicles track their successes and failures.

Called and Anointed

Called individuals were usually anointed to perform certain tasks. Some jobs were small; others were major endeavors like building an ark, delivering people from bondage, finding the Promised Land, defending a kingdom, or building a temple. One example is Samson who God called as a judge over Israel. His specialty was harassing enemy Philistines with feats of supernatural strength. He once used the jawbone of a donkey to kill a thousand adversaries.

Some of God's people held more than one calling. Moses was both priest and prophet. Melchizedek served as king of Salem and as high priest. God called Saul as Israel's first king, but Saul was also named among the prophets (see 1 Samuel 10:10–12). Jesus of Nazareth assumed the role of all three callings: prophet, priest, and king. After the Holy Spirit outpouring on the Day of Pentecost (Acts 2), the emphasis changed and so did the callings.

Ministry Callings

"And He Himself gave some *to be* apostles, some prophets, some evangelists, and some pastors and teachers, for the equipping of the saints for the work of ministry, for the edifying of the body of Christ" (Ephesians 4:11–12). These anointings are known as the fivefold ministry. Some theologians believe this passage shows a fourfold calling, equating the role of pastor-teacher as one. Either way, whether four or five categories, each calling is distinct and necessary for Christian growth.

When God calls us, our call is permanent and perpetual: "For the gifts and the calling of God are irrevocable" (Romans 11:29). If we continue in unrepented sin, God might replace us, even remove our anointing, but He will not take away our call. On Judgment Day, all of us will give account of what we accomplished or did not accomplish with these callings. "For we must all appear before the judgment seat of Christ, that each one may receive the things *done* in the body, according to what he has done, whether good or bad" (2 Corinthians 5:10).

Other Callings

The call of God is not limited to the fivefold ministry. God anoints believers with other callings as well. Nine are associated with spiritual gifts (*charisma* in Greek), also called giftings, where the Holy Spirit sovereignly selects certain individuals for specific ministry functions.[108] First Corinthians 12 describes the diversity, activity, and purpose of these gifts.

> Now concerning spiritual *gifts*, brethren, I do not want you to be ignorant:
>
> There are diversities of gifts, but the same Spirit. There are differences of ministries, but the same Lord. And there are diversities of activities, but it is the same God who works all in all. But the manifestation of the Spirit is given to each one for the profit *of all:*
>
> for to one is given the word of wisdom through the Spirit,

265

to another the word of knowledge through the
same Spirit,

to another faith by the same Spirit,

to another gifts of healings by the same Spirit,

to another the working of miracles,

to another prophecy,

to another discerning of spirits,

to another *different* kinds of tongues,

to another the interpretation of tongues.

But one and the same Spirit works all these things,
distributing to each one individually as He wills.
(1 Corinthians 12:1, 4–11)

Some callings seem more like God-given talents or attributes, such as showing mercy and offering encouragement. Like the giftings above, they also involve *charisma*. "We have different gifts, according to the grace given to each of us. If your gift is prophesying, then prophesy in accordance with your faith; if it is serving, then serve; if it is teaching, then teach; if it is to encourage, then give encouragement; if it is giving, then give generously; if it is to lead, do it diligently; if it is to show mercy, do it cheerfully" (Romans 12:6–8 NIV).

Although the Bible mentions many callings, one is different from the rest. Paul referred to it as the upward call of God. It is the highest call of all. In Ephesians 1:18, Paul wrote about the hope of His calling, and within that context, this calling belongs to the heavenly Father. It is a call God placed upon Himself. All the Father's plans from ages past until now have revolved around it.

The Upward Call

"Brethren, I do not count myself to have apprehended; but one thing *I do,* forgetting those things which are behind and reaching forward to those things which are ahead, I press toward the goal for the prize of the upward call of God in Christ Jesus" (Philippians 3:13–14).

The upward call of God is heaven's highest call. The Authorized Version translates it as *the high calling of God;* the New Revised Standard Version renders it as *the heavenly call of God;* and the New International Version defines the call as *heavenward.* The high call of God is higher than the call to preach or pray—or any other call. Embracing it was the one thing Paul wanted more than anything else, and within this call, he envisioned a prize and a goal.

Prize and Goal

In the passage above, Paul describes pressing toward *the goal for the prize* of this upward call (v. 14). The Greek word for press is *dioko.* It means to run swiftly in order to catch something, like a runner racing toward the finish line.[109] The New International Version calls it *the goal to win the prize.* The Authorized Version uses *the mark for the prize.* Regardless of wording, it sounds like an important challenge. But what are the prize and goal Paul mentioned?

For Paul, the prize was to "win Christ, and be found in him" (see Philippians 3:8, 9 KJV). The Greek word for win, *kerdaino,* can be translated win, gain, or acquire.[110] Like an archer in an archery contest, Paul aimed for the highest mark, the perfect score. Like an Olympic runner, he raced with resolve, striving to win the gold medal. He considered nothing greater or nobler than winning Christ.

If the ultimate prize was to win Christ, then Paul reasoned that the corresponding goal would be winning the more. Paul believed if he could become *all things to all people by all means,* then he could lead even more people to Christ. As seen in the passage below, Paul would make whatever changes were necessary to reach this goal.

> For though I am free from all *men,* I have made myself a servant to all, that I might <u>win the more</u>; and to the Jews I became as a Jew, that I might win Jews; to those *who are* under the law, as under the law, that I might win those *who are* under the law; to those *who are* without law, as without law (not being without law toward God, but under law toward Christ), that I might win those *who are* without law; to the weak I became as weak, that I might win the weak. I have become <u>all things</u> to <u>all *men,*</u> that I might by <u>all means</u> save some. (1 Corinthians 9:19–22, underlined emphasis mine)

The more people who found salvation in Christ, the weightier, more glorious God's inheritance would become. Paul realized the outcome of the greatest moment depended partly upon him. "The Spirit Himself bears witness with our spirit that we are children of God, and if children, then heirs—heirs of God and joint heirs with Christ" (Romans 8:16, 17*a*). Being a joint heir with Christ, he felt responsible, even accountable. Would he, like the servant who received one talent in the parable told by Jesus (see Matthew 25:14–30), bury his talent or do something great with it?

The more Paul thought about these truths, the more he realized something needed to change in his own life. What had been so important to him now seemed worthless when compared to the glory of the greatest moment. Moreover, what about the good things: his reputation, his religious heritage, or his educational accomplishments? If they interfered with the high call of God, then they would need to be removed, reckoned as lost, or considered as rubbish. Below is Paul's narrative on this matter, his rationale heartfelt, his words heavy with conviction.

Paul's Narrative: One Thing I Must Do

> Circumcised the eighth day, of the stock of Israel, *of* the tribe of Benjamin, a Hebrew of the Hebrews; concerning the law, a Pharisee; concerning zeal, persecuting the church; concerning the righteousness which is in the law, blameless.
>
> But what things were gain to me, these I have counted loss for Christ.
>
> Yet indeed I also count all things loss for the excellence of the knowledge of Christ Jesus my Lord, for whom I have suffered the loss of all things, and count them as rubbish, that I may gain Christ and be found in Him, not having my own righteousness, which *is* from the law, but that which *is* through faith in Christ, the righteousness which is from God by faith;
>
> that I may know Him and the power of His resurrection, and the fellowship of His sufferings, being conformed to His death, if, by any means, I may attain to the resurrection from the dead.
>
> Not that I have already attained, or am already perfected; but I press on, that I may lay hold of that for which Christ Jesus has also laid hold of me.

> Brethren, I do not count myself to have apprehended;
> but one thing *I do,* forgetting those things which are
> behind and reaching forward to those things which
> are ahead,
>
> I press toward the goal for the prize of the upward call
> of God in Christ Jesus. (Philippians 3:5–14)

A Change of Callings

Somewhere along the line, it happened—Paul's calling changed. I'm not saying he walked away from his apostolic call; rather, he stepped higher. He decided to make the high call of God, his call, and God's plans, his plans. The hope of the Father became his hope too. He would no longer strive after things that counted for so little. Paul would become all things to all people if it helped return the Father's lost inheritance. He would reach out to Jews, Gentiles, believers, unbelievers—to anyone who listened. If writing a few epistles advanced the cause, then he would do that as well. Paul did not want anyone to miss the greatest moment of all. And neither should we.

Maybe this mindset is what the Father wanted in the first place, but such changes have to be our choice. Higher callings entail greater responsibilities. Such commitments exact a toll and come at a great cost—just ask the disciples of Jesus. Still, we need to follow Paul's lead. "Even as I try to please everyone in every way. For I am not seeking my own good but the good of many, so that they may be saved. Follow my example, as I follow the example of Christ" (1 Corinthians 10:33–11:1 NIV). We do this by taking on a servant's heart, assuming responsibility for the harvest, and reaching out to lost souls with the gospel. With one simple act of faith, those who receive eternal life will become part of the Father's glorious inheritance. Is anything more important? Not according to Jesus. "I say to you that likewise there will be more joy in heaven over one sinner who repents than over nine-ty-nine just persons who need no repentance" (Luke 15:7).

Here then is the upward call of God: to become *all things to all people by all means* so *every person, tribe, and nation* has the opportunity to win Christ and be found in Him (Philippians 3:8, 9, 14; 1 Corinthians 9:19–22; Revelation 5:9). Will we, like the apostle Paul, make the high call of God, our call — so we may likewise, win the more?

Appeal from Heaven

In Revelation, we find a heartfelt appeal. What makes this message so unusual is that you as a redeemed believer are one of the speakers:

> *And the Spirit and the bride say, "Come!"*
> *And let him who hears say, "Come!"*
> *And let him who thirsts come.*
> *Whoever desires, let him take the water of life freely.*
> —*Revelation 22:17*

These words are from the future yet recorded in the past, written down in the Bible thousands of years ago. The Spirit and the bride are speaking from eternity. Everything is done, completed as planned. The greatest moment has come and gone. The new heaven and earth are now a reality. And we are in total unity with the Spirit of God.

Did you ever hear the song, "They'll Know We Are Christians," written by Peter Scholtes? In the 1960s, this song became synonymous with the Jesus Movement. As a teenager, I loved it—the words, the minor cords—and I still play the tune on my guitar today. It appears the composer was right; in eternity, we will share a special oneness with the Spirit.

271

On that day, the Spirit of God and every redeemed saint will prophesy together. Our words are unified, pointed, and revolve around one word. The appeal sounds desperate. Suppose you were stranded on an isolated mountaintop with only enough battery power in your cell phone to text a one-word message, what would you transmit? HELP or SOS? Those would probably be good choices, considering the circumstances. However, suppose you were in heaven and could only send one message to humanity, what would you say? Well, here is the word you will use: "Come!" Your message will be repeated three times, like a divine SOS to *save our souls*.

We have wasted too much time on religious stuff, missing the simplest, most important ministry call of all—reaching the harvest. Convincing people to come to eternal life is what matters most. *And the Spirit and the bride say, "Come!"* One word says it all: Come to eternal life; come to heaven; don't miss out. Anyone who hears this word needs to speak it as well: *And let him who hears say, "Come!"* Notice the exclamation marks in these verses. In writing, sometimes we use too many exclamation marks, and like overused clichés, they have lost their impact. But not here. You can hear this word shouted forth—sense its urgency. Time is running out. We need to listen to our own message from the future… and so does the world.

Then the word is repeated a third time: *And let him who thirsts come*. When the Bible repeats a word or phrase twice, it shows importance. When repeated three times, the significance increases. Someone is trying to make a point, get our attention. God's heavenly home is not a figurative place; we are there. Heaven is real; hell is real too. And we have a message for the world: anyone who is thirsty should come to the Father's house and be part of the greatest moment of all.

The Father has put everything on the line to recover His inheritance. The harvest is ready, and the lost and hurting sheep of God's flock are waiting. The greatest moment is waiting too. Will you help God's lost children come home?

We have a critical mission to accomplish and for this we need faith—not survival faith, not sit in the pew faith—but faith that moves mountains. Moreover, we must know how to release that faith. The final chapter explains *how to believe*. It could be the most vital chapter in this entire book.

CHAPTER 23

THE GREATEST WORK

Faith is deliberate confidence in the character of God
whose ways you may not understand at the time.[111]
—Oswald Chambers, Scottish minister

"Then they said to Him, 'What shall we do, that we may work the works of God?' Jesus answered and said to them, 'This is the work of God, that you believe in Him whom He sent'" (John 6:28–29).

Faith is the greatest work. Practically every book in the Bible contains a story or illustration on the importance of believing. The kingdom of God operates by faith (see Hebrews 11). Without it we cannot please God, be saved, receive healing, or impact the harvest. Faith is fundamental for everything. Ironically, the Scriptures tell us all about belief except one thing—*how to believe.*

This omission creates an interesting dilemma. Although the Bible commands us to believe (1 John 3:23), the *how-to* procedure is not readily explained. Furthermore, when we realize all things are possible to those who believe (Mark 9:23), the issue of how to believe becomes even more consequential. This predicament with faith is one many people have faced, among them, a Scottish pastor named John. Unique circumstances, combined with a divine sequence of events, draw this pastor to a critical moment where he finally learns how to believe. We can benefit from what he discovered. Here is his story:

Word Picture: Pastor John's Dilemma

Sometimes existence comes to a standstill. Our lives become ineffective, unchallenged, and all too predictable. Daily routines turn into a mix of boring errands, and soon the years pass by unnoticed. Life was like that for John, at least until the day he stopped at the bridge.

John pastored a small congregation located northeast of the loch, about a day's hike in favorable weather. His church members were scattered throughout the many hills and mint-layered bluffs common to this part of the Scottish Highlands. His closest neighbor, known only as Grandma, lived across from his parsonage on the opposite bluff.

The only clue to Grandma's identity was the plaid design on her tartan bonnet, suggesting kinship within the Farquharson clan. No one seemed to recall Grandma's age or how long she had lived in the single-room cottage atop the bluff. Rumor had it she was at least ninety years old, perhaps older.

Grandma was soft-spoken, gentle, and friendly. Communicating with her, however, presented a challenge, partly because she had never learned to read or write. A hearing problem, which made it hard for her to distinguish words and sounds, only made matters worse. Conscious of her disability, Grandma carried something resembling an old phonograph speaker that she plugged in her ear. She called it a hearing aid, but it only marginally improved her ability to hear.

Grandma had a broad smile and caring eyes, but these radiant features could no longer hide her failing health. She didn't attend church services or get out much, so Pastor John made it a habit to visit her when he traveled his rounds. Besides, Grandma grilled the best barley and oat bannocks in the village; she always had a few farls ready when the pastor came knocking. She covered her biscuits with some home-made crowdie cheese. Like most Scots, Pastor John loved bannocks and crowdie. With an open invitation for breakfast, he decided to start visiting Grandma every day.

Each morning, John dashed across the wood-planked bridge spanning the two bluffs, arriving early at Grandma's place. Mindful of her frail condition, he didn't let a single day pass without visiting her and sharing about his faith in God. Progress was slow and exhausting as he attempted to get his message past Grandma's deafened ears. The best he could hope for is that she understood a few sentences each day, adding to the previous day's conversation. After an hour of shouting into the hearing aid, John walked back across the bridge, wondering if his efforts were in vain. However, with the next dawn, refreshed and resolved, he ran back to try again.

Then one morning, an unexpected surprise awaited the pastor: Grandma understood her need for salvation and wanted to know what she must do. The pastor could hardly contain his emotions as Grandma grabbed the hearing aid and put it to her ear. Settling himself with a deep breath he said, "Well, Grandma, according to Bible, you must believe to be saved."

Grandma nodded her head, but asked in her Scottish brogue, "Laddie, how do I believe?"

"That's simple, just put your faith in God."

Nodding again she said, "Laddie, I know who to believe in, but how do I believe in Him?"

Taking time to speak clearly into her hearing aid the pastor answered, "You believe by having faith."

"How do you have faith?" she asked.

"That's easy; you have faith by believ..." Ending abruptly, he realized his answers were merely going in circles. *Could it be,* the pastor wondered, *I really don't know?*

Trudging back across the bridge, he noticed the shadows casting patterns on the stream below. Frustration pervaded a silent prayer: "All these years in the ministry and I've never been asked this question before; so Lord, how do I answer Grandma?" The more the pastor pondered the question, the harder it became. John paced around outside the parsonage until sunset—then he went inside, grabbed his Bible, and headed for the study.

What the Bible Says Concerning Faith

The Bible discloses many things about faith. The Scriptures explain how faith comes, how faith grows, and why everyone has a measure of faith. In Matthew 13:54–58, we see an example of people who did not believe: "Now He did not do many mighty works there because of their unbelief" (v. 58). Another example shows an individual before he believed (see story about the eunuch and Phillip in Acts 8:34–38).

Other Scriptures declare we must believe (Hebrews 11:6) and reveal the miraculous signs that follow when we do (Mark 16:17–18). One passage even describes a group of people as they discover their own faith: "Now we believe, not because of what you said, for we ourselves have heard *Him* and we know that this is indeed the Christ, the Savior of the world" (John 4:42b). There's even a passage showing a centurion commander in the very act of believing (Matthew 8:8–13), but it doesn't explain how he believed.

Finally, we encounter a Scripture in Hebrews 11:1, which interprets the substance of faith, but this verse is just a definition. Although the Bible explains everything conceivable about faith, it seems remiss on one matter: how to believe. The Bible's silence on this point, however, is not without reason, as the pastor soon discovered.

A Revelation about Faith

The next morning as the sun peeked over the hills, Pastor John crossed the stream, using the old weathered footbridge to Grandma's home. Sadly, today's results were no different from all the other times. John could not help Grandma understand the concept of faith. Leaving her cottage, the pastor hesitated at the bridge as a sizeable wind gust began tossing the bridge up and down, twisting the support ropes. He considered waiting for the wind to die down, then Grandma called out, "Nalibban the bridge, laddie!" Waving a hand in acknowledgment, Pastor John stepped upon the first plank, thinking aloud, "Grandma is right, of course; the bridge would hold fine; it always has."

Halfway across the footbridge, John paused for a moment. Soon the tears welled up in his eyes. He turned quickly and dashed back across the bridge. Speaking into the hearing aid with all his might, he cried, "Grandma, nalibban Christ." A final nod of her head and a deep smile revealed that Grandma finally understood what she must do, and how to do it.[112]

Faith by Experience

Pastor John and Grandma both knew that nalibban meant to put your full weight upon something (a footbridge in this case) and then show your confidence by crossing over it. Nalibban, a Scottish colloquial phrase of uncertain origin, might be a combination of the Gaelic words *a-nall* (over or across) and *abhainn* (river or stream). In this illustration, two individuals embraced faith by crossing a river, placing their full weight upon a bridge, knowing it would hold until they reached the other side. However, it was not until they experienced the same bridge, many times, in various situations, with absolute certainty, that they learned how to believe. How ironic! Although she didn't realize it at the time, Grandma possessed the answer to her own question about faith through experience.

The Confidence of Faith

We understand how to believe, not by learning some definition or memorizing certain Scriptures about faith, but by going through real-life experiences with God. Apostle Peter learned about faith through experience the moment he stepped upon the stormy sea, realizing he could walk on water just like Jesus. Faith often surpasses knowledge or ability and operates beyond the natural realm, using experience to provide confidence.

This supernatural confidence is evident in 1 John 5:14–15: "Now this is the confidence that we have in Him, that if we ask anything according to His will, He hears us. And if we know that He hears us, whatever we ask, we know that we have the petitions that we have asked of Him." Every time Apostle John stepped upon his bridge of faith, experience gave him more and more confidence. As a result, he received the petitions he requested.

Apostle John did not say I have, but rather *we have* this confidence and *we have* the petitions asked of Him. God wants everyone to have this assurance so all things pertaining to His will are *haveable*. As we nalibban our own bridges, every experience teaches us a valuable lesson—we are learning how to believe.[113]

Final Comments: Our Call, Our Mission, Our Destiny

Much is at stake. We need to make the upward call our calling, God's work our work, and His purpose our purpose. While there is still time left, we must reach out into the harvest with the message of redemption in Christ. Nothing is more important, more critical, no mission more essential than to invite everyone to come to the Father's house. If people could only comprehend how important they are to God and what He has prepared for them in heaven, they would all turn to Him (see Ephesians 3:18–19). But many do not—their eyes have been blinded from the truth. "And even if our gospel is veiled, it is veiled to those who are perishing. In their case the god of this world has blinded the minds of the unbelievers, to keep them from seeing the light of the gospel of the glory of Christ, who is the image of God" (2 Corinthians 4:3–4 NRSV).

Herein is the work set before us, and for this endeavor, we will need mountain-moving faith. Such faith, shared and demonstrated, will help draw others to eternal life in Christ (John 20:30–31; 1 Corinthians 2:4–5). And then one day they will stand with us before the Father at the greatest moment of all. "But how are they to call on one in whom they have not believed? And how are they to believe in one of whom they have never heard? And how are they to hear without someone to proclaim him?" (Romans 10:14 NRSV). You and I need to be that someone.

See you at the greatest moment. Invite as many people as you can. In this, I bid you Godspeed!

ABOUT THE AUTHOR

D r. Charles Earl Harrel is a Christian writer with more than 550 published works. His articles, inspirational stories, and devotionals have appeared in various periodicals and in thirty-five anthologies. He is also a five-time contributor to Chicken Soup for the Soul. Before starting the writing ministry, Charles pastored for thirty years, serving churches in California, Nevada, and Oregon. He holds his doctorate in ministry. In all these things, he credits God.

Charles and his wife, Laura, live in Portland, Oregon. They enjoy camping, hiking, leading worship, and teaching from God's Word. He invites you to visit his website, "The High Call of Writing," at charlesearlharrel.com.

BIBLIOGRAPHY

Achtemeier, Paul J., Harper & Row and Society of Biblical Literature. *Harper's Bible Dictionary*. San Francisco: Harper & Row, 1985.

Alexander, Pat, organizing editor. *The Lion Encyclopedia of the Bible*. Tring, England; Batavia, IL; Sydney, Australia: Lion Publishing, 1987.

Beers, V. Gilbert. *The Victor Handbook of Bible Knowledge*. Wheaton, IL: Victor Books, 1981.

Burnham, Robert, Alan Dyer, and Jeff Kanipe. *Astronomy: The Definitive Guide*. New York: Barnes & Noble Books, 2003.

Conner, Kevin J. *The Tabernacle of David*. Portland, OR: City Bible Publishing, 1976.

Easton, M. G. *Easton's Bible Dictionary*. New York: Harper & Brothers, 1893.

Guinness, Alma E., editor. *Mysteries of the Bible: The Enduring Questions of the Scriptures*. Pleasantville, NY: The Reader's Digest Association, Inc., 1988.

Harpur, James, editor. *Great Events of Bible Times*. Garden City, NY: Doubleday & Company, Inc., 1987.

Levitt, Zola. *A Christian Love Story*. Dallas, TX: Zola Levitt Ministries, 1978.

Levitt, Zola. *The Miracle of Passover*. Dallas, TX: Zola Levitt Ministries, 1977.

Logos Bible Software 6. Bellingham, WA: Faithlife Corporation, 2000–2016.

Manser, Martin H. *Dictionary of Bible Themes: The Accessible and Comprehensive Tool for Topical Studies*. London: Martin Manser, 2009.

Myers, Allen C. *The Eerdmans Bible Dictionary*. Grand Rapids, MI: Eerdmans Publishing Co., 1987.

NASA. "News & Features." https://www.nasa.gov/content/nasa-news-and-features-archive/.

Nestle, Erwin, and Paul R. McReynolds. *Nestle Aland 26th Edition Greek New Testament with McReynolds English Interlinear*. Oak Harbor: Logos Research Systems, Inc., 1997.

Singer, Isidore, managing editor. *The Jewish Encyclopedia*. New York: Funk and Wagnalls, 1901–1906. Online version. http://www.jewishencyclopedia.com/.

Sky & Telescope: The Essential Guide to Astronomy. http://www.skyandtelescope.com/.

Soter, Steven, and Neil deGrasse Tyson, editors. *Cosmic Horizons: Astronomy at the Cutting Edge*. New York: The New Press, 2001.

Space.com. "Science & Astronomy." http://www.space.com/ science-astronomy/.

Strong, James. *Enhanced Strong's Lexicon*. Woodside Bible Fellowship, 1995.

Swanson, James. *Dictionary of Biblical Languages with Semantic Domains: Hebrew (Old Testament)*. Oak Harbor: Logos Research Systems, Inc., 1997.

Swanson, James, and Orville Nave. *New Nave's Topical Bible*. Oak Harbor: Logos Research Systems, 1994.

The Open Bible Expanded Edition: The New Kings James Red Letter Edition. Nashville, TN: Thomas Nelson Publishers, 1985.

The Zondervan Parallel New Testament in Greek and English. Grand Rapids, MI: Zondervan Bible Publishers, 1980.

Vine, W. E., Merrill F. Unger, and William White, Jr. *Vine's Complete Expository Dictionary of Old and New Testament Words*. Nashville, TN: Thomas Nelson Publishers, 1985.

Wight, Fred H. *Manners and Customs of Bible Lands*. Chicago: Moody Press, 1980.

Wood, D. R. W., and I. Howard Marshall. *New Bible Dictionary, Third Edition*. Leicester, England; Downers Grove, IL: InterVarsity Press, 1996.

ENDNOTES

CHAPTER 1

1   "Single-Season Leaders & Records for Home Runs," Baseball-Reference.com, accessed April 2016, http://www.baseball-reference.com/leaders/HR_season.shtml.

CHAPTER 3

2   Tetragrammaton can also be rendered *YHVH*.

3   Erwin Nestle and Paul R. McReynolds, *Nestle Aland 26th Edition Greek New Testament with McReynolds English Interlinear* (Oak Harbor: Logos Research Systems Inc., 1997), Revelation 13:8*h*.

CHAPTER 4

4   "How Many Galaxies Are There in the Universe?" Sky & Telescope, http://www.skyandtelescope.com/astronomy-resources/how-many-galaxies/.

5   "How Many Stars Are in the Milky Way?" Space.com, http://www.space.com/25959-how-many-stars-are-in-the-milky-way.html.

6   NASA Exoplanet Archive, http://exoplanetarchive.ipac.caltech.edu/.

7   Robert Burnham, Alan Dyer, and Jeff Kanipe, *Astronomy: The Definitive Guide* (New York: Barnes & Noble, 2003), 206.

8   James Strong, *Enhanced Strong's Lexicon* (Woodside Bible Fellowship, 1995), Strong's Hebrew #7363.

CHAPTER 5

9   James Swanson, *Dictionary of Biblical Languages with Semantic Domains: Hebrew (Old Testament)* (Oak Harbor: Logos Research Systems, Inc., 1997), DBL Hebrew #5749. Also see *Enhanced Strong's Lexicon*, Strong's Hebrew #5193.

10 Strong, *Enhanced Strong's Lexicon,* Strong's Hebrew #7218.

11 Alma E. Guinness, editor, *Mysteries of the Bible: The Enduring Questions of the Scriptures* (Pleasantville, NY: The Reader's Digest Association, Inc., 1988), 24–25.

12 Strong's Hebrew #6376, #1521, #2313, #6578.

13 Strong's Hebrew #6963.

14 Strong's Hebrew #7307.

CHAPTER 6

15 *The Open Bible Expanded Edition,* Biblical Cyclopedic Index (Nashville, TN: Thomas Nelson Publishers, 1985), 39.

16 Strong's Hebrew #120 (noun, *'adam*), #119 (verb, *'adam*).

17 Strong's Hebrew #2332.

18 Strong's Hebrew #802.

19 Strong's Hebrew #376.

CHAPTER 7

20 T. C. Mitchell, "Moon," ed. D. R. W. Wood et al., *New Bible Dictionary* (Leicester, England; Downers Grove, IL: InterVarsity Press, 1996), 782.

21 Cult prostitution (also called temple, sacred, or religious prostitution) was practiced in Ur and throughout Mesopotamia. Fertility cult activities were an abomination to God.

22 Paul J. Achtemeier, Harper & Row and Society of Biblical Literature, *Harper's Bible Dictionary* (San Francisco: Harper & Row, 1985), 653–654.

23 Strong's Hebrew #8004 (Salem), #3389 (Jerusalem).

24 Strong's Hebrew #3458.

25 Islam's opinion of Abraham is a historical notation, not an endorsement of Islam or its doctrines.

CHAPTER 8

26 "Smoke Tree," DesertUSA, http://www.desertusa.com/flora/smoke-tree.html.

27 Strong's Hebrew #4872.

28 Mount Horeb is an alternate name for Mount Sinai (see Exodus 3:1–12; 19:1–2, 17–18; Deuteronomy 1:6, 19; 5:2).

29 Strong's Hebrew #430 (*'Elohiym*), #3068 (*YHWH*/יהוה) .

30 Strong's Hebrew #1961, #834.

31 Achtemeier, *Harper's Bible Dictionary*, 404, 957. Biblical writers refer to Mount Sinai by several names: the mountain, the mountain of God, Mount Horeb, the mountain of Horeb, and the mountain of God in Horeb.

32 Allen C. Myers, *The Eerdmans Bible Dictionary* (Grand Rapids, MI: Eerdmans, 1987), 84. Also called the Ark of the LORD, Ark of God, Ark of the Covenant of the LORD, Ark of the Covenant of God, and Ark of the Testimony.

33 Strong's Hebrew #3519.

34 Strong's Hebrew #2898.

35 Strong's Hebrew #8034.

36 Strong's Hebrew #6440.

37 D. Freeman, "Showbread," ed. D. R. W. Wood et al., *New Bible Dictionary* (Leicester, England; Downers Grove, IL: InterVarsity Press, 1996), 1098.

38 Achtemeier, *Harper's Bible Dictionary*, 1016, 1083–1084.

CHAPTER 9

39 "Kingmaker (board game)," Wikipedia: The Free Encyclopedia, http://en.wikipedia.org/wiki/Kingmaker_(board_game).

40 Kevin J. Conner, *The Tabernacle of David* (Portland, OR: City Bible Publishing, 1976), 127.

CHAPTER 10

41 Strong's Hebrew #2584.

42 Strong's Hebrew #1683.

43 Strong's Hebrew #7343 *(Rachab)*, same as #7342, taken from #7337.

44 Martin H. Manser, *Dictionary of Bible Themes: The Accessible and Comprehensive Tool for Topical Studies* (London: Martin Manser, 2009), 7388 kinsman-redeemer.

45 Strong's Hebrew #7327.

46 Fred H. Wight, *Manners and Customs of Bible Lands* (Chicago: Moody Press, 1980), 250.

47 The mention of Islam is a historical notation, not an endorsement of this religion or its doctrines.

48 Strong's Hebrew #6855, taken from #6833 *(tsippowr/tsippor)*, means little bird, fowl, or sparrow.

49   Strong's Hebrew #635.

CHAPTER *11*

50   Abraham married Keturah after Sarah died (Genesis 25:1). However, Keturah is not generally considered a matriarch from the patriarchal period.

51   "Patriarch and Patriarchate," *The Catholic Encyclopedia*, http://www.newadvent.org/cathen/11549a.htm.

CHAPTER *12*

52   Strong's Greek #3137, Strong's Hebrew #4813, taken from #4805.

53   *The Genealogy of Christ through Mary* (NKJV). Although Joseph's name is listed in Luke 3:23, some scholars believe this refers to Mary's lineage through her father Heli. Compare with the genealogy from Matthew 1:16 where Joseph's father is Jacob.

54   Strong's Greek #2501, Strong's Hebrew #3130.

55   M. G. Easton, *Easton's Bible Dictionary* (New York: Harper & Brothers, 1893), Jesus.

56   Myers, *The Eerdmans Bible Dictionary*, 573. Also see *Enhanced Strong's Lexicon*, Strong's Hebrew #3091 (Joshua), Strong's Greek #2424 (Jesus/Joshua).

57   V. Gilbert Beers, *The Victor Handbook of Bible Knowledge* (Wheaton, IL: Victor Books, 1981), 322–325.

58   Strong's Hebrew #6005.

CHAPTER *13*

59   Strong's Greek #3631*(oinos)*, Strong's Hebrew #3196 *(yayin)*.

60   Strong's Hebrew #8492 *(tiyrosh, tiyrowsh)*.

61   F. S. Fitzsimmonds, "Wine and Strong Drink," ed. D. R. W. Wood et al., *New Bible Dictionary* (Leicester, England; Downers Grove, IL: InterVarsity Press, 1996), 1242–1243.

62   Swanson, *Dictionary of Biblical Languages with Semantic Domains*, DBL Hebrew #9408.

CHAPTER *14*

63   "Badwater Basin," UntraveledRoad, http://death-valley.untraveledroad.com/Badwater-Basin.htm.

64   "Badwater Pool," UntraveledRoad, http://death-valley.untraveledroad.com/California/Inyo/DeathValley/Badwater/6NSign.htm.

65 Strong's Hebrew #2421 (live, alive, save, quicken, revive, restore).

66 Strong's Greek #859.

67 Beers, *The Victor Handbook of Bible Knowledge*, 510–511.

CHAPTER *15*

68 *Unto the Hills* by Billy Graham, copyright © 2010, used by permission, all rights reserved.

69 "The Transcript from the Apollo 13 Disaster Will Give You Chills," Business Insider, http://www.businessinsider.com/apollo-13-disaster-transcript-2013-4. (NASA generally considers Apollo-era records and documents as public domain information.)

70 "Apollo 13," NASA, http://www.nasa.gov/mission_pages/apollo/missions/apoll013.html.

    (For additional information about the Apollo 13 mission, see EP-76, a document produced by the Office of Public Affairs NASA, http://nssdc.gsfc.nasa.gov/planetary/lunar/apoll013.pdf.)

71 Strong's Greek #1695.

72 Matthew 28:9–10, 16–20; Mark 16:9–11, 12–13, 14–19; Luke 24:36–48, 49–52; John 20:14–18, 19–25, 26–29; 21:1–13; and Acts 1:1–11.

73 Strong's Greek #3306.

CHAPTER *16*

74 "Let no ma deceave you by eny meanes for the lorde commeth not excepte ther come a departynge fyrst and that that synfull man be opened ye sonne of perdicion" (2 Thessalonians 2:3). The Newe Testment by William Tyndale 1525–1526, 1534 edition.

75 Strong's Greek #646 *(apostasia)*, #868 *(aphistemi)*.

76 Cranmer Great Bible, Matthew's Bible, Beza Bible, and Geneva Bible.

77 Achtemeier, *Harper's Bible Dictionary*, 947.

78 "The Significance of the Shofar," Hebrew for Christians, http://www.hebrew4christians.com/Holidays/Fall_Holidays/Elul/Shofar/shofar.html.

CHAPTER *17*

79 Strong's Hebrew #1419, #3372.

80 Wight, *Manners and Customs of Bible Lands*, 165–166.

81 Ibid., 149–150, 166–167.

CHAPTER *18*

82 *The Zondervan Parallel New Testament in Greek and English* (Grand Rapids, MI: Zondervan Bible Publishers, 1980), 767.

83 Strong's Greek #1135.

84 Isidore Singer, managing editor, *The Jewish Encyclopedia* (New York: Funk and Wagnalls, 1901–1906), "Kiddushin," http://www.jewishencyclopedia.com/articles/9310-kiddushin.

85 Singer, *The Jewish Encyclopedia,* "Betrothal: In the Bible," http://www.jewishencyclopedia.com/articles/3229-betrothal.

86 Ibid., "Marriage: Betrothal and Nuptial Rights," http://www.jewishencyclopedia.com/articles/10432-marriage. Also see *Enhanced Strong's Lexicon,* Strong's Hebrew #4119 *(mohar).*

87 Ibid., "Betrothal: In the Bible," http://www.jewishencyclopedia.com/articles/3229-betrothal.

88 Ibid.

89 Ibid., "Betrothal: The Legal Ceremony, Gifts," http://www.jewishencyclopedia.com/articles/5843-erusin.

90 Strong's Hebrew #4976.

91 Singer, *The Jewish Encyclopedia,* "Betrothal: Betrothal and Home-Taking," http://www.jewishencyclopedia.com/articles/5843-erusin.

92 Ibid., "Marriage: Betrothal and Nuptial Rights," http://www.jewishencyclopedia.com/articles/10432-marriage.

93 Zola Levitt, *The Miracle of Passover* (Dallas, TX: Zola Levitt Ministries, 1977), 11–36.

94 The *Book of Common Prayer* is the short title for a number of related books that were first published in 1549 during the reign of Edward VI and was a product of the English Reformation.

95 Does the Lord's body have a heavenly inscription or tattoo? Revelation 19:16 seems to indicate that His thigh has the name, KING OF KINGS AND LORD OF LORDS, written thereon. For further consideration, compare Revelation 19:16 with Isaiah 49:16, where the people of Israel are inscribed on the palms of His hands.

CHAPTER 19

96 Strong's Greek #26.

97 Strong's Hebrew #6918.

98 Strong's Hebrew #2617.

99 Strong's Greek #5485.

100 Strong's Hebrew #3368.

101 Strong's Hebrew #7965.

102 Strong's Hebrew #3519.

103 R. E. Nixon, "Glory," ed. D. R. W. Wood et al., *New Bible Dictionary* (Leicester, England; Downers Grove, IL: InterVarsity Press, 1996), 414.

CHAPTER *21*

104 Strong's Greek #3875 *(parakletos)* Advocate, Helper, Comforter.

CHAPTER *22*

105 Strong's Greek #2822.

106 Strong's Greek #2564.

107 Myers, *The Eerdmans Bible Dictionary,* 902–903. Also see *Enhanced Strong's Lexicon*, Strong's Greek #40 *(hagios)*.

108 Strong's Greek #5486.

109 Strong's Greek #1377.

110 Strong's Greek #2770.

CHAPTER *23*

111 Taken from *Facing Reality* by Oswald Chambers. Copyright © 1939 by the Oswald Chambers Publications Assoc. Ltd., and is used by permission of Discovery House Publishers, Grand Rapids, MI 49501. All rights reserved.

112 *Nalibban* narrative adapted from Scottish story as told by Pastor Melvin Harrel.

113 "How to Believe: Nalibban the Bridge." Copyright © 2002 by Charles Earl Harrel.

CPSIA information can be obtained
at www.ICGtesting.com
Printed in the USA
FFHW021755151218
49861869-54426FF